Y0-BXH-020

TRAVELLING IN TROPICAL COUNTRIES

Jacques Hébert

Travelling in Tropical Countries

Guide for Africa, the South Seas,
Latin America, Asia, and the West Indies

Translated from the French by Gerald Taaffe

Hurtig Publishers
Edmonton

Copyright © 1986 by Jacques Hébert

All rights reserved. No part of this book may be reproduced or transmitted in any form by any means, electronic, electrical, mechanical, chemical, optical, or otherwise, including photocopying and recording, or by any information storage or retrieval system, with written permission from the publisher, except for brief passages quoted by a reviewer in a newspaper or magazine.

Hurtig Publishers Ltd.
10560–105 Street
Edmonton, Alberta
Canada T5H 2W7

Translated by Gerald Taaffe. Originally published as *Voyager en pays tropical* (Montréal: Les Éditions du Boréal Express, 1984)

Canadian Cataloguing in Publication Data

Hébert, Jacques, 1923–
  Travelling in tropical countries

  Translation of: Voyager en pays tropical.
  ISBN 0-88830-303-3

  1. Travel.   2. Tropics — Description and travel.   3. Developing countries — Description and travel.   I. Title.
  G151.H4213 1986   910′.2′02   C86-091292-2

Edited by Nancy Marcotte
Design by Tad Aronowicz/DESIGNWORKS
Typeset by Attic Typesetting Inc.
Printed and bound in Canada by Tri-Graphic Printing (Ottawa) Ltd.

For Maximiliano
my beloved grandson
from the Third World

Contents

Preamble

Travel is fatal to prejudice,
bigotry and narrow-mindedness.
            Mark Twain, 1867

I've written this book for everyone attracted to beauty and adventure, the unknown, and the exotic, for free individuals who intend to make the most of their freedom; for young men and women in a hurry to go out and discover the world before settling down; for old people who at last can set aside working responsibilities and travel to see how others live.

Between the extremes of youth and age are the businessman who wants to understand the people he meets in other countries, the diplomat who is something more than a civil servant, the overseas volunteer inclined as much to give as to receive, and the modest secretary who patiently saved up because she long ago decided that some day she would go and see Fez.

I've written also for the tourist who finally tires of the usual trip to Florida and sets off to discover a lost beach in The Gambia, Tobago, or Tunisia, the tourist who is fed up with organized tours and wishes to vacation under the sun and at the same time make some real contact with local people.

In short, this book is an open invitation to feel at home with oneself in this world of mankind and especially in the Third World, where no doubt the future of all mankind will unfold.

A good part of my life has been spent in travel across the five continents by air, sea, and land. In my younger days the conditions were most often wretched. Later, and less frequently, I experienced the luxury of large exotic resort centres. I know all of the joys of the road, the emotions that can be inspired by sea and desert, and the perpetually new joy of meeting an exceptional being at the far end of the world. As Baudelaire put it, "I have the memories of a thousand-year-old." And to top it off, I know all the tricks of the trade.

This may sound a little less than modest, but there it is. Put your trust in me and I assure you that the sailing will be smooth.

A real traveller is curious, a stickler for detail, careful in matters of health, patient in all circumstances, tolerant of others, and gifted with an indestructible sense of humour.

Some of the many pieces of advice in the following pages are of major importance, while others have the lesser goal of making you more comfortable. You would probably survive even if you didn't bring the recommended pocket flashlight or even remember to brush your teeth with boiled water. But you would be taking a needless risk of minor annoyance and, at worst, of finding yourself in hospital. Or in jail!

A certain amount of repetition is inevitable in a work of this nature. Because I have tried to hold repetition down to the minimum, I suggest that you read even chapters that don't seem to be of direct interest. You may find useful bits of information that won't be found in other parts. For example, the chapter on young travellers will be quite useful to tourists of a riper age, because responsible adults sometimes discover an amazing youthfulness in themselves once they've slipped out of their own country.

Now let's be on our way!

CHAPTER 1

The Tourist

Once the preserve of such citizens of the world as Somerset Maugham, André Gide, Graham Greene, and a few eccentric millionaires, travel to exotic places, last fantasy of our consumer society, is now within the reach of nearly all income groups.

Florida and California haven't lost their appeal for many Canadians, but by the 1950s people were beginning to venture to Mexico (although all too often no further than Acapulco), then to leave terra firma for Hawaii on the one hand and Bermuda or the Bahamas on the other. The lilting speech and good inexpensive French wines of Guadeloupe and Martinique soon attracted Québécois, while Ontarians opted for the sublime golf courses of Jamaica and the discreet charm of the islands inhabited by English-speaking people. Then charter flights began to carry the most timid of souls to Morocco, Sri Lanka, and as far as the enchanted island of Bali.

Most astonishing was that the charter flights weren't packed with the rich but with middle-income people: young couples, small-business people, thrifty typists, and groups of senior citizens.

For some developing countries, the substantial economic fall-out from this explosion in international tourism has literally meant rescue from bankruptcy. An example is the Seychelles, a group of islands in the Indian Ocean whose principal source of income is now the tourist trade.

THE INFLUENCE OF TOURISM

A great deal has been written and will continue to be written about the negative effect of thousands of tourists on simple societies and their traditional values. One sure thing is that these outsiders, pockets stuffed with money and on the lookout for every kind of pleasure, provide strong incentives for begging, picking pockets, the drug trade, and prostitution. I find myself staying clear of once cherished places when Club Med or a big, pompous Hilton moves in. Some countries still resist and discourage tourists. Burma is one of them and for that reason has retained its unique traditions unadulterated by Western values.

The fact has to be faced, however, that as long as there are rich countries where people shiver through long cold winters and poor countries with superb beaches and uninterruptedly delectable climates, travel to exotic places will continue to meet the desires of the former and serve the economic needs of the latter.

There is only one way to mitigate the bad effects of tourism on Third World countries, and that is to change the outlook of the tourists themselves, to show them that they can get more out of their expensive trips by opening up a little to the authentic cultural values of the host countries. This is no light task, and I'm not sure that the purveyors of guided, cost-inclusive tours will be converted overnight into cultural crusaders on its behalf.

GUIDED TOURS

It's not hard to understand why those of you new to Third World travel would consider this option. A guided tour gives you the feeling that you belong to a group; there are no surprises (alas!); the guide has all the answers. That much is soothing and calms more or less valid fears.

Some people really enjoy guided tours—folks who make friends quickly and easily, people who hope to meet the romantic figures of their dreams, retired people, bashful people, and people who get bored or fearful once they are by themselves in a foreign country.

Finally there are the tours for specialized groups: people under the age of sixteen, birdwatchers, Sunday archaeologists, butterfly collectors, safari-bugs, amateur photographers, pilgrims to the Holy Land, and so on.

Another decided advantage of guided tours is that they cost less than the equivalent in an individual trip.

Take this itinerary offered by a large travel agency: air travel to Peru and Bolivia with stopovers in Lima, Cuzco, Puno, La Paz, and Chulumani; day-trip to the (absolutely magnificent) ruins of Machu Picchu. Duration: eleven nights. Travel in a single class, equivalent to economy. First-class hotels, single room, all meals inclusive as well as transportation to the interior of Peru and Bolivia. Price per person: $2198. (A couple sharing a room in a more ordinary hotel can save $299 each.)

The same trip sold by the same agency to a single person travelling independently would easily have cost one thousand dollars more.

THE INDIVIDUAL ITINERARY

We move now to the more individualistic and daring tourist, willing to complicate his vacation a little in exchange for being sure of an enriching, unique, and unforgettable experience.

Preparing for the trip takes more time, but here the travel advisors of good agencies will be a great help to first-timers and even to others. They may have been in the country you intend to visit and be able to describe with confidence the climate, tourist sites, and hotels.

You should also discuss your itinerary with the travel agent. The first time give your dates of departure and return, name the cities (or villages) you wish to visit, and give the length of stay in each. Since there are always several ways to set up an itinerary, it is important to specify your preferences first thing, even before the agency begins to check seat availabilities on one or more airlines.

For example, you can go to Africa via New York, or via London, Paris, Brussels, and Frankfurt. Unless there is a big difference in fare, *stay away from New York*, especially on the return flight.

In a later chapter I will stress the enviable ease for Canadians of travelling to and from the United States. On the other hand, when you land in an American airport simply to change flights on your way to another country, or on return from another country en route to Canada, you will be treated like any other foreigner. American airports are the only ones I know of where transit passengers have to pass through all the customs and immigration formalities exactly as though the United States were their destination. This can be a long and painful process. It has taken me nearly two hours at John F. Kennedy airport, almost making me miss a connecting flight with Air Afrique.

There are other reasons for avoiding New York. If you arrive at La Guardia Airport and your connecting flight leaves from John F. Kennedy, there's a half-hour, fifteen-dollar taxi trip. And even if your flights arrive at and leave from Kennedy, don't forget that this is one of the largest airports in the world: there are nine terminal buildings, each of them housing a number of airlines. If, for example, you arrive from Mirabel at John F. Kennedy on Aerolineas Argentinas, you have to go to another terminal for the connecting flight on Air Afrique. There is a constant bus circuit between the various terminal buildings, but porters are a vanishing species, and you will end up carrying your own bags through a dense and jostling crowd...and again you will lose half an hour.

Finally, John F. Kennedy is one of the busiest of airports, and all too frequently planes trying to come in circle the city for an hour before receiving landing clearance. Even on the ground there is sometimes another hour's wait before the plane can come in to the terminal and unload passengers.

Other major American airports are also transfer points: Chicago, Atlanta, and Miami for flights to Latin America; San Francisco and Los Angeles for flights to Asia and the South Seas. These airports are often very overcrowded and, as in New York, Canadians in transit have to undergo all the formalities of immigration and customs.

As you will find out from the travel agent, it can happen that you have no choice. In that case, like millions of other Canadians who have had to pass through the United States, you will just have to endure it.

With the travel agent, go over your itinerary carefully *on a map*. You may see that at no additional cost you could stop over for a day or two in a country that hadn't even crossed your mind. If you are headed towards a country in the Antipodes such as Sri Lanka, you can go via the Pacific and come back via Europe and the Atlantic, making a round-the-world trip without paying more. Another advantage is that you would always be travelling westwards, which distinctly cuts down on jet lag symptoms.

A few days after receiving your instructions, the travel agent will send you an itinerary with all the necessary information: date, place, and time of departure and arrival of each flight; airline flight numbers and names; hotel names and addresses. Make sure that each flight is marked **OK**, meaning that your seat is confirmed. (For more details on airline tickets see Chapter 9.)

Because flights are sometimes infrequent, cancelled, or booked up, the suggested itinerary may be a little different from your original plan. If you are satisfied, the agency will then issue your ticket, which you should insist on having *in hand* at least a week before departure, or even sooner if it must be presented to get certain visas.

You will be given several copies of your itinerary, one of which should be left with your secretary or family so that you can be contacted in case of emergency. Keep another *with* your ticket; you will have to consult it often en route. Put the other copy in your flight bag. If you should ever be so unlucky as to lose your ticket, the detailed itinerary will help the travel agency or airline to replace it.

Unless there is a cancellation, the flight from your Canadian departure point and any connecting flights to your destination are automatically confirmed. This isn't the case for any of the other flights, each of which must be reconfirmed forty-eight and often seventy-two hours in advance. In Chapter 9 you will see the safeguards to take in this regard.

You may have noticed that the choice of a good travel agent—and they can be found in any responsible agency—is of prime importance, even to the seasoned traveller, who can fall victim, as I have, to bungled reservations, sometimes on non-existent flights.

One of the conveniences of travelling is that the often indispensable services of travel agents cost the traveller nothing. Their commissions come from the sale of airline tickets (approximately nine per cent) and the booking of hotel rooms (ten per cent). In fact, it is pointless and awkward to buy your ticket directly from an airline except for short domestic flights.

HOTELS

There are poor and rarely visited countries that have only a single decent hotel. An example is the Indépendance Hotel in Conakry, Guinea. At the other extreme is the great variety of hotels sometimes found even in tiny countries, ranging from an imposing Sheraton to a seedy little hotel that is best avoided, not because you wouldn't generally be safe there but because of the often deplorable sanitary conditions.

Personally, I take care to avoid the luxury hotels. But unless absolutely necessary I'm just as scrupulous about sidestepping cheap places where the kitchen may be unclean, the rooms open to mosquitoes, and the bathrooms swarming with cockroaches.

Writing as I am for travellers with no desire to sabotage their own vacations, I don't need to belabour the point. You will choose suitable, clean hotel rooms, even luxury ones if that is your wish.

Travel agencies have impressive guidebooks with descriptions of all hotels of any importance. Insist on consulting them yourself. You know your own tastes better than anyone, and a detail that might have escaped the eye of the travel agent could attract you straight-away. In Dakar the agent would have suggested the Méridien, a glamorous name but, as it happens, a boring hotel. At seaside next door, however, is the Village N'Gor: Senegalese huts scattered around a site wooded with palms and eucalyptus. A thousand times more interesting than the Méridien. To be sure the huts are made of concrete, there's galvanized iron under the pointed palm-frond roofs, and in each a bathroom and air-conditioning. It costs less than its next door neighbour, where you can nonetheless go to dine on French or Senegalese cuisine. There you have it. All the information was there, but how could your travel agent guess that you would rather live in a hut than a grand hotel?

Another detail to check out is the distance from the hotel to the town centre. Poorly advised once on a three-day mission to Lima, I found myself in a hotel that was forty kilometres from the Plaza San Martin, the centre of the city.

In the Dakar example, I took it for granted that you would be looking for a seaside holiday spot. The suggested hotel, the Village N'Gor, is about ten kilometres from the centre of Dakar. There's a bus service, and the modest taxis aren't expensive... provided you take the time to discuss the fare *before* getting in.

If for some reason you had to stay in Dakar proper, I would have suggested the Lagon II, a beguiling little modern hotel on the bay and in the center of town. For the thrifty, there's an old, somewhat decrepit hotel dating from colonial times, the Croix du Sud. There's no view, no luxury, and a lot of street noise, but the dining room is the best in the country.

That's the kind of information I would give the clients if I were a travel agent. I would also make sure that they made room reserva-tions and paid for the first night in advance. As a client, I would insist on having a copy of the confirming telex. With a hotel voucher and telex copy in hand, I would be better armed for an 11:00 P.M. showdown with the hotel manager who dared deny having ever received a reservation... having just given someone else the last room. At the peak of the tourist season—December 15 to January 15—even hotels are given to overbooking.

In some cities there's a chronic shortage of hotel rooms, so reservations must be made very far in advance. One of these cities is Algiers.

If you would like a hotel room that is comfortable, original, and sometimes historic, don't hesitate to say so to the travel agent, or you might very well find yourself in an American hotel of the "no surprise" kind. In Rabat, for example, there's a very luxurious Hilton with splendid gardens. On the other hand, there is also the lovely Hotel de la Tour Hassan, centred around an old Moorish palace with ceilings of carved cedar, ceramic walls, and marble floors strewn with beautiful hot-coloured Moroccan rugs. In a restaurant out of the Arabian nights, you will get roast lamb, *paella*, and *couscous* worthy of the pashas that guests of the Tour Hassan become for a few days. (Obviously the bathrooms are more modern at the Hilton.)

Another fine hotel with an interesting past is Shepheard's in Cairo, where, following the habit of Lawrence on his returns from Arabia, I never fail to at least go and have a gin on the terrace overlooking the Nile. At dusk, when the sun comes down slowly over the city and colours the minarets like white-hot spearheads, you can watch big brown butterflies sliding along the Nile, *feluccas* returning to port. Their slim masts rock, cross, and mingle against a tawny sky, knitting little white clouds for winter. (Take it easy, dear poet!)

The same holds true for Singapore, a city that has become ultramodern over the past few years, sprouting skyscrapers and many luxury hotels. In Singapore it's better to pick the famous Raffles Hotel, still comfortable and of which Rudyard Kipling wrote: "Feed at Raffles when in Singapore." You can go to the ground floor Long Bar and order a Singapore Sling on the very spot this dubious quaff was invented at the turn of the century and in time consumed by such as Somerset Maugham and Noel Coward. But if you don't want to make the waiters smile, simply say "Sling," or they will give the same reaction as a Parisian baker asked for a loaf of *French* bread.

TIPPING

A lot of people I know are made extremely uneasy by the tipping question. They dread not giving enough and, even worse, giving too much. What a relief it is for them when the bill shows that a gratuity is included. But even then, should they leave something? Except of course in China, where all forms of tipping are forbidden.

Personally I've solved the problem. In a modest restaurant, I leave a little more than ten per cent; in a more impressive one I leave a little more than fifteen per cent or even twenty per cent. Why a little more? Because I like to and also because this big Togolese, who is doing his best to serve me, is paid a starvation wage. Since he works while so many of his countrymen are unemployed, he has to meet the needs not only of his wife and four or five children but also those of his very extended African family, including parents and grandparents, cousins, second cousins, and great-nephews-once-removed.

According to my hasty calculation, a tourist who dines for three weeks at good and not-so-good restaurants in Lomé, Rangoon, or Rio de Janeiro and always leaves a little more than ten or fifteen per cent would be out about twenty-five dollars. The entire trip would cost between two and three thousand dollars. Worriers about the tipping question then can set their minds at ease for this modest sum. A bargain!

TAXIS

Almost without exception, taxis in the Third World have no meters. You will be told that there are fixed rates. This is rarely the case. In airports, rates for the town center are sometimes posted. But if you don't bargain *before* getting into a cab, before even deciding which one you will take, for competition is stiff, there is a risk that at the hotel the driver will ask double the rate posted at the airport. He may claim that after a certain time the rate goes up by fifty per cent, or that so much extra is charged per suitcase or extra passenger. After nine hours in flight, an hour in customs and immigration, and a half-hour in the cab, you are tired out . . . so you pay. To sidestep this widespread kind of scam, discuss prices *before* the trip rather than after.

The essential thing is not to let yourself feel bitter about such incidents, for which, as has just been shown, we bear some of the blame. All over the Third World, bargaining is an old tradition, almost a sport. Anyone who doesn't take this into account is considered at best naive.

Put yourself for a moment in the shoes of the taxi driver, a truly poor man, his shirt in tatters as is the bodywork of his indescribable jalopy. You are fresh from America. He knows that the airline ticket cost you around a thousand dollars. He guesses that your big overstuffed suitcase is full of fine clothes, cameras, and all sorts of little treasures, while your flight bag probably contains a carton of American cigarettes and a bottle of Scotch bought at the last duty-free shop. Since he's driving you to the Sheraton, he must know that your stay there will set you back another thousand dollars. All in all, the amount you spend on this trip plus the contents of your luggage come to ten times his entire fortune, including the wretched cab... and for the same reasons as the Togolese waiter, he has to support an enormous family. Yes, put yourself in his shoes. Wouldn't you try to impose a little tax of two or three dollars, chicken feed for this rich tourist?

This said, still learn how to bargain a little, if only so that all Canadians won't look like easy marks.

Rent a car? My advice is, absolutely not! Except perhaps in certain circumstances in certain countries which shall remain name-less so as not to lead you into temptation.

Yes, cars can be rented in almost all Third World countries. You even find branches of the big American companies, the multination-als of driving. But as a general rule you will be disappointed. The car reserved in Montréal or Vancouver will no longer be available in Abidjan. Instead of the promised Renault 16, you will be fobbed off with a somewhat battered Renault 4 of a less recent make than promised. Expect a flat or a motor breakdown. And rental prices are always exorbitant.

This little test might persuade you: ask the agency for proof of total insurance coverage if you crash into a dromedary, smash a cabinet minister's Mercedes or, worse still, kill someone. There will be lots of reassurances, but the proof will not be forthcoming. Risks you would not take in Canada should never be taken in Paraguay, Ethiopia, or Brunei. Take dozens of taxis if necessary, hire a taxi for a day or even two, but don't ever take on legal responsibility for a vehicle in countries where drivers are reckless and roads are dangerous and sometimes jammed with pedestrians, goats, mules, llamas, cows (sometimes sacred ones), and even elephants.

And to add to the complications, in former British colonies traffic is always on the left.

A first-time visitor to the Third World is often put off by the condition of many taxis: doors held in place by baling wire, smashed fenders, cracked windshields, loose brakes, angry-sounding mufflers, and tires worn down to the lining. But they always work. Don't be too nervous. The driver likes being alive as much as you do, and to him this heap of scrap is something precious: his means of livelihood and entire capital.

Just about everywhere you can use jitney cabs, buses, or minibuses crammed with cheerful passengers. Watch out for pickpockets and have a good time!

There are often jitney cabs for intercity travel, called *taxis-brousse* in French-speaking Africa. They leave when the cab is full, sometimes a little too full. You must not be in a hurry.

I must tell you about a cab ride in Katmandu, an anecdote that I have often dined out on. I have dug it out of a travel diary dated January 6, 1979:

> I arrive in Katmandu at about 8:00 P.M., dog-tired, thank you. The taxi at the airport is a wobbling rattletrap held together with baling wire. After hardly a kilometre or two it runs out of gas. The driver and his helper (all the drivers have helpers, and with good reason) make their excuses, say there's really no problem. From the trunk they then unearth an old Pernod bottle that's half full of gas. This they brandish about, joking all the time.
>
> There's hardly enough to moisten the bottom of the tank, much less fill the connector pipe to the carburetor.
>
> Diffidently I point this out. Still making jokes, the two Nepalese handymen show me a little rubber tube. They do their best to stuff one end in the carburetor. Passing the other end through one of the many holes in the dashboard, they stick it in the Pernod bottle. One of the two sucks up the gas at the end of the tube connected to the carburetor, while the other, from inside the car, blows with all his might in the bottle to make the gas go up the tube. And it works! I show the liveliest admiration for this new triumph of human ingenuity.
>
> After four or five kilometres, chug, chug, out of gas again. Once more I'm given reassurances, but this time with less joking around. Down there in the darkness there's a gas station....
>
> Painfully we push the *thing* to the gas pump. I sit back in the taxi

and tell myself that I'm done with breakdowns, since the two jokesters are going to fill her up.

And so they do—they fill the Pernod bottle! And the process begins again.

I was to arrive late at the hotel.

CHAPTER 2

The Young Traveller

Until the 1950s it was the exceptional young man (Young woman? Perish the thought!) who went off, knapsack on back, to seek adventure in far-off and exotic lands. A few daring ones sometimes wandered around Europe, perhaps saw Spain from a motorcycle and Italy from a train. Youth hostels, hospitable and cheap, began to proliferate. But these young people took care not to go and risk their lives in black Africa, Brazil, or India.

No doubt that's why I had a brief spell of notoriety in Québec between 1946 and 1954, when I took to the road on endless auto trips across most countries in Latin America, Africa, and Asia.

It isn't hard to account for the interest shown in the travel narratives of my younger days, published first in newspapers and then in book form. The world had just emerged from World War II, almost seven years in which Canadians, like people almost everywhere on earth, weren't able to travel great distances— unless they were armed forces personnel, who had no say in their itineraries.

Since then things have changed a great deal. Young people, at least those from affluent countries, have set off in discovery of the world and, more and more, the Third World. You see them every- where, in the most unexpected places: in a lost hamlet atop the Andes, beside a Sumatran lake, in a Hindu temple in Nepal, on a golden beach in the Ivory Coast.

I admit that young travellers are the ones of greatest interest to me. Because they are young, a trip that is at all successful can have a deep and lifelong influence. When you have trod the dusty paths of Niger under the sun, shared the tortillas of Guatemalan peas- ants, slept in a longhouse at the far end of Sarawak, you already have a better understanding of Third World countries than the best of the armchair experts. And you have a better understanding of yourself.

Again, the trip has to be a successful one. And that takes a modicum of preparation and discipline that all too many young travellers think they can do without.

I'm not thinking of the misguided youths looking for cheap drugs who often end up in squalid hospitals and even more squalid jails. For them there's nothing I can do except to feel badly about the stupidity and waste.

Other young travellers haven't the slightest inclination toward delinquency and still don't get much done except to pile up the kilometres. They expect that all sorts of things will happen as soon as they are away, but it isn't so. Not for the young and not for the old. Nothing really interesting happens to someone who sets off empty of head and barren of heart. Frustrated, they bring their frustrations with them. Ignorant, they drag their ignorance along everywhere, like a ball and chain.

HAVING A SUCCESSFUL TRIP

Any trip, large or small, has to be prepared for with all-consuming interest and enthusiasm. Everything isn't to be found in books, but a few good books will lead the way to the rest. How dare you, for example, travel across Saudi Arabia without having read T.E. Lawrence's *The Seven Pillars of Wisdom*? Visit India without knowing Mahatma Gandhi? Jerusalem without the Bible? Or the Sahara without Antoine de Saint-Exupéry's *Citadel* or *The Little Prince*?

Of course, not all the truth is to be found in books, and you often learn more about a country directly from a traveller just back from even a short stay. There are cities where I've lived for only a day, but within a very intense twenty-four hours, cities I thought I knew from my reading collapsed under my eyes, then to be rebuilt, different, not always better but finally with the true spirit of that city...for me at least.

But don't listen to travellers who have nothing but tales of woe, bad experiences, and depressing anecdotes. There is no perfect country, nor flawless people, nor mosquitoless tropics. The important thing is to have heart and mind wide open and to take in what is offered while, with discretion, rejecting the inevitable dross.

The young travellers who make me feel badly are the ones who slide across a country's surface, never stopping, never letting themselves be entranced by the serenity of a village, the beauty of an old person, the glee of a bunch of children who would dearly love to know what things are like in a snowy country. I've known some who go from town to town, youth hostel to cheap little hotel, making friends only with others like themselves, from Europe or America. After spending a small fortune, they come back from the heart of Africa with memories only of the nice young Germans in Timbuktu or Bamako and, above all, the unhoped for, providential *Canadian* in Marrakesh—no one they couldn't have met at the Café Campus in the heart of Montréal or at one of the Gastown bars in Vancouver.

At the age of sixty, it's always risky to give advice to young people who, in reaction against their elders, who are guilty of such a multitude of sins, would rather learn everything for themselves. Although I understand their feelings, I would still like to press the point. I have earned my travel scars. First, I myself was once twenty. Then too, as I said before, in my early days I did my share of moving around ... by foot, bicycle, canoe, barge, pirogue, freighter, train, camel, thumb, jeep, and, to be sure, plane, from wood-and-canvas single-motor to Boeing 747. I crossed the Andes six times in a 1931 Chevrolet, went down the Nile from Juba to Khartoum on a grain barge, crossed the Sahara from north to south by the Tamanrasset Trail and then by the Bidon 5.

The fact is that after my spell of adventurousness in the mid-1950s, I became the "expert" that the young sought out, generally in springtime, before leaving on a long trip.

With those who seemed to lack internal fortitude I was rather pitiless. I made no bones about the endless hardships of an extended camping trip to Asia or elsewhere. These hardships are so real, I told myself, that a novice traveller I was able to put off with mere words would never be able to survive them. And so I figured that the kindest thing I could do was to discourage completely the less-determined.

In other young people I could immediately see the divine spark. With these I would be endlessly patient, spending hours with them hunched over a map of Africa or pointing out various snares on that highway with the deceptive title of Pan-American, pointing out all the not-to-be-missed marvels.

THE IDEAL GROUP

Suddenly I would stop and put the question pointblank: "Do the three of you know each other well? Really well?"

Startled for a moment, they would answer, sure, Dave and Chris went to school together and Larry was Dave's neighbour and friend, and so on.

"That doesn't mean that you can *really* travel together for a year in Latin America. Travel is the best testing ground of friendship. If you are not absolutely sure of your group, sure that you will be able to bear with each other during long months of discomfort, hardship, doing without, and close daily contact inside and around your vehicle, it's better not to go at all. The trip would soon be hellish and undertaking it sheer madness."

I laid it on thick, but I knew from experience that on any trip the least bit complicated, the most important decision is the choice of travelling companions.

"Since you've decided to spend a year of your life travelling across the Americas, you're no doubt not leaving for another fifteen days? Good. Leave right away, the three of you, say for Abitibi or the Kootenays. Live for fifteen days the way you plan to live along the Pan American highway, camping out, cooking, group decisions, task-sharing. Being in your own country, on home ground, will make it all the easier. Come and see me afterwards, and we'll talk about Brazil again."

This odd bit of advice was followed by a few, and one day I would hear that the Latin American trip had been postponed or that Dave and Chris would go together, Larry having decided to stay home, or other variations.

Most of the others, of course, thought that I had gone a little daft and left straightaway with all the zeal of people who have been dreaming about adventure for a long time.

I got a few postcards from Mexico. None from Patagonia.

No one ever asked what was the ideal number for a group. This didn't stop me from volunteering that four is a lot, three is too many, and one just isn't enough. There are probably exceptions that prove this rule.

COST

Young travellers are often full of illusions about the cost of a trip to the Third World. They think that they can live on nothing, that nice ripe bananas or papayas will fall into their laps, and that if they run out of money they can always find some kind of work to get by.

You have to pay for the bananas, and more than local people do, which seems quite fair and normal to me. Working on the sly? It's forbidden by law. How, moreover, do you find work or even dare look for it in countries where half the population is unemployed and where to be unemployed really means to die by slow starvation? I've known young people who were occasionally hired secretly by some planter for the sugar harvest. They worked ten hours a day under the tropical sun, ate rice, slept mosquito-plagued on mats...and earned three dollars a day! It's not worth it. Better for a young person to hold off departure from Canada a little and work packing groceries at Safeway for a month. Earnings would be as much as from six months in the canefields.

"How much do you think a year-long trip in Latin America would cost each of us?" That was the question put pointblank by Dave, Chris, and Larry.

"It's easy to figure out, and you'll have a close enough figure when you come back from the Kootenays. First there's the gas for your car. Say that, except in the United States and Venezuela, it'll cost a little more than in Canada. If your trip is thirty thousand kilometres, then just add up the figures. During your fifteen days on the road in the Kootenays, try to live exactly as you plan to live along the Pan-American Highway: eat as little as possible, go easy on the chips, avoid little treats of the ice-cold Molson kind, shun restaurants like the plague. Add things up when you come back. Did it cost you three dollars a day each? Fine. Anywhere in the world then you'll be able to eat frugally for 365 days at a cost of $1,095.

This way of pricing the costs of a trip works as well now as it did then.

I know, I know. There are young travellers who boast about going all across Asia on five hundred dollars (and no doubt a plane ticket). That's possible. Everything is possible. A few years ago I met a young Frenchman who "went around the world on a franc." In Montréal, already halfway around the planet, he proudly showed us his franc. He was a naive kid, charming and disarming. People felt sorry for him. You couldn't just leave him to sleep outside in weather like that. So we found him friends.... Probably the French consulates and embassies had the same reaction, as well as Air France offices.

The young Frenchman succeeded in his exploit, and a year later he sent me a little book describing it down to the most embarrassing detail. The one thing this gentle dimwit didn't seem to notice was what hit me square between the eyes: he spent a year sponging off other people. I don't really object to his exploiting embassy secretaries and well-off compatriots, but he often had to depend on the hospitality of the poor. In Third World countries nothing could be easier. A foreigner travelling anywhere, most particularly perhaps in Muslim countries, is sure never to die of hunger; the most wretchedly poor Bedouin will give him a portion of his last dates and the bitter water of his *gherba*.

Sometimes this hospitality has to be accepted, and often it is even the beginning of a fruitful friendship. *But don't ever abuse it.* That is too easy and therefore too base. And your Bedouin friend, who expects nothing in return for his favours, will nonetheless be very pleased if you give him a package of tea or a can of condensed milk... either of which costs a little more than our young French friend's franc.

Sadly, it can happen that a careless young traveller finds himself suddenly penniless. Perhaps his traveller's cheques were stolen in a cheap little hotel. And don't fall for the television commercials and the smiling face of the American Express agent who replaces the stolen cheques on the spot. That can happen to Peter Ustinov if he's lucky enough to be in Hong Kong, Brasília, or London. But if your cheques are stolen in Hergeisa, in the north of Somalia, it is a disaster. By one means or another, by selling your jeans if need be, you have to go back to the capital, Mogadishu. Since there's no Canadian embassy, not much can be done there, and no doubt you should try to reach Nairobi, capital of the neighboring country of Kenya and quite a few kilometres away. There you can tell the embassy what happened, and in turn you will receive some good advice and a few shillings. They will send your family the telegram in which you plead for the money to continue your trip and promise to pay it back when American Express replaces your cheques. (You can easily have money wired to you in a large town such as Nairobi. Elsewhere the easiest thing is to have an international money order in American dollars sent by registered airmail.)

I've known even worse cases. For example, a young traveller had his plane ticket stolen and couldn't count on the help of anyone in Canada, so that he had to be repatriated at the Embassy's expense. Of course he had to commit himself to paying back External Affairs in short order.

In capitals with no Canadian embassy, Canadian citizens can have recourse to the British embassy or consular service in the event of natural disaster, problems with the police, civil disorder, war, and other kinds of emergencies.

DRUGS

Since we're on the subject of disasters, we might as well deal once and for all with other dangers facing the naive or foolhardy young traveller.

Just about everywhere in the Third World there is a lavish supply of a large variety of drugs from the softest, such as coca leaves, kwat, and marijuana, through hashish and hallucinogenic mushrooms, to cocaine and opium. In a very few countries, using or possessing these drugs is still legal. In most others possession is illegal and is punished with a harshness that can't be imagined by anyone who hasn't seen that frightening American movie, *Midnight Express*. Sometimes possession of a small amount of drugs is punishable by death. (Even in Canada the minimum penalty for importing drugs is seven years imprisonment.)

Again, these pages aren't intended in any way for the young drug addicts who hang around in Colombia or Nepal with the sole aim of debasing themselves at bargain prices. These candidates for suicide or jail call for psychiatric analysis. That isn't my field.

What I'm thinking of are young Canadians who, in Canada, might smoke a joint now and again. They *absolutely must abstain for the entire duration of the trip* despite the numerous opportunities. Drugs are offered on every street corner at rockbottom prices. Chance acquaintances will even give some away. Always turn them down absolutely, the risks being out of all proportion.

The fine sense of camaraderie amongst young travellers of the world is something marvelous. They do each other small favours,

pass on good tips, exchange a can of tuna for a pack of cigarettes. . . .
But it can happen that a young Canadian about to leave for Vancouver
is asked by a pretty American girl: "Hey, great! You're headed for
Vancouver? I just happen to have a letter and a little present for a
friend of mine over there. I can send him a telegram, and he'll come
and pick it up at the airport."

If there ever was a proposition that deserved absolute mistrust,
this is it. There's no doubt that thousands of young travellers have
been turned into drug traffickers for a few days. If the girl is really
stunning, one condition should be put squarely to her: let's see what's
in the rather thick envelope and the tightly wrapped little package.

If you are hitchhiking or let someone get in your vehicle, get out or
let your passengers out *before arriving at the border post*. If customs
officials should happen to arrest the other person for drug possession, you automatically become a suspect or, in countries where the
criminal code lists association as an indictable offence, an accused.

At this moment close to a hundred mostly young Canadians are
rotting away in dingy Third World jails, some of them through their
own fault and others because they wanted to help someone out.

In a great number of countries the prisons are horrible beyond
belief. By this I don't mean to cast blame on the authorities in
developing countries that lack necessary means and hardly know to
what to give priority. Should you invest in a little clinic that each year
will save the lives of hundreds of children, or should you rebuild the
local jail?

In 1970 I had occasion to visit fourteen Québec prisons. (In 1965 I
was even a prisoner in one of them.) As chairman of the Civil
Liberties Union of Québec at the time, I raised an outcry against the
inhuman conditions for the prisoners, including mere detainees. And
yet Canada is one of the eight richest countries in the world, one of
the most scrupulous about civil liberties, and one of the most
generous in providing social security. So what right do we have to sit
in judgement on the prisons of extremely poor countries where the
gross national product per person may be $475 a year, as in Haiti,
while ours is $18,478?

With this out of the way, I can say that for a young Canadian any
stay in certain Third World prisons is a nightmare and a sure menace
to physical and mental health. Often prisoners aren't fed and have to
rely on the help of relatives and friends.

A few years back I knew a third secretary at the Canadian embassy in Guatemala City. He had become a kind of social worker and every week had to go to El Salvador (where Canada had no resident diplomatic representative) to visit six or seven young Canadian prisoners at the San Salvador jail and bring them food parcels, along with some moral support. If they were convicted, these young Canadian citizens would have to serve their sentences in El Salvador, Canada able to do nothing for them except provide the ministrations of social worker-third secretary. In a great number of Third World countries the course of justice is vastly more cumbersome than here. An accused person runs the risk of rotting in a squalid jailhouse for two, three, or even six months before his case is even heard. By international treaty his only right is to communicate with his embassy or consulate.

My strongest advice is that before leaving Canada, you should see or see again *Midnight Express*, the true story of a young American who landed in a Turkish prison on drug charges.

So much for that. I don't want to dwell on these depressing subjects, but the case had to be stated clearly.

As a general rule the young traveller will go without let or hindrance through the lovely, marvelous, extraordinary countries of Africa, Asia, Latin America, and the South Seas.

And so, my young friends, set out for the far ends of the world without fear. Unsuspected joys lie in wait for you there: landscapes you will tear yourselves away from with great regret; birds so beautiful that their mere passing will make you shudder with emotion; fruits, spices, and flowers whose perfumed memories will come back to caress you decades from now; temples carved in rock by pious, mad hands; pagodas so fine that a gust of wind might have blown them away just before your time to admire them; yes, the Taj Mahal, Machu Picchu, Angkor Wat, but also the tiny red clay mosque at desert's end where prayer rugs are unfurled on a carpet of sand as white as salt. More marvelous still will be the men and women, our brothers and sisters, sometimes of such beauty of body and heart that you would like to gaze at them until world's end, live and die in the boundless peace of their frail village.

My young friends, set out in all confidence... but not before rereading my modest bits of advice!

CHAPTER 3

Other Kinds of Travellers

Most of the information in the previous chapters applies to every-one. This chapter contains information for travellers who call for special attention.

WOMEN ALONE

Travelling alone in the Third World is always difficult for a woman, even an older one. A very few countries such as Saudi Arabia flatly refuse entry to a woman alone. Human ingenuity being what it is, however, the strictest laws haven't stopped thousands of women, even young ones, from visiting the most closed societies on earth and some even from going to Mecca.

Women alone run no greater risk of rape in the Third World than in New York, Rome, or Montréal. But men harass them in a thousand different ways and often subject them to contempt. Unfair though this is, travel would be much easier for them with a woman compan-ion or better still a male.

Women can avoid calling unwanted attention to themselves by not wearing aggressively North American styles of clothing. Where women cover their arms or legs, do likewise. As a general rule dress as modestly as possible. Avoid jeans and, above all, shorts. Wear dresses with high necklines and, if possible, long sleeves. Roomy clothes are more comfortable in the tropics and make it possible to wear a moneybelt and passport holder underneath. Don't cross your legs in public; it is frowned upon, particularly in the Orient.

Whatever she does, a woman by herself will attract the attention of the macho men of this world. Their number is legion, and they seem thickest in tourist haunts—hotels, cafés, airports, and beaches. No matter how little she calls attention to herself, in some countries a woman alone is always hounded and the object of more or less insulting remarks.

Though the risks of rape are no greater in the Third World than elsewhere, they are nonetheless there. Women faced with a potential rapist, that is, an emotionally disturbed person, are advised not to provoke him with physical or verbal threats. *Talk non-stop* to him in a soft and self-assured voice, appealing to his sense of honour, his religious convictions, to the fact that you're married, pregnant, or not well. The formula is not infallible, but it has been a great help to many women travellers.

A woman alone is easy prey for thieves. Don't carry your purse, or, if you do, keep only a little money in it, just enough to satisfy a thief.

BUSINESS PEOPLE

More and more Canadian business people realize that the future of an exporting country such as Canada must come to involve the developing countries. No one can do business, sell a product or service, unless they spend some time on the spot and try to understand schools of thought and how to unravel the bureaucratic red tape that varies from country to country.

The Canadian government has several programs designed to help exporters. Information is available at Info Export, Department of External Affairs, 125 Sussex Drive, Ottawa, Ont. K1A 0G2. Telephone: (613) 993-6435 or 1-800-267-8376. An example can be taken from recent departmental publications:

The **Program for Export Market Development** (PEMD) is a means of sharing with the business community the financial risks of entering new foreign markets. The objective of this assistance is to encourage more firms to export and thus increase the export of Canadian goods and services.

PEMD is a dynamic program that has expanded to meet the changing needs of Canadian exporters in world markets. The program currently has nine sections that support a range of marketing activities in most world markets.

From 1971 to 1983 the PEMD assisted 15,000 business concerns. During the twelve-year period the amount of assistance rose to $165 million, of which only $85 million was claimed back. About $5 billion in sales resulted from PEMD assistance.

PEMD meets up to 50% of the cost of establishing new markets. The amount of assistance is repayable if export efforts are successful.

For more information, contact your regional office of the Department of Regional Economic Expansion. (See the list in Appendix G.)

More and more Canadian embassies are sprouting up in Third World countries and will prove most helpful if advised beforehand of your visit. Among other things, they can arrange meetings with local businessmen and, if need be, with high-ranking civil servants or cabinet ministers.

One thing has always struck me as amazing about the Canadian businessmen and delegates I've met in the four corners of the world. Travelling at the expense of their company or the government, it is their duty and to their interest to devote as much time as possible to their mission. For a few dollars more they could stop over during the going or return trip and discover another country, another culture. A serious case of jet lag, which can be averted with a stopover, cuts down physical and mental stamina and affects judgement and the quality of decision-making, all of which are of prime importance in closing an important deal. It is a rare businessman or delegate who seems to understand these things.

Each autumn over a ten-year stint as Chairman of the *Association des éditeurs canadiens* I led a delegation of participating publishers at the Frankfurt Book Fair, in the Federal Republic of Germany. I was travelling, of course, at the association's expense and tried to do my job as well as possible. After each fair, however, I took at least a week's vacation at my own expense in a country previously unknown to me. On departure from Montréal I bought a ticket to the furthest destination and paid the often minimal difference. In ten years of this I managed to visit all the eastern European countries as well as Malta, Cyprus, Tunisia, and Libya.

STUDENTS

My advice to young travellers (see the previous chapter) applies as well to students off for a year in a Third World college or university.

The student will, of course, have enrolled in advance. at the institution of his or her choice and reserved a room or a bed in a student residence. He or she will also be armed with various cards that bring sharply discounted prices for transportation, lodging, and admission to museums and entertainment.

You should get proof of student status from your school or student association, which in turn will get you an International Student Identification Card (I.S.I.C.), recognized in most European, American, Asian, and some African countries.

This card can be obtained (five dollars and a photo) from one of the non-profit travel agencies specializing in youth travel, such as Travel CUTS (Canadian University Travel Services), 44 St. George St., Toronto, Ont. M5S 2E4. Telephone: (416)979-2406. There are branches of this agency in Victoria, Vancouver, Edmonton, Saskatoon, Winnipeg, Toronto, Ottawa, Montréal, and Halifax.

The card of the International Youth Hostel Association (fifteen dollars) is available to all travellers less than twenty-six years old from the Canadian Hostelling Association, 333 River Road, Ottawa, Ont. K1L 8H9. Telephone: (613)746-3844. The association also has thirteen regional offices in cities across Canada. (See the list in Appendix H.) The card gives access to over five thousand hostels in sixty countries, including twenty-five in the Third World.

Students who would like to do part of their schooling in a Third World country should consult or obtain a copy of a UNESCO publication called *Study Abroad* from Renouf Publishing Co., 61 Sparks St., Ottawa, Ont. K1P 5A6. Telephone: (613)238-8985. At a cost of $16.50, this work gives useful details about two hundred thousand scholarships and courses offered students in more than a hundred countries, including admission, language, and age requirements, lodging, and cost-of-living.

A youth travel agency can provide information on the special student fares of various air lines.

You should not leave without an insurance policy that can avert financial disaster in case of sickness, accident, or sudden need to come home. Ask the agency to tell you about their costs and advantages.

YOUTH EXCHANGES

Rotary International is the pioneer in this area. For thirty years this service club has organized exchanges and paid travel costs for young people at the high school level. These young people study in another country while their counterparts from the exchanging country do the same in Canada. They stay free in families in which the father is a Rotarian. Long limited to the industrialized countries, these exchanges now include some Third World regions. Information is available from the president of the Rotary Club in your community.

Canada World Youth. Founded in 1971, this non-governmental organization (financed in part by the Canadian International Development Agency) has already helped nearly six thousand young Canadians to discover the Third World and six thousand young people from thirty Third World countries to discover Canada.

It is a highly demanding eight-month program (half in a Third World country) for young people between the ages of seventeen and twenty, accompanied by older, salaried group leaders and coordinators. The cost for participants is nil, but they must expect to work hard, often in torrid climates and under rough conditions.

Information is available at the head office, 4824 Côte des Neiges, Montréal, Qué. H3V 1G4. Telephone: (514)342-6880 or, preferably, at the regional offices. (See the list in Appendix I.)

Commonwealth Youth Bureau. There are a great number of youth exchange programs in Commonwealth countries, most of which belong to the Third World. Information is available from the *Commonwealth Youth Program*, Commonwealth Secretariat, Marlborough House, Pall Mall, London 5WIY5HY, Great Britain. In Canada, information is available from the Department of the Secretary of State, Terrasse de la Chaudière, 15 Eddy St., Hull, Qué. K1A 0M5.

MISSIONARIES

On my first trips to the Third World (not then given that name) the only Canadian volunteers you would meet were missionaries. Oblates or White Fathers, Anglican or Presbyterian ministers, teaching brothers or nuns—you would find them in the four corners of the world. Today still there are more than 3,650 Catholic missionaries spread among ninety-eight countries in Latin America, Africa, Asia, Europe, and the South Seas. A recent development is that a hundred of these missionaries are lay people. For information contact: Missions Office, 90 Parent Ave., Ottawa, Ont. K1N 7B1. Telephone: (613)236-9641.

Canada's Protestant churches also send out several hundred

missionaries to the Third World, most of them lay people. For information contact: Canadian Council of Churches, 40 St. Clair Ave. East, Suite 201, Toronto, Ont. M4T 1M9. Telephone: (416)921-4152.

VOLUNTEERS

There are many kinds of volunteers who practise their trades or apply their special skills to necessary jobs at the express request of developing countries. Among the non-governmental organizations that see to the presence of these volunteers with the help of private donations and grants from the Canadian International Development Agency are the following:

World University Service of Canada. Founded in 1957, this organization puts the resources of Canadian universities at the disposition of Third World universities and other learning institutions while advising Canadian universities of the problems faced by developing countries. The WUSC now has about 450 Canadian volunteers, or cooperants, in a dozen countries in Africa, Asia, and Latin America. Their rôle is to provide technical assistance to countries that have requested it. (1404 Scott St., Ottawa, Ont. K1Y 2N2. Telephone: (613)725-3121)

CUSO (Canadian University Students Overseas). Founded in 1961, one contribution of this non-governmental organization to international development is to send 860 volunteers to forty Third World countries in Asia, Africa, Latin America, the Caribbean, and the South Seas. (151 Slater St., Ottawa, Ont. K1P 5H5. Telephone: (613)563-1242)

CECI (Centre canadien d'étude et de coopération internationale). Not only does this organization maintain a hundred volunteers in thirty countries year-in and year-out, it also operates a public information center on international development. In addition, the CECI organizes courses and information sessions for future volunteers and persons due for a stay in the Third World. (4821 Côte des Neiges, Montreal, Qué. H3V 1G4. Telephone: (514)738-1999)

Canadian Crossroads International, founded in 1958, sends about 160 volunteers a year to twenty-five Third World countries. (31 Madison Ave., Toronto, Ont. M5R 2S2. Telephone: (416)967-0801)

OCSD (Organisation canadienne pour la solidarité et le développement), founded in 1983, is already sending out more than two hundred volunteers, mostly to French-speaking Africa and Latin America. (180 East Dorchester, 3rd Floor, Montréal, Qué. H2X 1N6. Telephone: (514)397-1753)

Several other Canadian religious or lay organizations support Canadian volunteers in the Third World. Information is available from the Canadian Council for International Co-operation, 200 Isabella St., Ottawa, Ont. K1S 1V7. Telephone: (613)236-4547.

CIDA (The Canadian International Development Agency), under the responsibility of the Minister of External Relations, makes grants to non-governmental organizations that send volunteers to the Third World. CIDA itself, moreover, sends out nearly six hundred experts, not to mention the consultants who yearly contribute about three thousand person-years.

CIDA's cooperants and consultants are specialists and experts who meet urgent needs at the express request of Third World countries. (Place du Centre, 200 Principale St., Hull, Qué. K1A 0G4. Telephone: (819)997-5456)

OLDER PEOPLE

A healthy older person, retired and free of family cares, must not think that Florida is the only warm place still accessible. The climate is much better in most Third World countries and possible discoveries much more stimulating.

Senior citizens, of course, shouldn't ever leave on a trip or make a permanent move to a tropical country without a complete physical checkup. They should be scrupulous about observing the rules of hygiene described in Chapter 8 and purchase insurance that covers all eventualities, as advised in Chapter 7. Medical care costs a mint in the Third World, and often a sick or injured person should go to a hospital in Europe for care or better still return in all haste to Canada.

All over the Third World, old people are treated with immense respect and the greatest kindness, something that never fails to impress travellers from the West. Our friends in Africa and elsewhere, however, are appalled at the way we treat our old people. To them it seems inconceivable that we put them away in institutions for their so called "golden age" rather than keeping them home surrounded by reverent care and love until their dying breaths.

Canadian Executive Services Overseas is an organization that began in 1967 and now has about 2700 qualified free consultants,

500 working in Canada with Natives and 2200 in the Third World—businessmen, manufacturers, and technicians.

It has been my privilege to meet some of these pensioners who began a new life at the other end of the world, sometimes at a very advanced age. One of them once told me, "I've been in Zaïre for two years, and I'll stay here as long as God grants me life. I feel that I've been more useful here than during all the other years of my life as head of my own business firm."

There are a great many branches of CESO throughout Canada. Information can be had from its headquarters at 350 Sherbrooke St. West, Suite 1130, Montreal, Qué. H3A 2M8. Telephone: (514)282-0556.

DISABLED PERSONS

The major airlines are most attentive to the disabled and people on restricted diets. On twenty-four-hours advance notice, the diabetic's own menu will be on board, and a wheelchair will be waiting at the airport for a paraplegic.

For people with some types of disabilities there may be a problem with the tiny lavatories on board aircraft. They can at least ask for the seat nearest the lavatory, refrain from drinking immediately before the trip, and get a urine-inhibiting prescription for use during the flight.

The air trip then will have as few complications as possible for a disabled person, but I would advise against other kinds of transportation in the Third World except, for those who can afford it, first-class train travel or a chauffeured car.

Except for group travel with others of similar needs, the solitary disabled person will hardly be able to travel in the country's interior and have to (sadly) do without the wonderful *souks* of Fez. But I know disabled people whose courage and imagination enabled them to overcome all the barriers.

CHILDREN

Except in circumstances beyond the traveller's control, I'm absolutely unconvinced that there's any need to drag small children along on a long trip to a tropical country. They get very little out of everything of interest to adults, miss their friends and their peanut butter, and have little resistance to all the germs, viruses, and parasites that gleefully lie in wait for them. A simple scratch can take a long time to heal in the tropics and easily becomes infected because of the dust, polluted water, and flies.

In spite of this, I know parents who would never go anywhere without their children, including infants. If that's what they want, they must be sure to take all the necessary precautions.

At least two months before departure, and after the pediatrician's checkup, begin a vaccination program adapted to each child's age, as prescribed by a specialist in tropical medicine. Some vaccines have no effect on very young children, and others must be given in small doses, as for anti-malarial medication. Bring a mosquito net for each child and, naturally, follow the rules of tropical hygiene down to the letter. (See Chapter 8.)

On the subject of vaccinations, be sure that the child is vaccinated against measles, one of the chief causes of infant mortality in the Third World. The vaccine is combined with one for mumps and one for German measles.

An advantage of travelling with children is that you don't spend your time worrying about what's happening to them back home. Most hotels accept them at no charge if they share the parents' room. On air flights, children of less than twelve go at half-fare, while infants travelling on a parent's lap go at ten per cent of the adult fare.

I've often seen parents at odds with their children on long flights, and I didn't envy them. During take-off and landing give infants a bottle as the sucking might ease the pressure that causes earaches. Bring the infant's usual food; the flight attendant will be happy to warm it up. Baby food will be provided on major airlines if notice is given twenty-four hours before departure.

Pregnant women should avoid flying during the first three and last three months of pregnancy... and even during the other three except in circumstances beyond control. Most airlines require women in their eighth month of pregnancy to provide a medical certificate stating that there is no risk of premature birth. Finally, some essential vaccines cannot be taken at any time during pregnancy.

In brief, as I said above, I don't encourage parents to make young children undergo the inevitable hardships of a long trip to the tropics. I nonetheless feel the urge to tell the following story.

Twenty years have gone by, and still it seems like yesterday. It began with a French missionary, Father Paul Riou, who at the time headed a small outlying hospital on the Ile de la Tortue, in the north of Haiti. We became friends, and he talked me into going for a visit ... with wife and children, five of them, all very young. Here are extracts from an article I wrote afterwards, so that future generations might remember this incredible odyssey:

4:00 A.M. The thermometer reads 0°F as the adventure begins. In the sleeping air terminal at Dorval I take roll call and inventory. Eleven pieces of luggage, four adults, and five children: Michel, 10; Pascale, 8; Isabelle, 7; Bruno, 5; and Sophie, 20 months. In addition to mother, Thérèse, and father, Jacques, there's Lise, the mother's helper, and Uncle Jean, the brother-in-law. Just getting a tribe like this to the airport has already been an adventure. So we think, in our innocence.

The children are over excited at the thought that soon, finally, they'll be on board a plane. But flying is less exciting than they had expected.

Ten minutes on a Boeing 707 would have been enough for the whole tribe, but it takes four long hours to reach Jamaica. There is real joy at the Montego Bay airport—the embrace of a damp, perfumed tropical breeze from a bold stand of palms. The older children spring back to life and celebrate; the small ones feel that it's just a little hot.

The arrival at Port-au-Prince is at about seven or eight in the evening; none of us has a very clear sense of time anymore. We only know that we've been on the move since four in the morning.

The last leg comes the day after next. Up at 5:00 A.M. Pineapple, papayas, mangoes, bananas, and Haitian coffee.

It takes seven long hours in a tiny bus over an extremely bad road to reach Port-de-Paix. It's one in the afternoon. We bargain strenuously with a gleeful captain, bare of foot and chest. For forty dollars he'll take us to the island in his sailing ship, anchored in the middle of the bay. Thrilled, the children step immediately into a Captain Morgan adventure. A black sailor in swimming trunks takes up each member of the tribe in his arms and wades through the surf to a dinghy loaded down to the waterline that will carry us to Captain Morgan's galleon. The mainmast, made up of two tree trunks, bears a sail patched with cement bags.

"With a good wind," said Father Riou, the optimist, "you can cross to Ile de la Tortue in less than an hour." Today's wind is good for nothing. Hours pass without the island, five miles off the coast, seeming any closer. The sun beats down on our heads until the sky sends us some big helpful clouds. It's the rainy season, winter. It's 75°F. Michel and Bruno have no better sea legs than their father, and the three of us stretch ourselves out, to the audible and well-earned amusement of the women. After more than five hours we arrive at the green carapace.

As we're being transferred to dinghies, the clouds burst all at once. Night falls, and the adventure takes on a more sinister face. Our little pirates aren't so very bold now as they're picked up by wet black arms and set down in the muddy bottoms of the dinghies. But Sophie remains unruffled, and the men pass her along one to the other like a bale of white cotton. The rain becomes a torrential downpour. The dinghies scrape bottom. The last leg is by human arm. In the dark we grope for each other like blind people.

"Where's Isabelle?"

"In the water there, on a sailor's back."

"Michel?"

"My purse!"

"Mom, I lost my hat!"

Total confusion! If our children weren't exceptional, gifted, and geniuses, they would have been howling in fear. Which would have helped us find them on the beach.

In the wet, mud, and darkness, lashed by an increasingly vicious torrent of rain, we head for a cabin inhabited by some friends of Father Riou. We take roll call. All present. The loud laughter of Father Riou, soaked to the bone, brings back our good spirits. Life is good, but we're far from thinking that the worst isn't yet to come. And it isn't Father Riou's style to warn us that we're still an hour and a half's trudge away from that hospital of his, perched fifteen hundred feet high.

"My people are coming with horses ... and it looks as though the rain is letting up." Good old Father Riou! At the end of an hour, two half-drowned mules arrive in the raging storm. Fortunately only Bruno still wants to "go horseback riding." Thérèse and Sophie can have the other mule. Let's be on our way! Father

Riou lunges behind the mules, goading them with the sharp edge of his tongue. "A little jaunt," he mutters. "Less than nothing! It'll give you an appetite." The rest of the flock does its best to follow on a track with nothing to distinguish it from the surrounding landscape. The path, in fact, is a mountain stream. The slope gets increasingly steep, and we move ahead stumbling over big, rough-edged rocks, tree trunks, and moss-covered roots. The undergrowth gets thicker, and we have to wade through seething water thickened with red silt and pebbles from the high plateau.

I've been in spots like this before, but I wasn't forty then. And a small eight-year-old girl wasn't asking me at every pebble's length, "Will we be there soon?" I can't see a thing through the thick sheets of rain. "Look, Pascale, it must be behind that tree down there!" She lifts her little head and works up courage again. "Daddy, I just now understand what it means to rain so you can drink standing up."

The mules and Father Riou are long out of sight. Seven of us remain in the sorry-looking rear guard. Three times Pascale falls down in the mud. I do my best to lift her up, and once I myself take a fall, right in the middle of the stream, which rips away one of the two enormous handbags the women had put in my keeping. I let myself tumble and plunge into the water to retrieve a few headscarfs and wallets. Up then, and on we go.

Now and again I say to the people ahead (with two flashlights for the seven of us, we can't spread ourselves out), "Hold it a moment! Pascale is tired!" I was the tired one, but the head of the family has to salvage his reputation as a seasoned traveller. To keep Pascale's spirits up, I let on that we're just doing it for fun. "When you tell your friend Josée, she'll never believe it." After a moment's hesitation and two mouthfuls of rain, my daughter gives a laconic response: "If she won't believe me, then what good is it to go to so much trouble?"

After an hour and a half of steep slope, mud, water, roots, and slippery stones, we reach the top of the monstrous tortoise that will stay so long in our memories. Even as we'll remember the moving welcome of Father Riou's numerous family. We're surrounded; we're warmed; we're brought to a wing of the rectory, a crude tropical affair that has seen better days. On this evening, it's a castle.

The children are soaking and filthy as never before. "Everyone to the shower!" Bruno doesn't agree: "What? Another shower?"
(*Le Magazine Maclean*, April 1964.)

CHAPTER 4

The Passport

Foreigners you mention it to are always amazed to hear that a Canadian citizen can go to and from the United States without a passport. A Canadian need only tell the immigration officer his name, place of birth, destination, and the purpose of his trip. Rarely is he asked to show any proof of identity, not so much as a driver's licence. We have always taken this for granted, but it is an exceptional situation in today's world, as is the right to go anywhere in our country without identity papers of any kind.

Canadians can nonetheless go to Mexico and some islands in the Caribbean without a passport, although a tourist card is required. However, despite its apparent superfluity, you should *always* have your passport in a foreign country, even if it's not required. It will come in handy if you run into serious problems. The same goes for any young children in your party, even though you can simply ask the passport office to inscribe their names in your passport. If an emergency arises and the child has to return to Canada without his or her parents, a passport is essential.

OBTAINING A PASSPORT

First get a passport application form from a post office, travel agency, or regional passport office (listed in Appendix C). Fill it in with great care, since the least mistake or the least omission can delay delivery of the passport.

A section of the application has to be filled in by a guarantor, that is, someone who is Canadian and who has known you for two years and occupies a position or practises a profession specified in the application form.

Attached to your passport request must be an original (not a photocopy) of your birth certificate (or other documentary evidence of Canadian citizenship), a money order or cheque made payable to the Receiver General of Canada for twenty-one dollars, and two recent passport photos. I should add that all of this is explained quite well in the application forms.

In Canada's larger cities you can go in person to the regional passport office (listed in Appendix C).

If that isn't possible, you can send in your application to the Passport Office, Department of External Affairs, Ottawa, Ont. K1S 0G3.

If your passport photo shows you with a beard and you decide to shave it off during your trip, you run the risk of arousing the interest of immigration officials, something to be avoided at all costs. The same goes for a woman who, during her travels, makes too radical a change in her hairdo.

Photos taken by a vending machine are not acceptable since they don't come from the same negative and aren't the required size. But just about any photographer can do a passport photo, most of which are unflattering. A good photograph costs more, but at least people won't burst out laughing every time they see it.

When you receive your passport, sign it on page 3 and fill in the personal information in the designated spot on page 4. It will take about fifteen days to arrive, presuming, of course, that you gave the right answers to the several other questions on the application form... and that the post office isn't on strike. If you are pressed for time, go in person or send someone to the passport office. A passport can be obtained in three days. A person in a great hurry to leave (and very patient) can get it even quicker if he or she can show the urgency of the situation by producing, say, a letter to that effect from an employer.

Everyone but the inveterate stay-at-home should always have a valid passport on hand in case an unforeseen trip comes up. After all, this vital document costs only twenty-one dollars and is valid for five years.

Before leaving for abroad, make sure that your passport will remain valid for three months after the end of your trip. Some countries will not grant a visa unless this condition is met. And who knows whether at some point you won't decide to extend the trip?

If you already have a passport (expired or filled up) and want a new one, you must return the old one. By registered mail, it goes without saying. The cancelled passport will be returned to you automatically.

Frequent travellers are better off with a *business passport*, which has forty-eight pages rather than twenty-four and costs only two dollars more than an ordinary passport. Considering that a visa takes up an entire page, and that the stamping frenzy of Third World immigration officials will waste another page or more in each country, the twenty pages of the passport reserved for visas might well be used up before its expiry date.

COUNTRIES IN CONFLICT

Before setting out on a trip with a well-used passport, be sure that this or that old visa won't prevent you from getting another because of ideological or political conflicts between the two countries. A South African visa will make it difficult if not impossible to get a visa for many Third World countries that boycott that last stronghold of apartheid and racism. With a visa for Israel stamped in, don't dream of going to most Arab League states, even if you have valid visas. The Kuwaiti visa, for example, says it in black and white: "This visa is considered void if bearer obtained an Israeli visa thereafter." (On request, however, embassies of Israel issue visas on sheets not attached to the passport.) There was a long period when a visa for Taiwan would exclude you from China. This is no longer the case, but I myself would avoid visiting China with a passport showing that I had gone to Taiwan or intended to go there. Which puts me in mind of a story I have to pass on....

In September 1960, five Canadians were invited by the government of China to visit that country, which to all practical purposes had been closed to visitors from the West since Mao's victory over the Kuomintang. The five privileged persons were all from Quebec: Micheline Legendre, Madeleine Parent, Denis Lazure, Pierre Elliott Trudeau, and Jacques Hébert.

At the time the People's Republic of China had not yet been recognized by Canada and would not be for another ten years, when one of the visitors had become head of the Canadian government. To get a Chinese visa you had to go through a country that maintained diplomatic relations with Peking. We were assigned to Great Britain.

Here is the incident of the visas as told by two of the participants:

London. Tuesday, 13 September 1960

Montreal to London by jet. A dull passage: we didn't even get to use the life-rafts. And Hébert wasted five dollars on a flight-insurance premium.

Why London? Because no country in all the Americas recognizes Communist China, except (just lately) Cuba. A letter from Mr. Chu Tu-nan, president of the Chinese People's Association for Cultural Relations with Foreign Countries, had notified us that our Chinese visas would be granted to us in London.

About five o'clock in the afternoon, then, we present ourselves at the office of the Chinese chargé d'affaires for this little formality. A young Chinese, all smiles and unction, admits us to the old house at 49 Portland Place. "Mr. Lin is waiting for you," he says.

We, as it turns out, wait for Mr. Lin—in a vast drawing-room that has known better days. Old furniture upholstered in green velvet, a large worn carpet: they haven't had occasion to throw a party hereabouts since the good old days of Chiang Kai-shek.

Mr. Lin is late. The furniture is mildewing, the carpet is fraying—along with our patience. "There's probably a plane leaving for Peking this very evening..."

We are exchanging criticisms on the immense Mao Tse-tung in technicolor enthroned above the fireplace, when a slender personage wearing a smile too big for him enters discreetly, on tiptoe: Lin himself!

Delighted to see us, of course. He runs from one to another, distributing friendly words, Chinese cigarettes, matches. We exchange commonplaces with the greatest possible conviction.

"You have been to China before?"

"No," says Hébert. "Hong Kong, Macao—they're not really China."

But Trudeau went to China in 1949.

"*Really?*" says Mr. Lin with lively interest.

"From Hong Kong I slipped into the territory still held by the Kuomintang. It was in a state of anarchy. I got myself as far as Shanghai while the Red Army was on the other side of the Yangtze. I would have liked to stay and watch the capture of the city, but a truce was proclaimed. It was not to last long, however; soon after I left, the Red Army entered Shanghai.''

"How amazing," says Mr. Lin, delighted. "*I* was in the Red Army at that time—in the very contingent that took Shanghai.''

"We might have met in 1949!''

The ice is broken. Mr. Lin sends for tea, which he pours himself, remarking that it's certainly a small world. The excellent jasmine tea leads to confidences. We learn that Mr. Lin has been in London for four years, that he studied English in Amsterdam—a lot of instructive facts like that. Not until the third cup do we get to the point of this friendly tea-party: the visas, and the tickets for China.

Mr. Lin hands out the visa application forms. The usual questions, plus two that we have also been asked in Spain, Argentina, and a few Arab countries: "Religion? Political party?" To the second question we long to answer "Social Credit," just to see the reaction in Peking.

Mr. Lin takes the forms and passports. "I'll be right back. Time to stamp the visas.''

On the table, near the teapot, are tickets from London to Peking. Bits of paper that will allow us to cross half the world and see China at last.

Mr. Lin is taking his time in coming back. Let's just glance at these tickets: "Departure 14 September, 0830 hours." Hell! that's tomorrow morning.

What *is* Mr. Lin doing? These Chinese! Still Orientals after all, never in a hurry, as we have always been taught.

Mao Tse-tung smiles down from his splendid gilt frame.

Mr. Lin at last! He is smiling too. He has the passports. His smile seems rather forced.

"There is a small difficulty for three of you," he says carefully, with the air of announcing to a group of invalids that they have small and unimportant cancers.

Mr. Lin takes his courage in both hands. "Look. In Miss Legendre's and Mr. Hébert's passports there is a note from the Canadian Department of External Affairs that—that—"

He says no more, but we understand. In recent years, when the Department issues a passport, it sticks a leaflet on the last page full of careful advice to Canadian citizens travelling to Communist countries. In brief, these travellers are required, before departure, to notify the Canadian government of their plans and to indicate the probable length and the purpose of their journey—all of which we had done. Then, on arrival in a Communist country, they are required to report to the nearest Canadian or United Kingdom diplomatic or consular officer.

Why not? However, that's not what is bothering Mr. Lin. The thing is that the Department of External Affairs of Canada has committed a terrible gaffe in the eyes of a Chinese official by using the term "Mainland China." The implication is that there is another China, an island one, that we call Formosa and the Chinese call Taiwan.

Micheline Legendre and Jacques Hébert suggest a way out: that Mr. Lin should simply tear the questionable leaflet out of the passport, especially as it is held only by a mere spot of gum. Mr. Lin's smile brightens: he must have foreseen this step, since the Chinese visas are already in the passports—except Trudeau's. "The difficulty is more serious in Mr. Trudeau's case," says Mr. Lin, no longer smiling. "A little more tea?"

No, thank you. Three cups are quite enough.

There is drama in the air. "A more serious difficulty?" inquires Trudeau (who already realizes the trouble).

"Yes. There is a Taiwan visa in your passport."

"That's true. I went to Taiwan two years ago."

"Hmm. What did you go to Taiwan to do?"

"I was travelling in that part of the world. Actually, I wanted to go to China, but your government hadn't given me permission. So I visited Japan, the Philippines—and Taiwan as it happened to be on my way. I had no sympathy for Chiang Kai-shek, but that was no reason for avoiding Taiwan."

"I regret to tell you that the policy of my government is explicit on this point: we do not give a visa to anyone who has been to Taiwan."

"But your government invited me to visit China."

"Did my government know that you had been to Taiwan?"

"I don't suppose so. But what does it matter? I could have got a new passport before I left, and you wouldn't have known anything about my earlier travels."

"True. But I do know now, and the regulation—"

"I could explain the matter to the Canadian High Commissioner's office here and get a completely new passport—possibly even today."

"I am heartbroken," says Mr. Lin, really looking heartbroken. "But my duty requires me to seek advice from Peking."

We parley for over an hour, each of us invoking new arguments to convince Mr. Lin that Trudeau is neither an agent of American imperialism nor an admirer of Chiang Kai-shek.

"Terribly sorry," repeats Mr. Lin, "but I have to ask for authority from Peking before I give you a visa."

There is no more point in insisting.

"In my telegram, however, I shall take your arguments into account. I will even add a word of recommendation."

"How soon will you have an answer?"

"Let us have at least two or three days," say Mr. Lin, glancing at the five tickets spread out on the table like a mandarin's fan. The icy wind that was tempered just now by a little warm tea makes its way back into the great drawing-room. "I could make a suggestion—" begins Mr. Lin cautiously. He hesitates. "A little more tea?"

No, really.

"Well. I suggest that Mr. Trudeau should wait for the answer from Peking and that the others should leave tomorrow morning as planned."

"And if the answer is negative?" asks Hébert.

"You will be in Peking in two days. There you will be able to put Mr. Trudeau's case."

We don't agree. The Chinese government ought to have informed itself sooner on the subject of Trudeau. "They invited him; let them accept him, Taiwan visa or no Taiwan visa," says Micheline Legendre categorically.

We decide to abandon the scheduled take-off and wait for the answer from Peking. In Montreal we had already elected Trudeau group leader—taking advantage of a meeting he wasn't at. The scene is becoming worthy of Corneille: "We shall go with the Leader or we won't go at all!"

Mr. Lin closes the fan and puts the five airline tickets back in his pocket. He seems annoyed with us, and we feel he has just learned something of the spirit of solidarity of the capitalists of the province of Quebec.

We leave him and go into the nearest pub; after all that tea a beer would be welcome.

Trudeau pays for the round: that'll teach him to go to Taiwan.

Wednesday, 14 September

London is a good town and Alec Guinness a wonderful actor; we see *Ross*, a play of Terence Rattigan's on the life of Lawrence of Arabia.

In the *Punch* that comes out today, a very amusing article about a traveller who has provided himself with two passports so as to go to China after visiting Taiwan. We thrust this timely article under Trudeau's nose; it begins, "A touch of schizophrenia is useful if you want to visit the two Chinas, Nationalist and Communist..."

No news from Mr. Lin.

Thursday, 15 September

A meeting in Trudeau's room to decide whether we will go to Brecht's *The Life of Galileo* or Chekhov's *The Seagull*. We debate for a good while before the Leader announces casually, "Mr. Lin phoned—"

"Ah!"

"Peking has answered."

"Ah!"

"I will have my visa in three hours."

Three hours. Mr. Lin is radiant. There is tea, and above all a magnificent album of photographs of China that he wants to show us. He turns the pages slowly, lovingly, as if it were a family album. Look, that's his grandmother! No, it's Madame Sun Yat-sen.

The flight is tomorrow night. We invite Mr. Lin to go out to dinner with us. We shake hands.

The war will not take place; we have settled all that, we and Mr. Lin.

(Jacques Hébert and Pierre Elliott Trudeau, *Two Innocents in Red China* [Toronto: Oxford University Press, 1968] pp. 6–11)

We had just squeaked by!

Sad to say, the major conflicts grinding on for decades are joined by new ones that spring up continually between hitherto friendly states. Overnight they become fierce enemies, breaking off relations and closing frontiers if they don't go openly to war. Examples are Ethiopia and Somalia, Iraq and Iran, Cambodia and Viet Nam, and Honduras and Nicaragua. Most of the close to a hundred and fifty wars since the end of World War II have been in the Third World.

Your preparations for a trip should include research in depth on all these conflicts so that, valid visa in hand or not, you won't try to cross a border where you will be turned back because conflict has suddenly arisen. Oddly enough, even when land borders are closed you can sometimes go from one country to the other through their international airports. If there's any doubt, check before departure with, in Canada, the Department of External Affairs (125 Sussex Dr., Ottawa, Ont. K1A 0G2) or abroad with a Canadian embassy. (See Appendix B for a list of Canadian diplomatic posts in Third World countries.) Also check with the embassies or consulates of Third World countries where the possibility of conflict is a concern. (Representatives of Third World countries in Canada are listed in Appendix A.)

LOSS OF PASSPORT

Inscribed in fine script on the inside cover of the passport is a formula that recalls the credentials borne with such care by travellers in bygone times; "The Secretary of State for External Affairs requests in the name of Her Majesty the Queen all those it may concern to allow the bearer to pass freely without let or hindrance and to afford the bearer such assistance and protection as may be necessary."

Soon afterwards comes the less lyrical statement that "this passport is the property of the Government of Canada" and that it "should be safeguarded in every way."

This is an understatement. While you are abroad, the passport is the basic condition of freedom. Without it you can no longer move around, check in at a hotel, cash a traveller's cheque, or leave a country. In brief, anyone who loses a passport or has it stolen in some far-off country is in a tight spot. It's a major disaster that can cause endless time lost and compromise a trip.

If you happen to be in a country with a Canadian embassy, you will be able to recoup your loss, perhaps within a few days. You will have to fill out the form, provide three photos, and pay the usual fee. It will save a great deal of time if you have proof of Canadian citizenship, the best being an original of your birth certificate, which is why I advise you always to take it along on a trip.

In the 1950s it was my baptismal certificate from the fine Montréal parish of St. Louis de France that enabled me to prove to an Egyptian immigration official that I wasn't Jewish. Without it I would have been held up at the Egyptian-Sudanese border on the Upper Nile.

Let us now imagine the worst case. You find yourself without a passport in a little African village at the end of the world. The country has no Canadian embassy, and so you call on the good offices of the British embassy. Again, you have to reach them, which can be a little complicated if the village has no telephone or telegraph and the chief of police won't let you go to the capital without a passport.

For all practical purposes you will be at the mercy of the chief of police, who could be understanding or, on the contrary, could decide you are an enemy spy. In brief, days or weeks could be lost before you get a new passport. It might make a good story back home, but it's never any fun to live through.

I'll come back in Chapter 7 to safeguards against the loss or theft of a passport. For now you should know that it's a misfortune that each year hits nearly ten thousand Canadians, our country's passport being in great demand and worth up to several hundred dollars on the black market.

Small practical tip: before leaving Canada, write the following information on the back of a business card or on a light, sturdy piece of cardboard:

- ☐ passport number.
- ☐ date of issue.
- ☐ expiry date.
- ☐ place of issue.
- ☐ issuing authority.

Always keep this card within easy reach. When you fill out an immigration form at a crowded counter in a busy airport, it will save you from having to handle the passport itself.

In cases of passport loss or theft, these few bits of information will be an invaluable help to the police and the Canadian embassy, to both of whom you are obliged to give immediate notice, although it would be better still to show them a photocopy of pages 2 and 3 of the passport that you were wise enough to carry in your travel bag.

Finally, this little card will enable you to fill in the inevitable hotel forms and sometimes even to cash traveller's cheques without taking your passport out of its hiding place.

Of course, there are people with good memories . . . .

CHAPTER 5

Visas, Immigration, and Customs

Passports have been around from time immemorial. Visas, on the other hand, are a modern invention, a pure emanation of our own bureaucracy-ridden, red-tape-bound, espionage-obsessed times.

In the past travellers with passports moved freely from one country to another. Times have indeed changed. The height of absurdity was reached after World War II, when most countries in the world required visas for all foreign visitors. Since then, and mostly to boost the tourist trade, a number of countries have let the requirement drop for nationals of friendly countries.

A Canadian today does not need a visa to enter many countries in Europe, several in the Caribbean, and most Commonwealth countries.

The Commonwealth connection has many advantages for Canada, one of them being that Canadians do not need a visa to travel to forty Commonwealth countries in Africa, Asia, the South Seas, and even America.

Once your itinerary is drawn up, however, you still have to check with the embassies (called High Commissions in the case of Commonwealth countries) or consulates. Even a Commonwealth country can, for reasons of its own, decide to require Canadian citizens to obtain a visa, as Australia did in 1975. This is also the case with the following countries: Ghana, Guyana, India, Maldive Islands, Nauru, Nigeria, Papua New Guinea, Sierra Leone, and Tonga.

I never cease to admire the obliging nature of Third World countries that we can still enter without visas even though we require one from their nationals on the pretext of curbing illegal immigration.

It's important to get all the needed visas for a trip as long as possible before departure. A great many complications can arise: the return of an improperly completed visa application, the loss of a visa-stamped passport in the mail, even a mail strike. And sometimes the nearest appropriate embassy is in New York. (See Appendix A for a complete list of Third World diplomatic representatives in Canada.)

Start applying for your visas a month or two before departure, particularly if you intend to visit countries with harder-to-get visas such as Nigeria, Libya, Iraq, Saudi Arabia, Yemen, and others. But beware of applying too soon; some visas are valid for only one or two months after date of issue.

There is no need for people vacationing in Hawaii or Martinique to worry, since neither France nor the United States requires visas from Canadians. Those going to Mexico to get a tan under the Puerto Vallarta sun need only a free tourist card that is handed out by the travel agency along with the air tickets, or by the Mexican embassy, consulates, or tourist bureaus in Canada. The same, with minor variations, applies for travel to several other countries, including the Dominican Republic.

The filled-in tourist card is handed over to the immigration official at the airport or border crossing. He will give you back a duly stamped copy, which should be guarded carefully since it must be turned in on departure.

Travel agencies will often obtain visas for their clients. That's one way of doing it, if there will be only one or two easily obtained visas, but I wouldn't leave it to an agency if the itinerary is at all complicated.

EXAMPLE OF A COMPLICATED ITINERARY

Let's imagine a six-week itinerary involving travel in the following countries: Morocco, Libya, Sudan, South Yemen, Sri Lanka, and the Philippines.

Morocco: No visa required for Canadians travelling as tourists.

Libya: Visa required. No embassy in Ottawa, the nearest being in New York. The identification information in the passport itself must be in Arabic. At the passport office in Ottawa (and in certain Canadian embassies) there are stamps that carry an Arabic version of all the Canadian passport's essential English and French texts. Also required are several filled-in copies of the application form, three photos, proof of possession of an ongoing air ticket, and proof that the traveller does not already have a visa for Israel or South

Africa. Even with a visa, you can't enter Libya without five hundred dollars (U.S.) in your possession.

Sudan: Visa required. It must be requested from the embassy in New York, the one in Ottawa having shut down in 1983. Provide three photos and fill in an application form in triplicate, including a section to be filled in by a guarantor who agrees to provide the funds necessary to repatriate the visa-holder in case the latter comes to be stranded and penniless in Sudan. It takes at least fifteen days before delivery of the visa-stamped passport, since Sudan requires the embassy to telex the application to Khartoum. Cost of visa: $14.50.

South Yemen: Visa required. No embassy in Canada. The nearest is in New York because the United Nations is there. Write a letter to the embassy giving the reasons for the visit and requesting application forms for a visa. Fill the forms out and return them by registered mail along with the passport, requisite photos, and a bank money order in *American* dollars.

Having said this, I will add that *never* have I sent my passport anywhere by mail, registered or otherwise. It's too much of a risk, especially when the departure date is fast approaching. If you have good reason to go to South Yemen (a fascinating place!) and the means, you should take the trouble to go to New York or send someone in your stead, or at least use a reliable courier service.

Sri Lanka: No visa required. Hurrah for the Commonwealth!

Philippines: This non-Commonwealth country requires no visas from several friendly countries, including Canada.

There you have it, a randomly selected sample. I could have devised an even more complicated itinerary, with a side trip to Israel, for example, or suggested an extraordinary round-the-world trip that wouldn't require *any* visas.

KINDS OF VISAS

A *transit visa*, usually the easiest to obtain, is needed by a traveller who has to land briefly in a country before catching the next flight out. Sometimes a traveller who wishes to spend a few days in a country is considered to be in transit, even for as long as fifteen days if he has a confirmed flight to another country. But each case has to be checked, the main feature of these regulations being that they change as often as possible and vary from one country to the next.

In a trip involving stops in many countries, you may have to pass several times through the same capital. In West Africa, Dakar is such a transfer point, as is Jeddah in the Mideast and Singapore in Southeast Asia. Ask then for a visa bearing the notation "Multiple Entry." If you are turned down, get the visas necessary as you go. Singapore, by the way, is a Commonwealth member, and you can stop by there as often as you like without a visa.

A *tourist visa* is valid for a period of one to three months or, sometimes, for the exact number of days or weeks specified in the application. It is wise to suggest a longer stay than is intended. Unforeseen events can easily happen, the most common being the missing of a flight because of the practice of overbooking. A visa for two months costs the same as one for three weeks, and an expired visa can bring on serious trouble.

A *business visa* is required for people who wish to close deals, convert large sums of money, or conduct other business.

A *residence visa or permit* is needed by a volunteer leaving for two years in Guinea-Bissau, an engineer going to live for a year in Niger or Indonesia to oversee construction of a bridge, and by a pensioner who decides to live out his days in Fiji or the Comoro Islands.

These last would be well advised not to sell their houses or cars before having settled the formalities with the immigration authorities in the land of their dreams. It's a long and complicated process. Third World countries are most hospitable but also too poor to do without guarantees when they take in long-term visitors who might prove unable to look after their own subsistence needs or even pay for a return ticket. (The one-way airfare from Fiji to Toronto is $1622.) Prospective residents are sometimes asked to provide proof of sufficient income.

A word to the wise: go as a tourist to the island in question for a few months, long enough to discover if you want to stay there forever; consult with local authorities; and find out firsthand about the experiences of other foreign residents.

VISA APPLICATION FORMS

These vary considerably from one country to another. Some are admirably simple, while others are so complicated that you would think they were designed to discourage any visitor still the least bit hesitant.

Answer *all* the questions, but not at any greater length than requested. Tourism is the most acceptable reason for a visit. If you have a vague intention of establishing a business contact, it may not be essential to point it out. In the case of a more or less official mission, you must do so.

You are always asked to name your occupation. Journalists, film-makers, writers, military people, and professors of Marxist philoso-phy arouse more worries than nurses, students, accountants, and mathematics teachers, but don't ever, ever say that you have no occupation!

If you give an affirmative answer to the question, "Do you intend to work during your stay in the country?" you are sure never to get a tourist visa, in some cases not even years later. You have to get a *work permit*, always a difficult thing, and a letter from your prospec-tive employer guaranteeing your job, before you can take a job in a foreign country. You can appreciate that developing countries bur-dened with unemployment rates that make ours seem like a laughing matter would not be eagerly forthcoming with work permits.

Finally, embassies or consulates of many Third World countries won't grant a visa before seeing your airline ticket to make sure that it includes a return to Canada or, at the very least, passage onwards to another country for which you have a visa.

MISCELLANEOUS TIPS

Unfortunately it isn't always possible to have all the necessary visas before leaving on a long trip, and, sadder still, you sometimes have to make sudden changes in itinerary while under way.

Get any missing visa in the *first* country in which there's an embassy or consulate. Don't hold off until you come to an adjoining country; if for some reason you run into problems at the embassy, you won't be able to try your luck in the next country. Consult with the Canadian embassy, which can give you good advice and perhaps intervene on your behalf. And watch out for tiny countries that can't afford to have more than three or four embassies (Djibouti, for example), generally located in neighbouring countries. They always have an embassy in New York since they have to vote in the General Assembly of the United Nations. (Djibouti's vote counts for as much as India's or Brazil's.)

Carry a good dozen passport photos with the documents in your travel bag. You will be asked for two or three for each visa, and the others will come in handy for exit visas or licences to take photographs, which are required in Somalia and other countries.

IMMIGRATION

While a very few countries issue visas at no cost, most charge between three and fifteen dollars. It's a bargain, however you look at it. It should surely impress the immigration official, this green-, pink- or blue-stamped document covered with foreign-language notations, seals, signatures, and sometimes magnificent stamps. He'll read it with the seriousness it deserves, giving you a quick professional once over between each line. Then there's a sudden burst of rapid-fire questions: "What brings you to Burma?" "You say you're an administrator...administrator of what, exactly?" "What business did you have in Qatar?"

Don't lose your cool. Answer the questions calmly, *not ever hesitating*. Hesitation is fatal! Above all, don't try to be funny.

Finally the immigration man grabs his rubber stamp and, *whomp!* he's given you the right to enter the country.

CUSTOMS

This leaves the customs: "Do you have anything to declare?" Don't *ever* say no. Customs men get mad when they hear that answer. They know very well that you have *something* to declare. It's up to them to decide what is going to get in duty-free.

Start with the premise that the following two items are absolutely forbidden: weapons and drugs. A whole lot of other things are considered just as dangerous, hence inadmissible: alcohol in some Muslim countries (notably Libya and Saudi Arabia); books and magazines deemed pornographic, including the latest issue of *Playboy* (in, for example, Malaysia); pets (even stuffed ones); food products; and plants.

"Do you have anything to declare?"

Answer frankly: "Yes...some souvenirs...handicrafts...personal items...a carton of cigarettes..." and, if it's legal, "...a bottle of whiskey, of course."

There's now a fifty-fifty chance that you will hear the liberating words, "Okay. Move on!"

Otherwise you will be more or less briskly told, "Open that

suitcase!'' Or nothing will be said but a finger will be pointed at your travel bag. Banish all thoughts of annoyance. After all, what could be more normal? Customs people are made for just that, rummaging through suitcases.

Open the designated piece of luggage yourself, and if it is full of zippered compartments, unzipper them without fuss. Don't move the contents around; leave that to the customs man. He's used to it; he *likes* doing it, and any help on your part would be suspect. If he messes up your neat arrangement, too bad! You will be emptying the suitcase at the hotel in an hour's time anyway.

The customs man is satisfied. You are not carrying a revolver, diamonds, opium, or *Playboy*. With his stub of chalk he scribbles a cabalistic sign that will bring you through the last stage: a doorway guarded by soldiers, often dressed in fatigues and armed with tommy guns.

I haven't brought up the declaration of currency required in some countries. This will be discussed in Chapter 7, in which there is a great deal about money.

A SLICE OF LIFE

In poorer countries it can happen that customs officials, surely underpaid, make things hard for you in an attempt to squeeze out a little *baksheesh*. Many travellers don't resist this kind of pressure very well, but they take the risk of finding themselves in deeper trouble ''for trying to corrupt a public servant.''

I myself have crossed hundreds of borders without any problem, and I've resisted to the end attempts to wring money out of me.

Once only have I left a few dollars for an immigration official, but the situation was a little ambiguous and I absolutely had to make a connecting flight. Here's an extract from my travel diary, Christmas Eve, 1982:

> I'm in transit at Dakar airport. A customs official asks me to go with him to an enclosed booth where, unwitnessed, he questions me about the amount of money on my person. My five hundred French francs, in particular, are counted and counted again. He looks put out. With extreme tact, I tell him that I have a perfect right to carry these French francs in addition to my American dollars. Again he counts them. ''Fine. I won't cause you any

problems, but surely it's worth a bottle of whiskey." I act innocent: "I don't have any whiskey," which is the unvarnished truth. Palpably disappointed, the customs man then gives me back the five hundred francs. I've won. "Ah!" he finally exclaims, "Your dollars are in travellers' cheques. That changes everything. I thought you had mostly bills. Now everything is in order. I had to check." And finally we leave the booth.

Another customs man, this one armed with a big rubber stamp, examines my passport after exchanging a glance with his colleague. His manner too is somewhat hesitant. My flight for Bamako leaves in a few minutes. He scrutinizes every page, and it's my bad luck to have a special forty-eight-page passport jammed full of interesting visas. Reading all the while, he opens a sort of folder in which I see about ten thousand CFA franc notes. He smiles. "You contribute to the customs charities?" A quick calculation tells me that a thousand CFA francs comes to $3.75. For a moment I think of telling him, "I already give to United Way." But then, what the heck! it's the holiday season, and I convince myself that the customs charities are surely worthwhile.

Once doesn't mean a habit.

Third World immigration officials and embassy and consular people can be unpleasant in the extreme to anyone who dares ask for a visa. In all cases we should be tolerant. Their teachers in these matters were European, and sometimes the students outdo their instructors. And remember that we have no more right to enter another country than we do to enter someone else's house. If it isn't a right, then it's a privilege. When it is granted, let's show both pleasure and deep gratitude.

ABOUT AN AFGHAN VISA

I'll tell about another incident that happened to me that can serve as an illustration of the advice given in this chapter. I was still an innocent in 1951 when I went around the world by jeep with a friend, Dr. Jean Phaneuf. We had gotten as far as India without a visa for its near neighbour, Afghanistan. New Delhi was the last capital city on our itinerary before the Afghan border. Twenty years afterwards I told this story in a book called *Blablabla du bout du monde*. I'm a little reluctant to quote myself for a rather odd reason. I had decided to write this work in the telegraphic style without which, according to Louis-Ferdinand Céline, there was no further hope for literature. Readers averse to the least whiff of Céline-isms can skip to the next chapter.

"You'll never get a visa for Afghanistan." So the spoilsports tell you, serious, journalists and all, still, know nothing, never rubbed up against Afghanistan, don't want to go there, don't want you to go, not worth it as they tell you again and who blah-blah-blah when you saw stinking, dirty poor in Calcutta, even Bombay, Madras if you want another, Benares if that's your pleasure, Kabul's old hat, don't take the trouble for nothing either, poor are poor, no poorer because Afghans, maybe less, on big wild high plateaus, you won't get a visa, sworn, nothing country, only one in world without train station or airport right now in 1951, when they can go to the moon, finally, it won't be long, believe us, you don't go to Afghanistan.

Remember, they said: no road, no gas, no garage, you'll leave your hide there, tacked on your jeep. And where do you expect to get this visa? You hear anywhere in world where there's Afghan consul? Monacan consuls, there's a real deluge of them, not to speak of Nicaraguan, there are armies of them in all capitals, nice black Chevrolets at the door, but a sweet little Afghan consul, you've ever heard of it, have you? No consul, no visa.

We ferreted out information everywhere, capitals, metropolises, seaports, holy cities; no Afghan consulate, much less embassy, so you wonder if there really is an Afghanistan somewhere, if the U.S.S.R. didn't gobble it up on the sly one day when the news agencies, newspapers, and radio stations were busy somewhere else, distracted to death by a really big story, birth of the Dionne quintuplets, Edward VIII's abdication, something colossal, really super-important, enough to keep a whole galaxy busy.

By the good Lord above, one day in New Delhi—it was high time, the Khyber Pass is next door, at the end of the street—we unearthed a brave little embassy behind a wall of mango trees, with a brave, oily little French-speaking ambassador, welcoming at first, sit down, smokes Turkish cigarettes stuck in silver cigarette-holder, slim, cold, dagger-like.

Our trip around the world is in this man's hands. If he says now, it's screwed up, go back to Karachi, find a freighter, slink back home with tail between legs. No room for mistakes, play it cautiously, he's suspicious, man of the world, bad sort. Above all no mention of visa the first time, risky madness, he says no and it's calamity, never will go back on no, not the way at his firm, some intelligent gossip, feel the man out, see it coming.

"So you're interested in Afghanistan?"

Studied briefly in Paris, knows London, even visited New York, Sorbonne, London School of Economics, Waldorf-Astoria: they take any old Afghan herdsman and make a gentleman out of him. You see him from here to Fouquet's terrace, His Excellency of the long cigarette-holder, looking good, talking Afghan literature to the little darlings, as if that's all every Afghan did, not scrape wooden plough over dry earth, not shiver through whole winter raising skinny sheep in snow, come back for details, lovely ladies. Not worried, the Afghan, no chance that they'll go and check on the spot between two lemon Perriers what it's like, in the dried mud huts, that "blue evening that falls like a velvet mantle on shivering Kabul," real nitwit poetry. "The beauties of Kandahar sing of their love in black tents poised like eagles in the valley," and so what else is new? Keep on talking, no one will ask you for a Champs-Elysées visa!

Even so, have to let understand, all discretion, that we dream vaguely of Afghanistan, little faraway dream, not to worry, still very vague, one day maybe, in five years, in ten years... Shit! We'd like to leave tomorrow. His Excellency sighs in relief, will be long gone in ten years, thousands of miles from wretched New Delhi, ambassador to Paris, no less, return to Fouquet's, literature, lovely darlings, couldn't care less about our microbes of dreams, that will pass like a bout of flu, fine, change the subject, it's turning sour, "no great cities like New Delhi, Paris, Ottawa," pounce on Ottawa, joke a little about it, not too much, all the same, bars closed on Sunday, oof! and Kabul then! lay it on thick for the Excellency, like it same as everyone, carry on, use third person....

"We're interested in Afghan literature, sixteenth century of course. Could Your Excellency help us find the excellent French-language magazine published in Kabul?"

Somewhat thunderstruck, the Excellency. We were ashamed,

especially about sixteenth century, bluff like that not fair, playing with dynamite, but we made a point, well worth the two hours at the New Delhi library, unearthed allusion to sixteenth, end of fine century in which poet saw blue mantle fall on snowy Kabul and blah-blah-blah, it could be the year Jacques Cartier came to the Gaspé to found the *Maison du pêcheur*.

"French culture," proclaims little ambassador, big voice, "is the finest legacy bequeathed to us by the West. Moreover, you Canadians who, that...." Forgot rest, just as well.

We're gagging on temptation to talk visas, better to leave while we're friends, give nothing away, say good-bye. An incredible story for a simple little visa, have to know horrors of visa turned down, irretrievable, real misery, consuls, ambassadors, distrustful little souls, have to know them....We then made a strange commotion in New Delhi, we knew a member of Nehru's cabinet through Capuchin Bishop, any port in a storm, get ourselves invited to the President of India's garden party, do without nothing, Rajendra Prasad, must be dead now, seems that the whole diplomatic corps will be there. Can't help but be there, ambassadors on down, cigarette-holder wouldn't miss it for the world. Naturally the Canadian side would be a help for once. Not a trace of our High Commissioner in presidential gardens, not a ghost of the Québec delegate, have to fall back on the High Commissioner of Great Britain, godsend, jolly old fellow, feels all paternal, calls us "my boys," around the world by jeep moves him, frightful, would do the same if he were young. Afghanistan? But you'll get them, all your visas, nicely phlegmatic, doesn't have a care in the world, even seems that the ambassador is an "old chap," they play cricket together, feed us any more and we'll burst. Big six-foot-six Englishman leads us to tiny Afghan who's downing one whiskey-and-soda after another, may Allah forgive him, in fine fettle, the Excellency, drooping cigarette-holder almost flute, expounds in all languages, inclined to give Afghan visas to all president's guests, come by tomorrow at ten, here's to Great Britain! France! Canada! Two more whiskeys and will shout, *"Vive le Québec Libre!"*

Ten o'clock next day. Hung over Afghan, not happy about day before, regrets all visas, that's sure, can only wait and see... gives us sickly spiel on the incredible Afghan winter, here in New

Delhi this heat, you forget that it's winter in the far-off plateaus there, most frightful, snow-blocked passes, impassable roads, avalanches, storms, snow squalls, ice everywhere, it makes him shiver, the nitwit, advises us to come back in spring. The Abominable Snowman falls flat! *Québécois* raised on an iceberg, we'll tell you about winter, Excellency, back home, your little snow squalls, we call them July, don't come in January, you'll turn into a chunk of ice when you step off the plane, to a *Québécois* your country is pure Florida, unvarnished Africa, don't worry, our ancestors all *coureurs de bois*, Excellency, Radisson my uncle, Eskimo blood on mother's side, half blood, half ice, Jeep all fitted up for North Pole, don't worry!

Didn't expect such an avalanche, the Excellency, embarrassed, sly, unhappy. Shouldn't have.

"May I see your passports?"

Leafs through, leafs through, begins again, compassionate, face lights up, glows, the cow!

"But you don't have a visa for Iran! I can't give you our visa before you have one for Iran. That's the rule."

Inning lost, don't press. And the Iranians, if they're as troublesome, complicated? Things going badly in that direction, a tinderbox among the oilwells.

At the Iranian consulate: "Yes, fine, but you have to get an Iraqi visa so that you can continue your trip westwards. Get an Iraqi visa first."

At the Iraqi consulate: "First get your Jordanian visa." And, of course, at the Jordanian consulate....

Receptions, cocktail parties, nice kowtowing, high-voltage diplomacy, it took ten terrible days of strenuous battle to satisfy Jordan, Iraq, and Iran. That left the other one....

Had forgotten all about it, the Excellency. Having us reapply so soon depressed him to death. Funny kind of mules, these Eskimos!

"Good. It looks as though it'll be all right. But I need a minimum of three photos each."

Photo-wise, we're ready, would like to see a greedy consul ask for forty dozen of them, we're beginning to know their tricks, are larded over with a thick, greasy smear of various documents, bundles of baptismal papers, vaccination certificates for every disease, bubonic plague, Indian cholera, trachoma, yellow fever, official letters coming out of our ears, Camillien Houde gold-engraved with *Concordia Salus*, R.C.M.P. all in English, Provincial Police, Chamber of Commerce, Union des Latins d'Amérique, Saint-Jean-Baptiste Society, good people all of them, gave us letters by the wagonload. Yes, we were coddled little heroes of *Le Devoir*, whole cloisters of sisters prayed for us, Richelieu Clubs put us on their programs eighteen months in advance, beautiful teenagers at the Outremont convent went to sleep at night dreaming of us, but all this glory hadn't reached the Afghan ambassador, fussy eater when faced with luscious documents, nonetheless tears away two letters and three certificates along with photos. Looks horribly put out, almost want to tell him there's a photo missing, just to be nice. You'd think he was going to apply his stamp.... You'd think.

"You don't mean it. Now I have to send your request to Kabul, to the Minister of Foreign Affairs. He's the one who makes the final decision. I don't expect he'll answer for three or four days...."

Don't look disappointed, find it least of problems, tough it out, smile, chat, about...French archaeological mission in Kabul... be cool down to the dregs.

You'll say that four more days in New Delhi isn't a no-survivor catastrophe, piles of historical monuments all around, in ruins or not depending on customer, enough to be cultivated for years to come, take Qutb Minar for example, modest-seeming, two-hundred-and-thirty-foot red stone tower, absolute architectural marvel, have to see it, if only leaned a little would draw charter-loads of Americans, still solid after so many centuries in the sun, unbelievable, built entirely by hand, at least a thousand years before St. Joseph's Oratory, these skinny Indians, they built things, tip of the hat. People are foolish, before our eyes we have Qutb Minar, impossible white palaces, unbelievable red palaces full of monkeys, Delhi unbelievable, India unbelievable...and we're obsessed with Afghanistan.

Ended by telephoning the ambassador-of-our-obsessions, who let us have his stinking visas. People are foolish: immediately we start to dream about the roses of Isfahan, further on, beyond another visa....

CHAPTER 6

Baggage

A tourist vacationing for two weeks in Barbados will not have the same baggage as a traveller going for a two-month stay in Africa or around the world by jeep. Nonetheless some basic rules apply to everyone.

THE SUITCASE

Everyone has his or her own ideas on the subject. I myself always use soft, heavy-plastic suitcases that bend in two. I prefer what is called the woman's style, in which the suitcase is taller and easier to carry when you have to stand in line for hours in certain airports.

Another advantage of soft over rigid suitcases is that they are less likely to break or pop open when dropped. They have outer pockets into which you can stuff the raincoat no longer needed once you arrive at the airport, or newspapers bought at the last moment to please Canadians "over there." Finally, you always feel that something more can be jammed into these flexible suitcases.

Nametags should be glued or attached to the inside and outside of each suitcase and travel bag, giving your name and address and the forwarding address in case they are misdirected.

Some major airlines no longer weigh baggage on long hauls, and *one* suitcase (or parcel) or even *two* are accepted: the weight of each must not exceed thirty-two kilos. This is shown on your ticket by the marking **1PK** or **2PK**.

On many Third World airlines there is still a weight limit of twenty kilos in economy and thirty kilos in first class. Anything over this and you run the risk of paying one per cent of the first-class fare for each extra kilo, which can be a sizeable amount not foreseen in your travel budget. One way to get around it is to have your baggage weighed together with that of another passenger whose luggage is under the limit—"We've travelling together."

If it appears that you will be over the limit, you can always stuff your travel bag with the heavier items—books, vulcanite Buddha, and travelling iron. They no longer weigh the travel bags the passenger brings into the cabin.

THE TRAVEL BAG

This too is made of thick, flexible plastic.

Equipped with several zippered pockets, it should be slung over the shoulder by a strap, preferably leather, that is long and wide enough. That way you will always have a hand free to hold passport, ticket, and boarding pass. It also helps protect against theft.

According to international regulations, the travel bag should be no larger than 450 × 350 × 150 mm (18 × 14 × 6 inches) so that it can be slipped under the seat ahead. With rare exceptions, slightly larger bags are tolerated, and your flexible bag, at any rate, can be squeezed down to regulation size.

The travel bag should hold the items listed below and nothing more so that you can add the bottle of cognac, carton of cigarettes, or Burmese doll purchased at the duty-free shop.

CONTENTS OF TRAVEL BAG

- ☐ shirt
- ☐ pair of socks
- ☐ underwear shorts
- ☐ small towel
- ☐ woolen vest or pullover
- ☐ toilet kit
- ☐ extra pair of glasses
- ☐ first-aid kit
- ☐ canteen
- ☐ alarm clock
- ☐ pocket calculator
- ☐ camera (and other valuables such as binoculars or jewelry)
- ☐ fragile or perishable items
- ☐ two or three ballpoint pens

☐ important papers
☐ paperback (and, if I dare suggest it, this guide, unless you have already learned it by heart)

This emergency gear (which women will have to modify slightly) will see you through if your baggage is lost or arrives a day or two late. What's more, the carrier refuses all responsibility for valuables, including papers, so it is just as well to keep them with you. (The above list is integrated into the basic list that you will find in the following pages.)

In *addition* to the travel bag you have the right to bring the following items on board if necessary:

☐ purse
☐ umbrella or cane
☐ reasonable number of books or magazines
☐ small camera
☐ binoculars
☐ coat or raincoat
☐ cradle or folding stroller (if accompanied by a baby)
☐ wheelchair (if disabled)
☐ crutches (if needed to get around)
☐ purchases from the duty-free shop

I myself carry nothing that won't fit into my travel bag so that my hands are always free and I have only one piece of luggage to look after.

CONTENTS OF SUITCASE

Pack your luggage at least a day before departure, leaving yourself time to purchase missing items that might not be available in Chad or Bangladesh.

It is forbidden by law to put hazardous substances, including such things as explosives, poisons, inflammable liquids and gases, acids, and aerosol cans, in your bags or anywhere on board an aircraft.

The only way not to forget anything is to draw up a detailed list and tick off each item as it is placed in the suitcase or travel bag. Naturally this list will vary with the individual and with the length and kind of trip.

By way of example, I submit a list that I use when I leave on a six-week mission to the Third World. The trip would include official meetings and receptions as well as forays into the bush. The list is followed by explanations that will help others adapt it to their needs. Finally I will add some extra suggestions for women and young travellers.

Clothes worn on departure are not included in the list. Taxis and airports are well heated, and even in February it is wise to dress lightly when you leave Canada for a tropical country. I wear a raincoat that I slip into an outside pocket of my suitcase on arrival at the airport, and, under my suit coat, a wool vest that will go into the travel bag in case, as sometimes happens, it gets cold on the plane. Finally, I wear laced, crêpe-soled shoes in soft leather, more comfortable in flight and eliminating the need for overshoes.

To keep in interior pockets on your person are:

- ☐ air ticket
- ☐ passport
- ☐ vaccination booklet (See Chapter 8)
- ☐ wallet
- ☐ list of traveller's cheques
- ☐ moneybelt (worn under shirt)

(The above list is integrated into the following basic list.)

Here then is the list of items to be carried in the baggage or on one's person and to be explained in detail further on.

(Women should substitute another garment or object for items marked with one asterisk (*). Young travellers should substitute for or carry fewer items marked with two asterisks (**). Items marked with a triple asterisk (*/**) should be replaced with substitutes by both women and young travellers, all the more so if the young traveller is a woman.)

1. dark suit */**
2. light-coloured suit */**
3. safari suit *
4. pair of pants
5. six shirts */**
6. three sports shirts
7. two neckties */**

8. six pairs of socks **
9. six underwear shorts **
10. shoes **
11. beach sandals
12. robe **
13. bathing suit
14. cap or beach hat
15. wool vest or pullover
16. small beach bag
17. beach towel
18. small towel
19. moneybelt
20. wallet
21. passport holder
22. canteen
23. pocket calculator
24. small alarm clock
25. small flashlight
26. document holder
27. pad of paper
28. airmail envelopes
29. two or three ballpoint pens
30. roll of transparent adhesive tape
31. some paperbacks
32. small gifts
33. glasses (or contact lenses) and sunglasses
34. three-metre length of line
35. camera
36. binoculars
37. first-aid kit (See the rules of hygiene in tropical countries in Chapter 8.)
    - ☐ chloroquine (for malaria)
    - ☐ mild soporific (to help you sleep on the plane)
    - ☐ mild antidiarrhetic (in the order of Kaopectate)
    - ☐ aspirin
    - ☐ antacid (in the order of Eno)
    - ☐ antiseptic ointment (or, for humid climates, healing powder)
    - ☐ Halazone pills (emergency water purifier)

- ☐ liquid mosquito repellent
- ☐ petroleum jelly (Vaseline)
- ☐ Mercurochrome or iodine
- ☐ small quantity of absorbent cotton
- ☐ sunscreen lotion
- ☐ calamine lotion or Noxzema
- ☐ vitamins and minerals
- ☐ thermometer
- ☐ contraceptives
- ☐ usual medication that might not be available on the way

38. documents
- ☐ passport
- ☐ vaccination booklet
- ☐ birth certificate
- ☐ photocopies of above documents
- ☐ photocopies of travel insurance policies
- ☐ dozen passport photos
- ☐ copy of list of traveller's cheques
- ☐ calling cards
- ☐ road maps of countries to be visited
- ☐ basic information on countries to be visited
- ☐ address book

39. money and credit cards (See Chapter 7.)
40. day's newspapers
41. toilet kit
- ☐ good leather or soft plastic bag
- ☐ comb and brush
- ☐ toothbrush (in plastic container)
- ☐ toothpaste
- ☐ dental floss
- ☐ razor (if electric, with appropriate converter)
- ☐ razor blades
- ☐ shaving soap
- ☐ shampoo (in plastic bottle)
- ☐ deodorant
- ☐ soap (in plastic container)
- ☐ nail cutter
- ☐ tweezers (handy to remove splinters)
- ☐ paper tissues

☐ Swiss army knife, medium size, with two blades, cork-
   screw, bottle opener, can opener, and pick
☐ disposable lighter
☐ small sewing kit (the kind provided by large hotels)

SUGGESTIONS FOR WOMAN TRAVELLERS

Women can use the following as replacements or additions to as-
terisked items on the basic list:

1. two dresses
2. skirt
3. blouses
4. two pairs of trousers
5. two bras
6. headscarf
7. shoes and sandals
8. plastic raincoat
9. tampons or sanitary napkins
10. contraceptive medication
11. cosmetics
12. travel iron **
13. hair dryer **

SUGGESTIONS FOR YOUNG TRAVELLERS

For young travellers, two-asterisk items on the basic list should be
replaced or left out entirely, depending on the type and length of trip.
(Young women should do the same for one-asterisk items as well.)

No doubt young travellers prefer a knapsack to a suitcase. But
unless you plan to hitchhike or walk long distances, a suitcase is a
better choice. Your clothes will wrinkle less, and that will help to
make a better impression on immigration and customs officials.

Finally, if you plan to cook occasionally and stay in youth hostels
and small hotels, you should add the few things listed below:

1. safari suit or light suit (for women, a dress)
2. two pairs of pants (for women, trousers or skirts)
3. two shirts
4. running shoes
5. light poncho-style raingear

6. sleeping bag liner
7. sleeping bag
8. alcohol burner
9. mess kit
10. toilet paper
11. unbreakable plastic cup

DISCUSSION OF THE BASIC LIST

1. *Dark suit*. Made of lightweight, wrinkle-resistant fabric. Why dark? Because even in tropical countries dark clothes are worn to receptions, theatres, and other partly formal occasions. And it's frequently forgotten that winters can get rather cold in many Third World countries, particularly at night. This is true of places such as north China, Nepal, and North Africa. A very light-coloured suit would look absurdly out of place in such high-altitude cities as Bogotá, Quito, or La Paz, where the climate is temperate and winters even rather cold.

2. *Light-coloured suit*. In very hot countries a lightweight, light-coloured suit in so-called wrinkle-proof fabric is more comfortable.

3. *Safari suit*. Even two of them if you plan to spend more time in the bush than in offices and at social gatherings. This kind of garment, made of lightweight, mostly cotton material, is just right for the tropics. In some countries Safari suits or bush jackets are worn even at business meetings and receptions.

4. *Pair of pants*. Roomy, lightweight, in light-coloured cotton.

5. *Six shirts*, three of them short-sleeved. High percentage of cotton in the fabric.

6. *Three sports shirts*. In Indonesia and Malaysia, the long-sleeved batik shirt and any long pants is the male national dress and can be worn on all occasions, as can the elegant national shirt of the Philippines, the *barong tagalog*, usually white and embroidered, most authentically in pineapple fibre.

7. *Two neckties*. One would do, of course, since the one worn on departure isn't included in this list.

8. *Six pairs of socks*. Absolutely no nylon, which is uncomfortable and unhealthy in hot countries. Pick a fine wool or a mostly cotton mix.

9. *Six underwear shorts*. Cotton, for heaven's sake!

10. *Shoes*. A pair of dress shoes, preferably black.

11. *Beach sandals.* In addition to beach and poolside use, they are good for wear in your room or, in small hotels, for going down the hall to the shower. Never wear sandals on muddy or overgrown terrain; they give the feet scant protection against snake- or scorpion-bite and certain skin-penetrating parasites.

12. *Robe.* Very lightweight cotton. Karate style. Useful for going to the toilet down the hall or the swimming pool area, as some major hotels forbid going through public areas in bathing suits.

13. *Bathing suit.* A very modest one, for both men and women. Women on Third World beaches should avoid two-piece suits . . . except at Club Meds.

14. *Cap or beach hat.* In lightweight fabric. Perforated to allow evaporation, easy to wash. Pick a sober style that you won't be embarrassed to wear on the street, where the sun beats down as hard as on the beach.

15. *Wool vest or pullover.* For Third World countries where winter evenings get colder than you expect.

16. *Small beach bag.* Nylon for once, that is, very strong, very light, and easy to carry. It can also serve as a shopping bag in markets and shops, which rarely provide bags.

17. *Beach towel.* Can also be used to give yourself a rough clean-up in transient accommodation, which is often bereft of soap and towels.

18. *Small towel.* For in the travel bag. It can be used to refresh yourself during long waits at airports. Very useful in the bush.

19. *Moneybelt.* Absolutely essential item to prevent the theft of

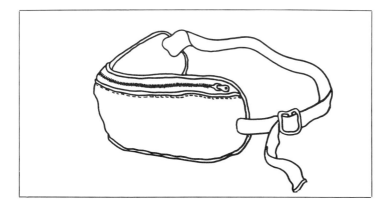

your money. There are many kinds, the most practical of which includes a plastic-lined cloth pouch for traveller's cheques and banknotes, sweat- and rain-proof to protect the signatures on the cheques. The zippered pouch is held around the waist by a sturdy belt that buckles firmly over the stomach. Along with the money you can slip in a credit card and small pieces of jewelry.

20. *Wallet.* Credit cards and papers you won't need during the trip should be removed from your wallet. Keep in it a single credit card and a small number of dollars.

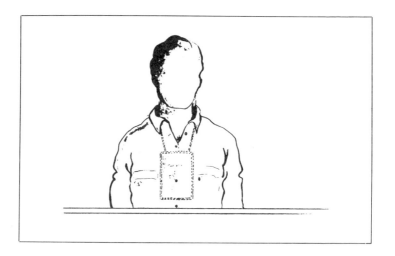

21. *Passport holder.* I made my own in Nigeria in 1949, and I still use it. I christened my invention A Tropical Safety Passport Holder. It is a plastic-lined pouch held around the neck by a cord and worn under the clothes. The passport can easily be taken out and put back through the neck opening of the shirt. In tropical countries you almost always wear lightweight pants and a shirt. Since you must *never* be without your passport, the only way to keep it with you obviously is to carry it under your shirt in a little pouch.

22. *Canteen.* Plastic, with three-quarter-litre capacity. It should be filled with boiled or mineral water for drinking or brushing your teeth. When I fly directly to tropical countries, I fill my canteen in Canada. If the plane stops over for hours late at night and the café is shut, my canteen of drinking water will be very handy, as it can be on

arrival at the hotel for brushing my teeth or taking my two chloroquines.

23. *Pocket calculator.* Very handy for converting dollars into ru-
pees, cruzeiros, or zaires and vice versa, and to keep track of
expenses in dollars as you go along.

24. *Small alarm clock.* Don't rely exclusively on the hotel's front
desk if you have an early morning flight to catch.

25. *Small flashlight.* Power failures are very frequent in many
Third World countries, and small villages rarely have electricity.
There *may* be some candles in the drawer of the bedside table, but
you will need a flashlight to get to the toilet or to walk at night over
grass that might harbour sleeping snakes.

26. *Document holder.* For business trips or official missions, a thin
plastic document-holder carried in the bottom of a suitcase is less
cumbersome than the traditional black attaché case. In principle you
will not be allowed to carry an attaché case on board the aircraft if
you already have a travel bag.

27. *Pad of paper.* And even more than one if you intend to write a
book about Dogonland.

28. *Airmail envelopes.* You will find them everywhere, but why
waste an hour looking for some in an unfamiliar city?

29. *Two or three ballpoint pens.* Wrap them in plastic and keep
them in the travel bag. They tend to leak in the unpressurized
baggage holds of older aircraft.

30. *Roll of transparent adhesive tape.* Scotch Tape kind. Smallest
size. Needed, among other things, to piece back together the
tattered banknotes cheerfully fobbed off on you by shopkeepers,
who will just as cheerfully turn around and refuse to accept them.

31. *Some paperbacks.* A good-looking book is liable to be damaged
during a trip. After you have read them, you can spread joy by
offering books to people for whom they are a rare commodity. For
reasons explained earlier, avoid books that could cause problems at
customs.

32. *Small gifts.* In certain countries the custom is to exchange
gifts with foreign visitors, particularly those on an official mission.
Choose handicrafts that aren't too cumbersome.

33. *Glasses (or contact lenses) and sunglasses.* If you need them,
be sure to have a spare pair. Keep in the travel bag.

34. *Three-metre length of line.* Nylon. Very handy to hold together

a suitcase whose straps have come loose, replace a broken handle, send a parcel to Canada, or dry laundry.

35. *Camera*. If you are not an expert, consult with someone familiar with photography in tropical countries about what filters to use, special wrapping for film, and other particular needs.

36. *Binoculars*. For birdwatchers, and even for others. You run the risk of being converted into a birdwatcher in bird heavens like the tropical countries.

37. *First-aid kit*. Keep the component items in a zippered transparent plastic bag. Buy the smallest possible sizes of all the suggested items. I've had the same tiny bottle of iodine for ten years. Keep the kit in your travel bag.

38. *Documents*. Before departure, have photocopies made of pages 2 and 3 of your passport, the first coupon of your air ticket, and the essential pages of your vaccination booklet. Put them in a large envelope along with the other documents on the basic list. The envelope goes in your travel bag.

39. *Money and credit cards*. See the recommendations in Chapter 7.

40. *Day's newspapers*. You can't imagine how happy you can make your Canadian friends or embassy staff by offering them the previous day's *La Presse* or *Globe & Mail*.

41. *Toilet kit*. Absolutely must be kept in the travel bag. You are sure to need it during the trip, particularly if you are going from Toronto to Kinshasa, a twenty-four-hour trip. And if your suitcase is lost, it is sweetly consoling to have at least the fifteen or so items in your kit.

DISCUSSION OF THE LIST FOR WOMAN TRAVELLERS

1. *Two dresses*. Just about everywhere in the Third World and particularly in Muslim countries, low necklines, sleeveless dresses, and of course very short skirts are considered unacceptable. Wear dresses of mid-calf length. All your day clothes should be cotton, although a dress in wrinkleproof synthetic can be very practical for evening wear.

2. *Skirt*. More than one if you visit countries where women in trousers are frowned on. Mid-calf length. Light colours. Cotton. Preferably with pockets.

3. *Blouses*. Roomy, long enough to cover the behind, one at least

with long sleeves that can be rolled up as circumstances dictate. Light colours. Cotton. Bring two of them. On the way you will find inexpensive ones that are better attuned to local custom.

4. *Two pairs of trousers.* Roomy. Cotton. Light colours. Deep pockets in front. Trousers on women are unacceptable in some areas.

5. *Two bras.* Cotton, if possible.

6. *Headscarf.* Provides protection against the sun or the grit in trains and buses. Enables you to cover your hair in countries where women are required to do so, or during visits to Lima's colonial-era churches.

7. *Shoes or sandals.* Leave with a good pair of crêpe-soled walking shoes. Also bring a pair of shoes or sandals for evening wear. Avoid high heels, if possible.

8. *Plastic raincoat.* In addition to the raincoat worn on departure from Canada, bring one of those raincoats in ultrathin plastic. They take up little space and will be of use during the rainy season.

9. *Tampons or sanitary napkins.* Very hard to find and very expensive; in some countries, nowhere to be found.

10. *Contraceptive medication.* Some available just about everywhere, but no doubt not the specific kind prescribed by your physician.

11. *Cosmetics.* Bring only the absolute minimum, and that in smallest format.

12. *Travel iron.* You can have your laundry and ironing done easily and cheaply in even the most modest of Third World hotels. If you can't leave home without your iron, check on the kind of voltage and plug used in the country to be visited. Purchase the needed converter and plug in Canada.

13. *Hair drier.* Smallest size possible. Same comment as above with regard to voltage and plugs.

DISCUSSION OF THE LIST FOR YOUNG TRAVELLERS

1. *Safari suit.* Or a lightweight suit or dress for going out in society, which can be a pleasure after three weeks in the desert! Wear your best clothes on the plane, where they will get less wrinkled than if they are rolled up in a ball at the bottom of your knapsack. A well-dressed young traveller will also have fewer problems with immigration, get through customs more easily, and be better received by people in general.

2. *Two pairs of pants.* Cotton, roomy, safari-style, with lots of deep pockets. Young women should have at least one skirt and even more in areas where women in slacks are frowned upon. Men as well as women should at all costs avoid shorts, which are generally not well regarded in the Third World, and are too greedily liked by mosquitoes. Derrière-hugging jeans are just as dimly viewed and not at all comfortable in hot countries. (They can cause skin rashes.) Jeans fanatics should at least avoid the traditional blue colour, which is a reminder of the hippies, whose reputation still unfairly tarnishes young travellers everywhere in the Third World.

3. *Two shirts.* Cotton, light-coloured, roomy, reaching to below the hips. You will find good, inexpensive batik shirts along the way.

4. *Running shoes.* You will be wearing comfortable, crêpe-soled walking shoes at departure. Since you can't wear them all the time, particularly in hot countries, you will also need a good pair of running shoes. Avoid white ones!

5. *Light poncho-style raingear.* If you left Canada in cold weather, you will have worn a raincoat or a windbreaker. Also take along a lightweight plastic poncho. It can serve equally well as a rain-cover for the knapsack and, if you sleep under the open sky, as a ground-sheet or improvised tent.

6. *Sleeping bag liner.* A single sheet folded over and sewn on two sides and inserted into the sleeping bag. You slip into it when the sheets in the inexpensive little hotel are of dubious cleanliness. This is a necessary item in youth hostels where sheets are not provided.

7. *Sleeping bag.* As lightweight as possible.

8. *Alcohol burner.* If you camp or travel by car or even want to save money by doing a little cooking now and then, get a small folding stove. I suggest the kind sold for use with Sterno fuel, which is rather expensive and hard to find in the Third World. When the Sterno is used up, keep the can and cover. Then refill it with alcohol fuel, which is cheap and available everywhere.

9. *Mess kit.* Camping goods stores sell various kinds of very compact mess kits, which include a tin saucepan with a frying pan that serves as a lid, a plate, and utensils.

10. *Toilet paper.* Always keep a roll in your knapsack and, at all times, a mini-roll in your pocket. It is very seldom provided in public toilets, practically never in Muslim countries.

11. *Unbreakable plastic cup.*

CHAPTER 7

Money, Mail, and Other Practical Matters

How much money should you take? Hard question. It depends not only on what kind of traveller you are, but also on the countries where you are going. In some the cost of living for a foreigner is extremely high, among them Ivory Coast, Libya, Hong Kong, and some small Persian Gulf states, while you can live on very little in Morocco, Mexico, and Sri Lanka. Before setting up a budget, get detailed information from your travel agent.

Having money sent to a remote part of the world is always difficult and time-consuming, so it is better to set out with more than you think you will need. In large cities, of course, credit cards can be used to avoid certain cash outlays.

TRAVELLER'S CHEQUES

Don't wait until the last moment. Getting two thousand dollars worth in small denominations and signing them one by one in front of the clerk can take time.

Banks affiliated with Visa or Master Card will try to get you to take cheques offered by one or the other. Some banks will even tell you that they no longer sell the Thomas Cook or American Express cheques. If you insist, however, they will end up by finding some. Until I'm shown otherwise, I'll pick American Express as the easiest to exchange everywhere and the easiest to get reimbursement for in cases of theft or loss.

Get your cheques in *American dollars*, which are better known and more highly prized abroad than Canadian dollars.

Avoid high denominations. It is annoying to have to exchange a hundred-dollar cheque at the end of a stay in a country when a fifty-dollar one would do. Theoretically you can always exchange your pesos or Rwanda francs for dollars before leaving the country, but that is always hard going and often impossible; the banks may be closed, including the one at the airport, as I have often discovered. And the chances of exchanging your Burmese kyats in Canada are quite slim.

If, for example, you have two thousand dollars (U.S.) in traveller's cheques on departure and plan to visit three countries over three weeks, here's what I suggest:

Six $100 cheques	=	$600
Twenty $50 cheques	=	$1,000
Twenty $20 cheques	=	$400
Total		$2,000

There would be no risk in exchanging a $100 cheque on arrival in a country.

At the end of your stay, however, cash only small denominations and figure out your final needs down to the last rupee.

The bank will give you receipts listing the numbers of your traveller's cheques. Be sure to safeguard these with your other documents in your travel bag.

It is still much handier to keep a list of your traveller's cheques that indicates how much cash you have in American dollars, Canadian dollars, and francs. This list, a copy of which should always be carried on your person (the other remaining in the travel bag), will enable you to cross off the amounts of cheques cashed or reduce the totals for your other currencies as you go along. You will always know how much money you have left for exchange. With the list, moreover, you will be able to fill in the currency declaration required in some Third World countries without having to count your money on the plane or, worse still, amidst the bustle of the airport.

The reason behind currency declarations is the curtailment of black market operations. Whenever you exchange money, make sure to have it written in on the form provided by customs, to whom it must be handed in when you leave the country. Spot checks can take place then (as happens in Algeria), and if your form doesn't show that you exchanged money only in authorized places (hotels, banks, certain stores), you can find yourself in hot water.

Another good thing about a list of traveller's cheques is that in cases of theft or loss, you will know immediately which cheques were stolen and be able to give the numbers to the police and the American Express office.

LIST OF TRAVELLER'S CHEQUES

RH	251	392	625	$100	JA	822	321	140	$20
			626	$100				141	$20
			627	$100				142	$20
			628	$100				143	$20
			629	$100				144	$20
			630	$100				145	$20
								146	$20
FX	422	451	820	$50				147	$20
			821	$50				148	$20
			822	$50				149	$20
			823	$50				150	$20
			824	$50				151	$20
			825	$50				152	$20
			826	$50				153	$20
			827	$50				154	$20
			828	$50				155	$20
			829	$50				156	$20
			830	$50				157	$20
			831	$50				158	$20
			832	$50				159	$20
			833	$50					
			834	$50					
			835	$50					
			836	$50	BANKNOTES				
			837	$50					
			838	$50	U.S. dollars				$150
			839	$50	Canadian dollars				$150

On the reverse side of the list you should write down various other information needed in cases of loss or theft:

CREDIT CARD NUMBERS:

American Express 4261-344-251-826
Visa 9461-480-521-326

AIR TICKET NUMBER:
4334-321-426-832

PASSPORT NUMBER:

SA 052841
Issued in Ottawa 4/11/1983
by the Department of External Affairs
Valid until 4/11/1988

```
TRAVEL INSURANCE COMPANY:
    Name . . . . . . . . . . . . . . . . . . . . . . . . . . .
    Address . . . . . . . . . . . . . . . . . . . . . . .
    Telex. . . . . . . . . . . . . . . . . . . . . . . . . .
    Telephone. . . . . . . . . . . . . . . . . . . . .
    Policy number . . . . . . . . . . . . . . . . . .
```

You will most probably cash your first cheque on arrival, at the front desk of the hotel. Get more information afterwards. Rates are often better in banks or, where they are allowed, currency exchanges.

Don't *ever* exchange money on the black market, mostly because it is profoundly immoral to do so in countries facing tremendous economic problems, but also because you face a high risk of being robbed. If you are, the police can't help, except perhaps to accuse you of trafficking in currency.

When you exchange your dollars, insist on getting the smallest denominations possible and lots of coins, which are always scarce in the Third World. Shopkeepers won't accept big bills because they can't make change.

CASH

Along with your traveller's cheques bring about a hundred and fifty dollars (U.S.) in cash, as follows:

ten $10 bills	=	$100
five $5 bills	=	$25
twenty-five $1 bills	=	$25
Total		$150

On arrival you might not be able to exchange money at the airport itself, and it can happen that even if a currency exchange is open, you will be quickly put off by the long lineup.

The porter who carries your bags will be overjoyed by an American one-dollar bill. When you negotiate a fare with the taxi driver, ask him if he will accept U.S. dollars. If not, he can wait by the door while you exchange your first traveller's cheque at the front desk of the hotel. But rarely will he refuse! If you travel a long distance by air across Africa, there will be many stopovers. Passengers are usually invited to get off and wait in the transit lounge when there is a stopover of an hour or more. I've had occasion to vegetate in one for six hours. At times like that, it is a great comfort to have your pockets stuffed with American greenbacks that no one turns down. You will be able to have a beer, buy a snack, and send a telegram.

When you settle the hotel bill, a five-dollar or ten-dollar banknote can save you from having to cash a twenty-dollar traveller's cheque and then have to convert the change back into dollars.

Finally, I advise you to carry a small amount in Canadian dollars. You can use it to pay the taxi or limo to and from the airport in your home city. And if you return at a time when the banks are shut, it is nice to have a few Canadian dollars in hand. Finally, a few quarters can pay for phone calls in the departure lounge or, on return, while you are waiting for your luggage.

CREDIT CARDS

Accepted by large hotels, airlines, large stores, and tourist shops, credit cards make it possible to carry less money and travel on credit, at least for a few weeks. Still, if your trip lasts for longer than a month and you don't arrange for your bills to be paid while you are gone, you run the risk of having your American Express card cancelled while you are in remotest India. To forestall this, send a cheque for the amounts you expect to charge to each credit card company before leaving.

Bring with you only the cards you are sure to use, leaving the others behind in a safe place. With a Visa card (accepted in over 155 countries) and an American Express card (accepted in over 150 countries), I've been able to get by in big cities all over the world. But I have nothing against Master Card (accepted in over 165 countries) or even Diner's Club (accepted in over 150 countries).

If you have two credit cards, keep one in your wallet and the other in your moneybelt. In cases of theft or loss, advise local police and the company by telephone or, if there's no office nearby, by telegram. Also advise the Canadian embassy. They will send you back your card if it happens to be found.

Exchange your traveller's cheques and dollars only as the need arises so that you won't have to exchange local currency back into dollars at the time of departure. Nonetheless, put aside enough gourdes, bolivars, or pesos for the last hours of the stay. (See Chapter 14.)

THEFT

The best of trips can be spoiled by the theft or loss of your money, not to mention your passport and air ticket.

All things considered, I don't think that there are any more thieves in the Third World than elsewhere, which I find amazing in view of the boundless wretchedness weighing down on so many millions of human beings in the developing countries. How justifiably envious they must feel at the sight of these expensive-camera-bedecked tourists who spend in a few minutes what represents the earnings of a month's hard labour for a Bolivian *campesino* or Guinean peasant.

Travellers should at least not flaunt their wealth and also take all useful precautions against theft, particularly in cities notorious for it, for example, Bogotá, Lima and Dar es Salaam.

The safeguards I recommend can't be too bad, since not once have I been robbed during my innumerable voyages... except for a shirt in Nairobi in 1953.

What thieves want most, of course, is money—cash or even traveller's cheques, for which there is a black market. My advice is to divide up your money as follows:

1. Put the bulk of your traveller's cheques and dollars in the moneybelt worn under the shirt. Also put one of the two credit cards there.

2. In your wallet should be a small sum in traveller's cheques and dollars and the other credit card, in brief, everything that could be stolen without causing grave inconvenience. Stuff your wallet deep in a front pocket. Women should keep no valuables in their purses.

3. In another deep pocket should go local coins and bills, which you will never carry in large quantities since you will be stingy about cashing in your traveller's cheques.

Don't, above all, ever leave money in your hotel room or unguarded on the beach. If you go to beaches or pools, you would be well advised to leave your money in a safety deposit box, found only in better hotels.

You should never bring jewelry or even an expensive watch along on a trip. In dense crowds you can be jostled free of your watch or gold chain. If you find yourself in uncomfortably crowded spots, slip even your wristwatch into your pocket. And it is very easy to find room in your moneybelt for a gold chain or an engagement ring.

If you absolutely must wear jewelry, be sure that it is insured.

Since Canadian passports are in great demand on the black market, keep yours well concealed in your passport holder under your shirt, in which should also go your air ticket, folded in two.

I've never been mugged during my trips, but I know people who have been, often as a direct result of their own unwise behaviour. You don't walk around alone at night in the old sections of Bogotá, Kingston, or Jakarta any more than you would in New York, Chicago, or London.

If you are mugged, don't put up any resistance unless you have a black belt in judo. Hand over your local money and hope that the thief won't insist on taking the wallet from your left pocket. He should make his getaway before giving you a more thorough going-over and finding the moneybelt and passport holder.

Don't put off filing a formal complaint with the police, and ask them for a copy of it. Advise the company that issued your traveller's cheques, giving them the numbers of the stolen cheques, thanks to the list of which one copy at least remains in the travel bag even if the other was stolen. Advise your insurance company and the Canadian embassy.

Earlier chapters have dealt with the steps to take in cases of theft or loss of the passport or air ticket.

TRAVEL INSURANCE

Baggage and personal effects insurance protects against loss, theft, or destruction of your baggage and personal effects. If you already have fire and theft coverage, a small extra premium should cover your baggage. A floating policy will provide $1,000 coverage on personal effects for a year at a cost of about $50. If you do not have this coverage, you can get from your travel agent for about $27.50 a special policy that gives you $1000 coverage for the duration of a fifteen-day trip.

Cancellation insurance. A few dollars buys protection against the loss of money paid in advance for an organized trip or cruise in case you have to cancel before departure.

Traveller's life insurance. There was a time when no one would get on board a plane without having purchased (for a minute sum) life insurance of $50,000 or more. With plane crashes becoming less and less frequent, this type of insurance has passed out of fashion, although it still exists. Tickets purchased with certain credit cards (American Express, enRoute, Diner's Club) automatically include $100,000 insurance. For an additional $2.50, enRoute will insure you for $250,000, which makes you think that the risks aren't all that awful. Your travel agent will sell you flight accident insurance of $350,000 for the modest sum of $11.

Emergency medical and hospital travel insurance. I recommend this kind of insurance to all travellers, including people going no further than Europe or even Florida.

Doctors' bills and, above all, hospital costs are exorbitant in certain countries. People have met financial ruin as a result of serious illness or accident abroad. Of course *part* of your expenses will be re-imbursed by your province's medicare plan if you provide them with the following: names and addresses of the doctors who administered treatment, the nature of the treatments, and the place and date of hospitalization. But you will receive only the amount that would have been paid for the same services in your home province, which can be only a fraction of actual costs. And in some urgent cases a gravely ill person must be sent home accompanied by a nurse and physician.

All expenses not covered by medicare will be met by emergency medical and hospital travel insurance, whatever your destination, on the condition that your trip does not last for more than 180 days. A $54 premium for a fifteen-day trip, for example, includes emergency medical and hospital costs ($1,000,000), life insurance ($250,000), and baggage and personal effects insurance ($1000).

Keep a copy of your insurance policy with your other basic documents and copy the basic information on the reverse side of the list of traveller's cheques: name of the company, address, policy number, and telephone and telex numbers.

BEFORE LEAVING CANADA

On the day before departure, you should check off the list of things to be done before leaving home for several weeks or months:

☐ *Car.* Don't wait until the last minute before finding a place to park it while you are away.

☐ *Newspapers.* Because a pile of newspapers by your door is an invitation to burglars, have your subscription transferred to a friend or relative. When you come back, hungry for Canadian news, it will be nice to thumb through a stack of *Vancouver Sun*s or *Toronto Star*s. Begin with the most recent. The grave problems set out in the old copies might have been resolved.

☐ *Home security.* If your trip is going to last some while, it is wise to advise local police and a neighbour.

☐ *Credit cards and other identification.* Leave the credit cards you aren't taking in a safe place, along with your medicare and social security cards, driver's licence, and other vital papers. Why risk losing documents you won't need during the trip? Do the same for your keys; take only the one you will need to let yourself in when you get home.

☐ *Refrigerator.* If you will be away for several weeks, don't leave any perishables in it. If the absence will stretch into months, it is better to empty the refrigerator completely, unplug it, give it a thorough cleaning, and leave it with the door open.

☐ *Pets.* Leave them with friends or board them at a kennel. If the cat or dog is going along on the trip, inquire about needed inoculations at embassies or consulates.

☐ *Plants.* For an absence of three weeks to a month, you need only water them thoroughly, shut the drapes to screen the sunlight, and trust in nature. For a longer absence, you can leave your key with a neighbour or relative who can come and water your African violets, or come to an agreement with the superintendent. At any rate, tenants are responsible for their apartments during absences and should arrange to have visits at three-week intervals, more frequently during cold weather.

☐ *Garbage cans.* Don't forget to empty them before leaving.

☐ *Heating.* Economize by reducing it to the minimum consistent with the well-being of your tropical plants.

☐ *Hot-water heater.* Don't waste gas or electricity—shut it off.

☐ *Kitchen stove.* Be sure that the oven and elements are turned off.

☐ *Windows.* Lock them securely.

☐ *Travel itinerary.* Leave a copy with your secretary or a relative so you will be easier to reach in an emergency.

☐ *Mail.* In a great many cities you can have your mail addressed to the American Express office or, in capital cities, the Canadian embassy. They will keep your mail for a reasonable length of time but won't forward it. Unclaimed mail will be returned to the sender. In cities where there is neither an American Express office nor an embassy, use the general delivery of the General Post Office (*Bureau de poste central* in French-speaking countries and, in Spanish-speaking countries, *Central de Correos*). Your address would be like this:

> Mr. John Smith
> Poste restante
> Central de Correos
> *Montevideo*
> URUGUAY

The French phrase *poste restante* is used and understood the world over. This service is generally effective.

Still, I can remember how surprised I was when I came to pick up my mail at the general delivery (or *poste restante*) in Managua, Nicaragua. The mail clerk invited my friends and me into a room with a stack of letters at least two metres high. "Help yourself!" he told us with a broad grin. It has to be said that this was back in 1946.

CHAPTER 8

Rules of Hygiene in a Tropical Country

I learned the hard way. Before I left Canada for the first time in 1946 to go to South America (fourteen months' camping by car), no one was able to give me the information I needed on the health hazards that lay ahead. I left without a good number of the necessary shots, didn't even know that quinine was then the only effective way to prevent malaria... which I caught before even reaching Panama.

We are more fortunate now. The International Association for Medical Assistance to Travellers, a non-profit organization founded in 1960 by a Canadian physician, Dr. Vincenzo Marcolongo, provides a great deal of medical information free of charge for travellers, including a list of hundreds of recommended English-speaking doctors in more than a hundred countries. The Canadian address is 128 Edward St., Room 725, Toronto, Ont. M5G 1E2.

It goes without saying that I won't rely exclusively on my own personal experience to give advice on so vital a subject. For the past fifteen years, Canada World Youth has been privileged to have a medical director particularly well versed in tropical medicine, Dr. Richard Morisset, head of the department of microbiology and infectious disease at the Hôtel-Dieu hospital in Montréal and professor of microbiology at the Université de Montréal.

Over the years, Dr. Morisset has put together a program of inoculation and preventive measures against tropical illness adapted to the needs of young volunteers who have to work in rough conditions in unhealthy climates. Over this fifteen-year period more than six thousand young Canadians have each lived for several months in thirty Third World countries in Latin America, Africa, Asia, and the South Seas.

On their return these young people were given all the relevant checkups under the guidance of Dr. Morisset, who has even, thanks to them, identified a new bacteria, known today as *Salmonella montréal*.

This prominent specialist has been kind enough to read over the present chapter, for which I thank him in the name of all the travellers who will owe him a problem-free trip.

Someone going for a long stay in a country that is particularly rife with health hazards will need to take more precautions than a tourist going for a two-week vacation at the luxurious Hôtel Ivoire in Abidjan.

Some general rules apply nonetheless to all travellers to tropical countries, and one of them is "better one vaccine too many than one too few." It's no problem, moreover, to take two chloroquine pills a week even if you hear that malaria is no longer a problem in a particular country. If it recurs, travellers will find out—perhaps—six months too late.

There's an understandable tendency for natives to deny that a certain disease occurs in their own country, while admitting freely that it is a problem in all the neighbouring countries. And this is one subject on which you can't trust travel agencies, tourist offices, and embassies, all of which are rather inclined to be reassuring. Take due care and before departure contact a specialist in tropical disease, a specialized clinic, a Travel Information Office (see the list in Appendix E) or a Health and Welfare Canada immunization centre (see Appendix F).

Travellers who are careful to observe this chapter's recommendations have nothing to fear from even the most extended of stays in any Third World country. *The following advice is not intended to frighten but rather to lend confidence.*

I have friends who have had rotten times in absolutely marvelous countries, laid low from day one by a serious case of diarrhea or even dysentery. The same friends, finally persuaded to take the most elementary precautions, have since made trouble-free trips to the same countries in the same circumstances.

BEFORE DEPARTURE

☐ Have a *complete medical checkup* and tell your doctor what countries you will be visiting. People with cardiac or respiratory problems should mention if they are going to Mexico City, Quito, La Paz, or Addis Ababa, which are among the highest-altitude cities in the world. Certain physical and even mental disorders can be aggravated by high altitudes or sweltering climates.

☐ See your *dentist* and have all needed work done. Certainly there are good dentists in the Third World, but they are found mostly in the capitals and don't have the sophisticated equipment ours do. In Hong Kong some years ago a Vietnamese dentist filled a tooth of mine without local anesthetic and with a foot-driven drill.

☐ *Ophthalmologists* and *optometrists* are also hard to find outside large cities. Travellers who wear glasses (or contact lenses, which, I should say, are ill-adapted to certain tropical regions) should bring along an extra pair and, if their eyes are sensitive, prescription sunglasses. An added precaution for a long stay is to take along the ophthalmologist's prescription, in English or French, depending on the destination.

☐ Begin to take *anti-malarial medication* two weeks before departure. (See below for further information in this regard.)

☐ Take out *emergency medical and hospital travel insurance*, as described in Chapter 7.

☐ *Two and a half months* before departure, the specialist in tropical medicine or the Centre for Immunization should have set up your immunization program.

IMMUNIZATION PROGRAM

You should ask an Official Centre for Immunization or a travel agency for an international immunization certificate, commonly known as a vaccination booklet, published by Health and Welfare Canada in accordance with international specifications.

Only inoculations duly inscribed in the vaccination booklet are recognized abroad. All the necessary inoculations can be very well given by the family doctor, the exception being the one for yellow fever, given only at the Centres for Immunization. The certificates the family doctor issues should be inscribed in the vaccination booklet and approved by a physician at the official Centres for Immunization.

Keep the vaccination booklet with your passport, since certain Third World countries still require proof of inoculation against yellow fever and cholera.

The simplest thing is to get all the needed inoculations at the same centre. Follow the immunization calendar to the letter, noting that some of them must not be administered at the same time. (A list of official Centres for Immunization is given in Appendix F.)

Ideally a complete immunization program stretches over eight or nine weeks. (See the Sample Immunization Calendar in this chapter.) Where the need is pressing, the program can be shortened to as little as three weeks, but this is less advisable.

RECOMMENDED IMMUNIZATIONS

Certain inoculations have fallen out of use over the years either because they are no longer deemed effective, as is the case for typhus shots, or because the illness has been wiped off the face of the earth, as with smallpox. Smallpox vaccine has been known since the end of the eighteenth century, but it is only quite recently that, thanks to the efforts of the World Health Organization, the need for it has gone.

Yellow fever and cholera shots are the only ones still required by many Third World countries. But there are a good many others that absolutely must be taken for protection against other equally serious illnesses that await the traveller to tropical countries.

☐ *Yellow fever.* This terrible disease has long wreaked havoc, particularly in Central America, South America, and central Africa. Thanks once again to the immunization program of the World Health Organization, inoculated travellers are no longer at any risk. Good for ten years, the vaccine is neither required nor necessary in all Third World countries. Check with the Centre for Immunization.

☐ *Cholera*, still rampant in Asia, has also made recent incursions into Africa and even Europe. A minor epidemic occurred in Naples as recently as the 1970s. Sadly, the vaccine isn't effective. Despite this, some countries still insist on it, and a small dose (0.5 cc) will meet their requirement.

☐ *Tetanus.* Travellers are more injury-prone, and each injury brings a risk of tetanus, an often-fatal disease. The vaccine gives complete protection.

☐ *Diphtheria.* The first requirement is a Schick test to determine your immunity to this disease. Persons not sufficiently protected will then be given the vaccine.

☐ *Poliomyelitis*. Although this disease has disappeared in the West, it is still rampant in the Third World. Persons who have not been inoculated against it for ten years must take the three required injections. Others need only take a booster shot.

☐ *Typhoid fever*, very common in tropical countries, is now guarded against effectively by a new typhoid vaccine. (The older TAB and TABT are no longer administered in North America.)

☐ *Infectious hepatitis* is a most irritating and debilitating disease, even though it is rarely fatal. Gamma globulin injections help protect against it, not as a vaccine but rather as a source of protective antibodies.

☐ *Tuberculosis*. A tuberculin test will tell if you are immune to this disease, conquered in the West but still endemic in the Third World. If the test is negative, BCG vaccine is recommended. Some people prefer to take the test when they come back home, willing to risk treatment if need be. To us it seems smarter to take the test and be inoculated before leaving.

☐ *Rabies* is still rampant in certain Third World countries, but not necessarily the same ones from year to year. You can't do without the vaccine (three injections at seventy-five dollars a shot) if you are going to stay in these countries and particularly if you expect to have contact with animals as, for example, in the case of veterinarians. At any rate, you have to be inoculated again or take a serum immediately after being bitten by an animal suspected of having rabies.

In addition, children should be immunized against other illnesses that could be fatal to them:

☐ *Measles*, always a serious disease, sometimes fatal. The vaccine is absolutely essential.

☐ *Mumps*, a disease with very serious complications—meningitis, encephalitis, meningoencephalitis. Children twelve months and older should be given the vaccine, which is usually combined with the one for measles and German measles (M.M.R. II).

SAMPLE IMMUNIZATION CALENDAR

VACCINE OR TEST	1st wk.	2nd wk.	3rd wk.	4th wk.	5th wk.	6th wk.	7th wk.	8th wk.	9th wk.
Tuberculin test[1]	X								
BCG									X
Schick test[2]	X								
Diphtheria		X							
Tetanus		X							
Poliomyelitis		X			(X)[3]			(X)[3]	
Typhoid		X (0.25 cc)			X (0,5 cc)			(X)[4] (1 cc)	
Cholera*					X (0,5 cc)				
Yellow fever[5]*								X	
Hepatitis									X

1. This test tells whether the subject is immune to tuberculosis. If not, the vaccine must be administered.
2. This test tells whether the subject is immune to diphtheria. If not, the vaccine must be administered.
3. The 2nd and 3rd doses are required by persons who have never been inoculated for poliomyelitis or have not been for five years.
4. The third dose of this vaccine is optional but recommended.
5. Yellow fever vaccine may be received between the fifth and ninth weeks, but at least two weeks before or after a dose of poliomyelitis vaccine, or at the same time.
*This vaccine is required in certain countries.

IMMUNIZATION CALENDAR

The table on the facing page is a sample immunization calendar telling the order and spacing of all immunizations for maximum effectiveness and a minimum of side effects.

When time is short, at least the essential shots can be given in as little as three weeks' time, although this is not advisable.

An eight- or nine-week calendar is ideal. Certain people who react badly to one vaccine or another might run a low fever for a day or two. Better that it doesn't happen on board the plane!

OTHER COMMON DISEASES

Malaria. A disease that is rampant in almost all of the world's tropical countries. An estimated 250 million cases occur annually. It is more dangerous still for Westerners who have not built up resistance, and it can be fatal. Although there is no vaccine, there are effective preventatives.

The medication recommended for most tropical countries is chloroquine, which is sold under various brand names. You should take two 250-mg pills once a week. I do it on Sundays, since that's the easiest day for me to remember. You take a grave risk if you miss a week. Begin this régime two weeks before departure and continue for eight weeks after return.

You could, in fact, take your first chloroquine pill on arrival in the contaminated country. But by beginning two weeks earlier, you will find out in time if you have an allergic reaction to the prescribed medication.

In certain countries malaria is chloroquine-resistant. In this case, you should also take other medication, such as sulfadoxin-pyrimethanin, fortunately sold under the less tongue-twisting name of Fansidar. Some people are allergic to this drug.

You take one Fansidar pill a week, still on Sunday, in addition, of course, to the two chloroquines.

An added and very important safeguard is to protect yourself against mosquito bites, malaria being spread by the bite of the anophele. Clothes worn after dark should cover the body well. You should smear yourself with mosquito repellent and sleep under a mosquito net, preferably after having sprayed the room with an insecticide.

Diarrhea is a great trial for travellers in tropical countries. Even if you take all the safeguards, certain physical effects have to follow an abrupt change in eating habits compounded by travel-weariness and the stress of arrival. A day or two of diarrhea without fever (*la turista*) is in the natural order of things and shouldn't trouble you unduly. At such times avoid all solid food, drink copious amounts of liquid to avoid dehydration (fruit juices, boiled water, and carbonated drinks, including Coca-Cola). You can also take a mild antidiarrhetic such as Kaopectate, which at least has the virtue of not being harmful.

But if the diarrhea persists after two or three days, don't put off seeing a doctor recommended by the embassy. Your case of diarrhea could be a serious illness of bacterial or parasitic origin, particularly if it is accompanied by nausea, if you are running a fever, or if your stools are blood-streaked.

Venereal disease. Very prevalent the world over, it is a sure danger if you indulge in casual sexual contact. Venereal disease is resurgent in industrialized countries and more frequent still in the Third World. The only sure safeguard, of course, is total abstinence from sex with anyone other than your regular partner.

WHEN YOU ARRIVE UNDER THE SUN

We'll talk about how to keep travel fatigue down to a minimum in the chapter on air travel.

When a Canadian traveller coming from the cold gets off the plane, he will be delighted at finding himself under radiant skies in a country where the mean temperature is 30°C (86°F). It will nonetheless be a shock to a system already stretched taut by the long hours in flight, not to speak of jet lag.

Here are some rules to follow for a quick and problem-free adjustment to your new environment: .

1. Rest at least for the first few days, resisting the temptation to set off in conquest of the new city. If you have passed through a good number of time zones, schedule absolutely no immediate business or other meetings; you risk making the wrong decisions.
2. For the first few days avoid exposure to sun, heavy exercise, alcohol, and overeating.
3. Diarrhea can be brought on by overconsumption of iced drinks, alcohol, and fruit.

4. To counteract the effects of excessive perspiration (weakness, nausea, headache), particularly in the early part of your journey, you should take lots of liquids—boiled water, tea, coffee, carbonated beverages, beer. Drink to the point where your urine is almost colourless. Make a notable increase in your intake of table salt.
5. You may feel unusually nervous and irritable for the first few days because of fatigue brought on by the long air journey, jet lag, the brusque change in climate, excessive perspiration, and sometimes diarrhea. The shock of a new environment and a radical change in routine can sometimes affect your outlook. Forewarned is forearmed against this transition period. We will discuss another effect of travel, cultural shock, in Chapter 13.

EATING PRECAUTIONS

Water. Copious amounts of liquids should be consumed in tropical countries, but this liquid intake must be clean. You are often told that the water in this hotel or that city is drinkable. That might well be for local people, but practically never for a Canadian with a different intestinal flora.

Missionaries and volunteers who stay for several years in the same country often end up by ''getting used to the water.'' In fact it is their intestinal flora that changes, which does not make them immune to water-borne disease. If you are in one or several countries for relatively short stays, drink only water that has been held at a brisk boil for three to five minutes. Improve the taste by letting it cool in sterilized bottles, and drink it within the half-day. This precaution is worth the effort involved.

Take absolutely no ice-cubes or any beverage made with unboiled water, and remember that certain fruit juices may be ''stretched'' with untreated water.

Don't trust the thermos jug of ice water brought to your room. Of course you will be told that it is drinkable, but even if it were, it wouldn't be for long unless the thermos itself had been sterilized.

Naturally you should brush your teeth only with boiled water or bottled mineral water.

When it is impossible to boil water, it can be disinfected by adding Halazone tablets (four 4-mg tablets per litre) or two drops of two per cent tincture of iodine per glass. These should be given half an hour to do their work. But this is much less dependable, and the treated water has a terrible taste.

Some of the various water filters are partially effective. Filtering improves and clears water by removing suspended particles, but that alone isn't good enough. After filtering you will still have to boil it, the only real way to purify water.

If you are not absolutely sure about the water, take carbonated drinks without ice, fruit juice that has not been diluted with water, tea, coffee, beer, wine, or coconut milk.

Fresh vegetables. As a general rule, eat only cooked vegetables. Eat absolutely no lettuce or other raw, unpeeled vegetables; they often cause intestinal disease.

Lettuce can be made fit for consumption by washing each leaf in boiling water. As a last resort, it can be given a twenty-minute soaking in Halazone-treated water. But take my word for it, you can get along very well without lettuce.

Fresh fruit. Peel all fruit (including tomatoes) after giving your hands a thorough washing.

Dairy products. They are scarce in tropical countries and rarely pasteurized. Best to avoid milk, butter, cheese, and ice cream. Make do with powdered milk, canned condensed milk, or boiled milk.

Sweets. Admire but don't eat the candies and pastries for sale on the street and thereby open to flies.

Meat and fish. Eat no pork. (Mohammed knew what he was talking about!) Eat only well-cooked meat and fish. Don't ever eat raw shellfish and be wary even of cooked ones; they could have been out in the sun too long beforehand.

Restaurants. Don't ever succumb to the lure of a quaint little greasy spoon, especially if it is abuzz with flies; there will be ten times as many in the kitchen.

GENERAL PRECAUTIONS

Travellers would do well to follow the local custom of many tropical countries and take a siesta, not venturing out in the sun between noon and 3:00 P.M.

As I've said so often, your clothes should be cotton (not nylon), lightweight, roomy, and light-coloured.

Don't go bareheaded under the sun. In colonial times whites held firmly to the belief that it was courting disaster to go out without the renowned *topee* or pith helmet. It took decolonization to open eyes to the fact that a plain beach hat or cloth cap will do as well.

The tropical sun beats down much more fiercely than ours. Take no more than ten or fifteen minutes' exposure the first few days on the beach. Increases in time of exposure should be gradual.

Beware of heat stroke, which occurs when the body temperature is between 40°C (105°F) and 40.5°C (106°F) but there is no perspiration. See a doctor as soon as possible and, while waiting, get into the shade. Have your forehead sponged with cold water and fanned to increase evaporation.

Speaking of shade—stay away from the shade of the coconut tree. One day in Mogadishu I had a peaceful meal under the coconut trees on the patio of a small hotel. A gust of wind shook loose three big coconuts, which duly crashed to the ground not two paces away from where I was sitting. Falling twenty metres onto a human skull, a coconut can bring instant death.

Excessive humidity often causes skin rashes. Take showers, dry yourself well, and apply talcum powder. And always wear light-weight, roomy, cotton clothing.

Humidity slows down the healing of scratches and cuts. Wash them thoroughly, apply generous amounts of iodine or Mercuro-chrome, leave them unbandaged, and avoid dust and flies.

Swimming. In tropical countries, don't go into the waters of lakes, ponds, rivers, or streams. Bodies of fresh water swarm with parasites that enter the body through the skin's pores. If you absolutely have to go barefoot in fresh water or mud, or if you absent-mindedly let your hand trail in water while travelling by pirogue, you should rub the moistened limbs briskly with a dry cloth. That should prevent penetration by microscopic parasites.

Be wary of swimming pools except in the large hotels. And even there, often they don't put in enough chlorine because of its high cost, and at any rate it evaporates quickly in tropical climates.

You can always swim in the sea, providing that the water is safe: not near the mouth of a river or a municipal sewer outlet; not infested with sharks, sea-snakes, or jellyfish; and not made hazard-ous by a tidal bore or an underwater current.

Traffic. The medical director of Qantas, Dr. Harvey Dakin, has said that more travellers are hospitalized because of traffic accidents than by tropical disease. The comment may be over-simplified, but do be especially careful crossing streets, particularly in cities with traffic on the left. Take the first opportunity to get out of any vehicle whose driver gives clear signs of recklessness, which isn't unusual in the Third World, or seems drunk, which also isn't unusual.

Insects. In certain areas, it is essential to sleep under mosquito nets. Most hotels in these areas supply them. As has already been seen, this is a necessary safeguard against malarial mosquitoes and others at least as voracious as the black flies and no-see-ums of the Laurentians and the Yukon.

Don't chase away the charming little lizards that abound in some countries and can be found even in hotel rooms. Their daily consumption of insect pests is phenomenal. But show no mercy to the common, germ-carrying houseflies.

Other insects such as chiggers, which make their nests in a skin pore near the toenail, and ticks, which cling to the skin, are more a nuisance than a danger. It was because of a chigger and its budding brood that I suffered and limped for two months during a trip to Africa. You protect yourself against these insects, as well as scorpions and snakes, by never going barefoot and by wearing shoes and pants tied around the ankles while walking through high grass. A nurse at any bush dispensary can show you how to get rid of these parasites.

Scorpions that are disturbed are quick to give a very painful sting. Wear shoes, and in the morning shake them out before putting them on, since scorpions like the warmth of a shoe worn the day before, as do certain chilly snakes. However, I admit that I've never found anything in my shoes except a panic-stricken roach. Application of very hot water will reduce the pain of a scorpion- or spider-bite.

Snakes. Despite the stories you hear, very few travellers will catch sight of a snake during their stay in tropical countries. In my five years in the tropics I saw four of them. Generally they are timid, people-fearing creatures. The greatest danger is the possibility of treading on a sleeping snake, which is why it is important to wear shoes or even boots and always watch where you put your feet. Don't ever walk in the grass at night without a flashlight.

If snake-bite occurs, see a doctor or, failing that, the nurse at the nearest dispensary. Avoid panic and all unnecessary movement. Don't make a cut to "suck out the venom" the way they do in old adventure movies. Apply a dry dressing. Put a tourniquet above the bite and loosen it every fifteen minutes. Take two aspirins for the pain. If the snake was killed, bring it to the doctor or nurse for identification. In most instances an antivenom serum won't even be needed.

Jellyfish. During a swim in the sea, the skin may come into contact with a jellyfish, whose venom can cause a dangerous reaction. It is important to remove the little tentacles clinging to the skin. These can be loosened by sprinkling them with alcohol or, failing that, sand. Don't rub your skin. In serious cases, stretch out in the shade and have someone apply a tourniquet, as for snake-bite.

CONCLUSION

No one should be put off by this chapter, since it provides the traveller with proven ways to avoid health problems. I can't emphasize too much that *the recommendations in it must all be followed down to the letter*, even the ones that seem excessive.

Having learned a great deal through hard experience, I have become extremely careful during my journeys to the tropics, and, except during the very first, I've never had the least touch of tropical disease nor even been bitten by a snake or the smallest of scorpions.

Along the way I have met some Canadian travellers who boast about always being in great shape without taking any special precautions. "After all," they tell me, "local people don't take any, and they're none the worse for it."

The answer to that is that the great majority of people in the Third World suffer from a variety of ills such as malaria, bilharziasis, trachoma, and amoebic and parasite-borne diseases. In the long run survivors end up by developing partial immunity.

Let bold travellers recall that life-expectancy in the Third World can be as low as twenty-nine years for men and thirty-five for women, as in Chad, while in Canada it is seventy-two for men and seventy-nine for women.

CHAPTER 9

Air Travel

The most practical and often the most economical way to travel in the Third World is by air. The large airlines and local carriers serve all countries in Africa, Asia, and Latin America, as well as the major islands in the Caribbean and the Pacific.

Some of the smaller carriers use ancient aircraft that in rich countries would have been consigned to the scrap heap long ago, but the pilots are almost always first-class. In Latin America, for example, aviation traditions are of very long standing. The transition from pack-animal to plane was made before most countries even had national road or rail connections. In the early 1930s, Mermoz, Guillaumet, and the other heroes of the Aeropostale were already making jaunts across the Andes in their strange-looking flying machines.

AIR FARES

There is great variety in the cost of going from one point on the globe to another. Fares change constantly, and it would be useless to set them down as I write these lines; somewhere a new set of rates will be announced tomorrow.

A wise traveller will be in no hurry to agree to the first suggestion made by the travel agent, who may tend to suggest the highest rates. There are always ways to save money. For example, you may save by buying the ticket far in advance, by leaving on one weekday rather than another, by staying two days longer or two days less in a country, or by taking a bus to a nearby American city for a bargain flight to your first transfer point.

Normally you don't decide overnight to go to Ecuador. Take the time to discuss all the possibilities.

The very wealthy traveller or the business person with a flexible expense account will most probably choose to go first-class on a well-known airline. I don't fall into either category, but I've nonetheless happened to go first-class on several long hauls with companies such as Swissair, Air France, Singapore Airlines, and Air Canada. It makes all the difference in the world: the seats are roomier and more comfortable and sometimes change into what is almost a berth. (Some airlines do have real berths, but they are very, very expensive.)

Impeccable service, Iranian caviar, free champagne,... What's more, you get to wait for your flight in the V.I.P. lounge and your baggage allowance is thirty kilos rather than twenty. But when you are young and poor, or old and fit, it isn't worth the expense of paying twice the economy fare.

As for the "business" or "club" class touted so extravagantly these past few years, they don't always offer enough in extras to be worth the twenty-five per cent hike in fare. On certain flights, however, the cost can be minimal. The seats are sometimes the same as economy class (Air Canada uses first-class seats), there's more leg-room, the food is better, and alcoholic beverages are free. Still, some companies such as Qantas and Singapore Airlines reserve the upper flight deck on Boeing 747s, which can be very nice.

Do the same prices always bring the same service on all the international airlines? Certainly not. I hope I'm not unleashing an international incident by reporting that it's better on, for example, Japan Airlines and Swissair than on Iberia or Sabena. But that can change from one year to the next.

The major airlines of Southeast Asia that are not members of IATA (International Air Transportation Association) compete strenuously with the prestigious European and American companies. They ply travellers with more and more extras, offering them free earphones, slippers, alcoholic beverages, cigarettes, and little gifts. The service is impeccable and nicely attentive, reflecting Oriental courtesy. For a long time that was the hallmark of Singapore Airlines, but recently Thai International and Cathay Pacific have shown themselves to be no slouches either. On the other hand, these companies sometimes touch down more on long hauls and so take longer. But since it's a little insane to go non-stop from Paris to Hong Kong, why not stop over on the way, for a few days rather than a few hours, which these companies allow you to do at no extra cost? On arrival in Hong Kong, you will feel less dazed by the length of the flight and the severity of the jet lag.

You can save a great deal by taking charter flights. Winter sees droves of them heading towards the sunny countries. The problem is that they go and come back on set dates, which, with few exceptions, means that you have to stay in the same place for one to three weeks. If you cancel for anything short of urgent necessity, you may be out the price of the ticket unless you have taken out cancellation insurance. (See Chapter 7.)

Finally, young travellers with time to spare may choose to go stand-by, saving up to half of the economy fare. This is worth the risk of turning up several times at the airport before you obtain a seat to your destination. Information is available from travel agencies specializing in youth travel.

THE PLANE TICKET

When you receive it, make sure that all flights are marked **OK**, which means confirmed. The initials **RQ** means requested, which is definitely not confirmed. Don't ever leave a flight unconfirmed—unless you love adventure and have time to kill. Still more dangerous are the initials **WL** for waiting list. Are there two people on this list...or two hundred? You will find out in some remote corner of the world, where you will be told in the same breath that the next flight with an available seat leaves in three weeks' time. Finally, if you want to know it all, the word **OPEN** means that you haven't asked for a reservation on a given leg of your journey; you are in no hurry and will decide on the way.

It is taken for granted in North America and Europe that *at least* an hour is needed between connecting flights. As we've seen in the first chapter, this is certainly not enough time between flights at certain major airports in the United States. With a very few exceptions, I allow two hours for a connecting flight, and preferably three in Third World countries, where flights are very often late. In brief, check the times of arrival and departure of all flights before accepting the itinerary suggested by your travel agent. Don't accept a transfer in Dacca or Lima that *theoretically* leaves only one hour between flights. You might make it, but in all likelihood your baggage won't—and will catch up to you Allah knows when!

NAME OF PASSENGER / NOM DU PASSAGER

HEBERT / J. MR

ORIGIN / ORIGINE YUL

DESTINATION YUL

PASSENGER COUPON / CAS. 2008

PLACE OF ISSUE – AGENCY
LIEU D'ÉMISSION – AGENCE

FROM / DE MONTREAL
TO / A MIAMI
TO / A PUERTO PLATA

	CARRIER TRANSP	FLIGHT VOL	CLASS CLASSE	DATE	TIME HEURE	STATUS RESERV
BlueSlic	DL	302	Y	08JUL	0700	OK
BlueSlo	KC DL	307	Y	08JUL	1300	OK

FARE / PRIX 528 00
TAX / TAXE 12.50
TOTAL 540 50

FORM OF PAYMENT / MODE DE PAIEMENT CHEQUE

DELTA AIR LINES, INC.

3290871298 1

Let's take another look at the air ticket. You will notice that it has as many coupons as there are flights. The ticket is issued by the company responsible for the first flight.

Your surname and the initial of your first name are written in the top left-hand corner of the coupon. They should be legible and not misspelled.

When you check in at the airport, make sure that the clerk takes the proper coupon and doesn't mistakenly take two of them, thereby depriving you of your ticket for the next flight.

All the needed information is given. You should take the trouble to read it.

In plain language it means that this part of your ticket is valid to bring you by regular fare from Puerto Plata to Miami. You have a right to one piece of baggage of any weight. (Other airlines allow you to bring two bags, or only twenty kilos of baggage. The travel bag you carry in the cabin doesn't count.)

Your carrier is Delta Air Lines, identified by the code letters **DL**. (Ask your travel agent to write out the full names of the various airlines, since some code letters bear no relation to their initials.)

Your flight number is 302, and you are travelling in economy class, indicated by the **Y**. For first class, **F** is used.

You leave at 7:00 A.M. on July 8, and your reservation is **OK**, on the condition, of course, that you reconfirmed it forty-eight or seventy-two hours in advance, depending on the company's regulations.

In the upper righthand corner you will see the ticket number, the place and date of issue, and the name of the travel agency.

Finally, in the lower lefthand corner is some information that you would just as soon forget: the price of the ticket.

When you check in at the airline's counter at the airport, the appropriate coupon will be removed and you will be given a *boarding pass*, which is the equivalent of a ticket until you have taken your seat on board the plane. After baggage check-in, you will be given a baggage stub, generally stapled or glued to the ticket itself.

In almost all Third World countries, there is an *airport tax*, payable in local funds. Sometimes American dollars are accepted, or you may be asked to have them exchanged at the currency exchange. The airline makes sure that this tax has been paid before they hand out your boarding pass. (In Canada, the airport tax is included in the price of the ticket.)

Immigration officers will want to see the boarding pass before giving your passport the final stamp of approval. You will be asked for it if you make purchases at the duty-free shop and, when the moment comes, it will clear the way for you to board the plane.

Here is a sample of one:

The boarding pass contains more information than appears at first glance. You are travelling economy class on Air Canada's Flight 741 on the seventeenth day of the current month. When your flight is announced or, if no announcement is made, at the designated time, you will go to gate 18A. You are in Row 23 on board the plane and your Seat D is on the aisle in the smokers' section. The plane leaves at 7:50 A.M., and you should go to gate 18A about half an hour before then. You are travelling from New York to Montréal, and you will arrive at Dorval airport (**D**).

FLYING IN COMFORT

A Zairean cabinet minister whose duties involved frequent travel about the globe once confided to me in hushed tones: "After years of difficult and exhausting trips, I've finally discovered the magic formula for going long distances without the least tiredness, even when there's a big time lag."

I was all ears! "It's a very simple formula," whispered the minister. "First I get as much sleep as possible before leaving. I eat nothing in flight, I don't smoke, and I take no alcohol or any other drink except uncarbonated mineral water. I take off my shoes, undo my collar, and loosen my belt. Now and again I walk around the cabin. Mostly I relax and sleep. When that no longer works, I bury myself in an absolutely fascinating book. There you have it! I always arrive at my destination as fresh as a daisy."

I have every reason to believe that my Zairean friend's method is the best one. It is based on common sense and the advice of the leading experts. And it has worked quite well for me every time that I've tried it. But too often you let yourself be tempted by the mediocre steak, watery carrots, and slightly stale pastry, not to speak of the whiskey that "won't do any harm."

Speaking of whiskey, people are too prone to forget that altitude multiplies the effects of alcohol. When you are flying at twelve thousand metres, the air pressure in the cabin is the same as at two thousand metres or more on the ground, that is slightly less than in Mexico City.

This rarefied air drains the system of energy to a greater or lesser degree, depending on the individual. And the air you breathe is polluted, notably by smokers.

Finally there's the jet lag.

The earth is divided into twenty-four time zones, and Canadians who go from Halifax to Vancouver are very aware of the effects of a jet lag of only four hours.

Obviously there's no jet lag when the direction travelled is north or south. Nonetheless, if you left Canada's far west, say Vancouver, and went to Rio de Janeiro, on South America's east coast, there would be a five-hour jet lag, which is considerable. (There would be an eleven-hour jet lag if you went from Montréal to Colombo via the Pacific.)

The body has to make an abrupt adjustment to a new rhythm. The usual signals come at all the wrong times—sundown when we feel like sunrise, meals when we want to sleep, and fatigue compounded by sleeplessness.

In flight it's best to wear roomy clothes and very comfortable shoes, since the feet tend to swell at high altitudes.

Some people take a mild sedative to make it easier to sleep. On principle I never do, but I envy travelling companions of mine who can cross the Pacific sleeping like babies while I can hardly get my eyes to close.

The abrupt pressure-changes in the cabin during takeoff and landing sometimes cause discomfort or even ache in the ears, particularly among cold-sufferers. It will go away if you yawn, pinch shut the nostrils and exhale, and energetically swallow your saliva.

If you suffer from airsickness, which hardly ever occurs on to-day's larger aircraft, or stomach-upset, the flight attendant can provide medication.

To sum up, you will stand up better under the combined onslaught of jet lag, shortage of oxygen, and the weariness inherent in a long voyage if you follow my Zairean friend's advice and don't smoke, eat as little as possible, and abstain from alcoholic and carbonated beverages.

The ideal seat? I prefer one by the aisle (you can move more freely), in front of the emergency door (there's more room to stretch your legs), and at the rear of the plane... where there's a better chance of surviving an accident.

In this regard, listen carefully to the flight attendant's instructions before takeoff (unless you know them by heart) and read the ones you find inserted in the pocket on the back of the seat ahead. Locate the emergency exits nearest your seat. Your life could depend on what you do in the seconds following an order to leave the plane. Finally, make a discreet check to see whether there is a life belt under your seat.

Keep your seat belt fastened at all times, particularly if you intend to sleep; that way you will avoid being wakened by the flight attendant if the order to buckle up is given.

Then worry no more. It is safer to cross the Atlantic by Boeing than to cross St. Catherine or Yonge Street on foot.

Whatever you do, you are not going to be "fresh as a daisy" after ten hours in flight, unless you happen to be a Zairean minister who does yoga exercises between cabinet sessions.

Eat lightly and get as much rest as possible in the twenty-four hours following arrival. The Pyramid of Cheops has been waiting for you for four thousand years; it will wait another day.

Towards the very end of the flight, the flight attendants will sometimes hand out a customs form and always a *disembarkation card*, which should be filled out with care, particularly with regard to the name of the hotel in which you expect to stay. If it happens that you don't have a reservation, have the name of a good hotel in mind or, failing that, write in Canadian Embassy, if there is one. Immigration officials are always troubled by passengers who don't know where they are going to stay.

Some countries require a *currency declaration*. The flight attendant will give you the appropriate form. (See Chapter 7.) To avoid having to count out your money on the plane or, worse still, in the airport, always keep handy a copy of your list of travellers' cheques, as described in Chapter 7.

RECONFIRMING FLIGHTS

As was seen in Chapter 1, only the first leg of your trip is automatically reconfirmed. In going from Montréal to Kinshasa via Brussels, for example, your seat is reconfirmed to Kinshasa if the two flights are marked **OK**. If, on the other hand, you wish to stop over in Brussels for a few days' rest, you should reconfirm the Brussels-Kinshasa flight as soon as you arrive in Brussels, at the airport itself if possible.

The golden rule of travelling is that the first thing you should do on arrival in a city is to go to the airline responsible for your next flight and reconfirm it. Don't let anyone else do it in your place, and don't rely on a telephone call, whatever you are told and whatever you are used to doing in Canada. Make sure that it is written in on your ticket that your flight has been duly and truly reconfirmed. These painstaking precautions are important in the Third World, where overbooking is rampant and computers, where you find them, are not always in working order, and where some governments assume the right to requisition seats for cabinet ministers, highly placed civil servants, or official visitors.

While at the airline counter ask for the following information:

- ☐ amount of the airport tax due on departure
- ☐ means and cost of transportation between the city and airport and
- ☐ airport check-in time on the day of departure

As I said before, arrive at the airport at least one hour before the time suggested by the airline. That way you will avoid the rush, have a better choice of seats, and have time to exchange your remaining pesos or spend them wisely in the shops. Finally, you can relax over a coffee and newspaper... while casting a pitying eye on the other passengers pushing and shoving for an hour to get a boarding pass.

Obviously you can't reconfirm a flight seventy-two hours in advance if your stay in a city is limited to a day or two. In that case you have to look after it in the preceding country, where the airline company will promise to send a telex ahead to its office or that of another company, as the case may be. Don't put too much faith in it! When you arrive in the city from which the flight in question leaves, reconfirm, or rather *re-reconfirm* it, even if there is less than twenty-four to seventy-two hours until flight time.

When you arrive at the hotel, find out the airline's address and its office hours, which vary from one country to another. And don't forget that each country has different holidays, independence, the revolution, or the coup d'état not having all taken place on the same day in every Third World country. Finally there are a great number of Muslim countries in Africa and Asia in which Friday is a holiday while Sunday is not.

There are still countries such as Guinea that require an exit visa. Apply for one on arrival or, at the latest, three or four days before departure.

BAGGAGE LOSS

The airlines have highly effective ways of protecting themselves from the complaints of unhappy customers. And the smaller the company, the less chance you have of being compensated for the trouble and expense caused by a last-minute flight cancellation, a connection missed because your flight was an hour late, or falling victim to overbooking. The most you can hope for is a meal voucher, or possibly a night's hotel lodging if the next flight doesn't leave until the next day. One sure thing is that you will get more by insisting than by keeping quiet.

The same goes for baggage that is misdirected or lost outright. In this latter case the airlines will pay you about twenty dollars (U.S.) for each kilo checked in to a maximum of thirty-two kilos. When it is found and arrives on a later flight, it is rarely delivered to you at the hotel, since customs insists that you go and pick it up yourself at the airport.

Once you are sure that your baggage hasn't arrived, advise the airline *before* leaving the airport. They will have you fill in a form, a copy of which you should insist on keeping. Don't *ever* hand over your baggage check before you have all of your luggage in your possession.

You can understand the reluctance of the carriers when you know that on IATA members alone an estimated fifty thousand pieces of baggage a year don't arrive at their destinations at the same time as their owners.

You will then have to insist that the airline tell you exactly how much it gives travellers deprived of their luggage for several days. Generally they pay back only direct and necessary expenses (keep your receipts) if it takes forty-eight hours for your luggage to catch up with you (one hundred per cent for toilet articles up to twenty-five dollars; fifty per cent for other necessary items). Some companies offer you an emergency toilet kit.

If after three days your baggage still hasn't arrived, ask the company for a *claim form* and send it back as soon as possible—no more than three weeks after the arrival date.

Above all, don't give up! Airline companies of any stature end up by giving in to a persistent client who is in the right. And most important, take out baggage insurance before leaving Canada if your suitcase and its contents are worth more than twenty dollars (U.S.) a kilo. (See Chapter 7.)

My baggage has never been lost, but it has been misdirected three or four times and caught up with me the next day or the day after. I have always put in a claim for compensation and more often than not won my case.

Once I was on the way back from India to Paris on Air India. While I made a (too close) connection in Bombay, my baggage was left behind and delivered the next day to my hotel room in Paris. On arrival at the airport in Paris, I went to the Air India counter and explained the serious difficulties this mistake on the company's part had left me in: that same evening I was due at a reception at the Canadian embassy and could hardly turn up in unpressed pants and a sports jacket. Without further discussion the clerk gave me the sum of a hundred and fifty dollars on the spot, easily enough in the 1970s to buy a navy blue serge suit at the Galeries Lafayette. Don't tell Air India, but I still wear that suit!

When there are several connecting flights, it is best to look after baggage-transfer at each airport yourself, even if the airline suggests checking it through to the final destination. It tires you out more, but you will be sure that the transfer has been made, and your baggage will arrive at the same time you do. This is another reason to turn down too-slim transfer times.

If you have to go just once without your luggage, even for only twenty-four hours, you will realize how important it is to have survival gear in your carry-on travel bag: a toilet kit, shirt, shorts, pair of socks, all important papers, and other essentials.

LOSS OF PLANE TICKET

Advise police and the embassy if your air ticket is lost or stolen, and go to the issuing airline or, if it has no office in the city you are in, the company responsible for the next flight.

If you have taken the precaution of making a photocopy of your ticket, formalities will be that much easier, and you should be given a new ticket after a check by telex with the company that issued the original ticket.

In Canada and the U.S. you have to pay costs and buy a new ticket, for which you will get a refund if the original ticket isn't used later.

If the difficulties prove to be insurmountable, you can always wire or telephone relatives or friends who will have a prepaid ticket sent to you. Or you can buy a new ticket (by credit card if you are short of cash) and the price of the lost ticket will be reimbursed on your return home.

CHAPTER 10

Automobile Trips

My favourite means of transportation is the automobile, particularly for long journeys in the Third World. In my youth I made four major trips of a year or more in duration by land: one in Latin America, two in Africa, and one around the world, including passage through most Asian countries. You will find that most of the information in this chapter also applies to motorcyclists. They need only adapt certain recommendations, particularly the ones dealing with equipment.

Cars and motorcycles give you freedom. You stop anywhere, whenever and for as long as you like; you change itineraries as the fancy strikes; you go off the beaten track to discover places where tourists never set foot.

You will be still freer if, as I strongly advise, you set up your vehicle so that it can be slept in, which, as will be seen further on, is quite easy for two people. This is a fine way to save a lot of money, since you don't have to stay in (very expensive or very dirty) hotels except once in a while when you feel an irresistible urge to take a hot bath. I advise against sleeping in tents, which make you much more vulnerable to thieves and other undesirable night visitors such as snakes, scorpions, and spiders.

You can bring along more supplies when you travel by car, including food and a small cooking set-up. That way you can avoid restaurants, which is good for both your health and your wallet.

AUTOMOBILE CLUBS

My first recommendation is that you become a member of an internationally recognized automobile club. There are a hundred of them all told in Canada's major cities, united under the banner of the

Canadian Automobile Association, itself affiliated with the American Automobile Association, the International Touring Alliance, and the Fédération internationale de l'automobile, which ensures reciprocal services for members in most countries worldwide. (See Appendix J.)

Your annual dues to one of these clubs entitle you to a great many services, all the more so when you travel abroad. Here are some of them:

—emergency road service twenty-four hours a day, 365 days a year (at least in theory)
—consumer protection service
—network of recommended garages
—advantageous car financing
—travellers' cheques at no charge
—free personal accident insurance

The clubs are empowered to issue two documents that are absolutely essential for automobile travel in all African, Asian, and Latin American countries: the International Driver's Licence and the Customs Driver's Permit. This service is offered even to drivers who do not belong to a club.

You nonetheless have to belong to a Canadian club to qualify for reciprocal services by affiliated clubs outside Canada. (See the list of Third World automobile clubs in Appendix K.) On request your club will give you a special card of introduction.

THE INTERNATIONAL DRIVER'S LICENCE

Any club affiliated with the Canadian Automobile Association will issue you this licence if you present a valid provincial licence, provide two passport photos, and pay a fee of $7.50. The International Driver's Licence comes in handy even in countries that don't require it, since all the information on it is printed in ten languages.

THE CUSTOMS DRIVER'S PERMIT

This document serves as your car's passport. With it you can bring your car or motorcycle for a temporary stay in most countries of the world. Western and Eastern European countries, the United States, Mexico, and the countries of Central America do not require this document.

To get a Customs Driver's Permit, apply to the nearest CAA-affiliated club. It's a rather long and costly process.

1. Fill in and sign an application form.
2. Supply two passport-size photos of yourself and a photo or illustration of the vehicle.
3. Pay a fee of $50 (for members of a club) or $60 (for non-members) as well as a returnable deposit of $100. The Permit is valid for a year from the date of issue and can be renewed annually for a fee of $10.
4. Provide a guarantee in the form of a letter of credit, a certified cheque, or a negotiable certificate of deposit. Obviously the letter of credit is the most advantageous. The purpose of the guarantee is to insure the countries visited against your selling the vehicle without paying taxes and customs duties, which are always high and sometimes out of this world. Assuming that you did so, the automobile club holding your security deposit until your return would reimburse customs.

This guarantee, at an amount set by the national office of the CAA, is now a major roadblock in the way of long international journeys. It must in fact be set as high as the highest duties imposed in the countries visited, that is from one to four times the value of the vehicle.

Let's suppose, for example, that you leave for Asia with a 1983 Chevrolet Suburban, valued in 1986 at $6,500. Since some countries levy duties of four hundred per cent on vehicles, your automobile club would require a security deposit of $26,000. An informed traveller can arrange his trip so as to stay away from the greediest countries and choose a car given the lowest possible evaluation in the countries to be visited.

Each page of the permit is divided into three segments, of which two are detachable. The customs official at the border will take the first segment and put all the needed information and stamps on the two others. When you leave the country, no doubt at another border crossing, customs will lift the second segment and write in the date of your departure on the stub.

The Customs Driver's Permit is almost as important a document as your passport, and you should have a photocopy made of its first page and keep it apart, with your other documents. If it is lost or stolen, advise police and the embassy, and then your club, which will provide a duplicate, sometimes through a local affiliated club, if there is one. At any rate, it will take a long time. The loss of a Customs Driver's Permit is a disaster. Guard it as closely as you do your passport.

I didn't know that there was such a thing in 1946, when I went without one on a trip across fifteen Latin American countries. There were no problems at the borders of Mexico and the Central American countries, but I was made abruptly aware that I was missing an essential document because when I came to Cartagena, Colombia, it took thirty-six hours and the help of a sort of lawyer to get the car through customs.

It was a real nightmare getting the car through at every border from Colombia to Argentina. It took long hours of talk, but in the end we made it through, particularly if the customs official had seen our picture in the day before's newspaper.

We came close to meeting our Waterloo at the Argentine border. After two days of discussions with Argentine customs, it was time to face the fact that there was no way we could get our wretched 1931 Chevrolet through short of a decree from the then-President of the Republic, General Perón.

Here's how I described the situation in my journal starting on March 11, 1947:

> Mendoza, towards noon. Everything about the customs superintendent says hypochondriac—nervous, clerkish, unlikeable.
>
> First he reads my friend and myself the letter of the law: "The government requires a Customs Driver's Permit before allowing a foreign car to enter the country in transit." No permit, no entry, unless we leave Mr. Superintendent a security deposit of two thousand Argentine pesos, that is, three times the value of the car. What to do? Try without success to get permission to continue by car to Buenos Aires, where the Canadian embassy might be able to get us out of this mess. The janitor at customs confides in us: "It's no use. Don't press it. The superintendent is afraid of losing his job. You know...the new government...Perón... ssh!"
>
> There's only one remaining solution: one of us can go by train to Buenos Aires (nearly a thousand kilometres) to pull a few strings.

March 13

It's chilly this morning on the train platform at the Pacifico station. A chilled, silent crowd jostles around the ticket booth. I wait my turn holding a little package with toothbrush, razor, pen, passport, and shirts all wrapped in yesterday's *La Prensa*.

All aboard! Fat, out-of-breath men loaded down with travel bags and parcels make a dash for the doors. Nervous, weepy women are hugged: "You'll get your sleep, won't you dear?" The train begins to move: "Will you write?" And the stolid boyfriend answers in a voice as sombre as Louis Jouvet's: "You'll be on my mind all the time. I'll send you postcards."

Now I'm gliding through the greens, browns, and yellows of the pampas, whose gentle monotony will see me through to Buenos Aires. Second-class coach, of course. I'm jammed between a talkative older woman and her for-the-moment silent daughter. A privileged position that I no doubt owe to a quirk of the railroad, which assigns every passenger a reserved seat. I have 21B, the respectable lady 21A, and her daughter 21C. Nothing could be simpler. I'm in between the two of them, which they feel is as it should be.

My companions hold back at first because of my presence, discreet as it is. But little by little they get more sociable. At barely fifty kilometres from Mendoza, Mrs. Lopez ends by saying: "Make me some *maté*, will you?" And Lucia, a docile child and, heaven knows, a lovely one, takes a smelly little alcohol burner from her bag. She boils a little water and pours it in her mother's *maté*, already jammed with green leaves, *Yerba del Paraguay*. A much-liked infusion throughout eastern South America, *yerba maté* is taken hot or iced, with or without sugar, in a little oval container. You drink it with a silver straw, *la bombilla*. While passing the *yerba* to her mother, Lucia spills a drop on my gray trousers.

"Santa Catarina! How dreadful! Look what you've done now, poor Lucia! Really, sir...."

Mrs. Lopez is ecstatic. At last we can talk freely. The ice is broken. "So you're Canadian! Lucia, the gentleman is Canadian! And is there lots of snow where you live? And the Northwest Police? A marvelous police force, isn't it? But those Redskins give you so much trouble."

Snow, Mounties, Indians, in brief, all of Canada! What's known about Canada all comes from American movies. And it's too bad that we are still a British colony. "When will you have your revolution and become the twenty-second American republic?"

Mrs. Lopez sips at her *maté*. Around noon she reaches into a deep bag and pulls out a big bologna, onions, bread, and cookies. Now that I'm a family friend, I'll get my share....

God, how huge the pampas is! Mendoza-Buenos Aires is a little like North Bay-Edmonton....We arrive in Buenos Aires exhausted and dazed at about 11:30 in the evening. I end up in a *muy barato* little hotel. A myopic Syrian rents me a bed in a room for four at a rate of two pesos (fifty cents).

March 19

By now I must have gone to fifty officials to solve the problem of the car, still back in Mendoza. Every one of them assures me, but without conviction, that all will be settled by tomorrow. *Mañana.*

The Canadian ambassador is getting things moving on his side. To boost my morale, he invites me to a cocktail party at his home at five o'clock. The guests, ambassadors of Britain, Australia, and perhaps New Zealand, exchange London society gossip while I stay in a corner and drink a gloomy Scotch-and-soda toast to the health of the Empire. A lady is told that I came from Canada by car. She aims her lorgnette: "Good for you, young man! Was the weather nice?"

March 24

At last! After long discussions with ministers of state—who no doubt consulted Perón—we were just given permission to go across Argentina in our old heap. I am quick to wire the three prisoners back in Mendoza. Their letter this morning sounded less than reassuring. "Hurry up! We're running out of money, and only grapes are cheap in Mendoza. But two weeks on grapes...."

Ah, yes! Our car was held up two weeks at the Mendoza border post because we didn't have a Customs Driver's Permit. Q.E.D....

As has been shown, it is in fact possible to cross borders without a permit. All you have to do is leave a deposit at the border of a sum of money equal to a hundred per cent or more of the car's value, which sum is theoretically returned when you leave the country. Obviously it was this requirement that lay behind our discussions with South American customs officials.

This was one solution that we couldn't conceive of, for the simple reason that we didn't have the money. What's more, in those days it would have been illusory to think that customs officials a thousand miles away from the ones who took our deposit would give us back the money, particularly in American dollars, without a struggle.

I say without hesitation that the great exploit in that Latin American journey wasn't going through seventeen countries in fourteen months in a 1931 Chevrolet, but rather doing it *without* a Customs Driver's Permit.

INTERNATIONAL INSURANCE

It used to be that Lloyd's of London offered an insurance policy that gave motorists liability coverage in practically every country in the world. This happy state of affairs no longer prevails, and nowadays just about every country gives recognition only to insurance bought in their own territory. It is often sold at customs posts.

The green, orange, or brown cards offered in some countries are valid in certain others that recognize such-and-such a card.

In the case of Mexico, temporary insurance can be bought from the automobile clubs in certain border towns. Since Khomeini, it is even simpler in Iran, which now has an outright ban on the entry of foreign vehicles. In brief, the situation has become so complex that only the automobile clubs can provide up-to-date information.

What is sure is that you should *never* travel in a foreign country by car or motorcycle without insurance. I have never had a traffic accident in my years of travel, but I know drivers who have been ruined by a car accident or gone to jail because they were the cause of serious injury to someone.

CHOOSING A VEHICLE

This choice depends, of course, on the kind of trip planned. Any kind of vehicle will do to go to Panama or even Buenos Aires, cross the North African countries, or make a circuit in India.

If, however, your plans include crossing the Sahara by the Mauritanian trail, or Central Africa from Dakar to Djibouti, especially during the rainy season, I advise you to drive a four-wheel-drive, all-terrain vehicle. There is a good selection of them on sale these days, but you should choose the make that is the best seller in the countries to be visited. That makes it easier to find spare parts and mechanics used to doing repairs on vehicles of your make.

SETTING UP THE VEHICLE

As I have said, you shouldn't leave for a months-long camping trip in a Third World country without setting up your vehicle so that it can be slept in. The illustrations below show, as examples, how I modified the Jeep used in my trip around the world and the Jeep Station Wagon driven on my second African trip so that two people could sleep in them.

These very simple changes were done at low cost by a small-town bodywork man.

All your vehicle's doors should lock by key. If possible have a double system to protect the baggage section. Finally, get a tamper-proof cap for the gas tank.

Springs. Before leaving, have *heavy duty* springs and shock ab-
sorbers installed. They may be uncomfortable for the motorist, but
they are essential on very poor roads, all the more so in that your
vehicle is very likely to be carrying a heavy load.

Tires. Leave with four new tires, two spares, and as many inner
tubes, tubeless tires not being advisable. Take along a good pressure gauge and use it often. Tire pressure should be lowered in very
hot weather or when the vehicle is travelling on a sandy track. And
don't forget to reinflate them after a cool night or when you go from
a sandy track to a rocky one. Rotate the tires every eight thousand
kilometres.

SPARE PARTS

Get a list of dealers for your make of vehicle in the countries to be
visited. But even if there is a garage in Tanzania that repairs Land
Rovers, don't count too heavily on its having the parts you need.

Fewer spare parts are needed, of course, for a new vehicle or one
in perfect working order. But a certain number will surely break
down in the course of a long trip over rough roads. Have a good long
talk with your dealer's chief mechanic and chief buyer. The combined experience of the two of them will enable you to draw up a list
of parts most susceptible to breakdown.

Among other things, the list will include:

- [ ] gas pump
- [ ] set of joints
- [ ] two fanbelts
- [ ] set of spark plugs
- [ ] condenser
- [ ] coil
- [ ] rotor
- [ ] set of points
- [ ] set of fuses
- [ ] set of light bulbs
- [ ] set of radiator tubes
- [ ] oil filters
- [ ] set of brake linings
- [ ] maker's repair manual

Additions to this very brief list will be made on the advice of your two experts. And if your dealer is a nice guy, he might agree to take back unused parts after your return.

TOOLS

- ☐ two good jacks (for rotating tires and helping free your car when it is stuck in a rut or sand dune)
- ☐ flat-tire kit (wrench to unscrew wheels, three tire-levers, innertube-patching kit)
- ☐ very complete set of wrenches (including adjustable ones and a spark plug wrench)
- ☐ set of screwdrivers
- ☐ hacksaw
- ☐ hammer
- ☐ two pairs of pliers
- ☐ metal file
- ☐ assortment of screws, nuts, bolts, cotters, and washers

GENERAL EQUIPMENT

- ☐ chemical fire extinguisher
- ☐ set of electric cables with clamps
- ☐ spool of steel wire
- ☐ two-metre length of electric wire
- ☐ spool of tape
- ☐ oil reserve (for motor, brake, etc.)
- ☐ two jerry-cans with spouts for gas (more for crossing the Sahara)
- ☐ jerry-can for water
- ☐ funnel
- ☐ short length of rubber tubing
- ☐ two ladders or two flat surfaces for putting under the tires when getting out of sand (indispensable for crossing deserts and other sandy areas)
- ☐ shovel
- ☐ pressure gauge
- ☐ good air pump
- ☐ long length of cable with a solid grapnel at each end (for being towed and for towing others)

CAMPING GEAR FOR TWO

- ☐ two sleeping bags
- ☐ roll of five-cm thick foam rubber (to put over the plywood board that serves as a bed)
- ☐ two small pillows
- ☐ alcohol burner
- ☐ a five- or six-litre thermos jug with tap (to hold drinking water)
- ☐ two small folding stools
- ☐ hatchet
- ☐ large plastic basin (for washing hands and dishes)
- ☐ two dishrags
- ☐ two saucepans with lids
- ☐ frying pan
- ☐ small coffeepot
- ☐ butcher knife
- ☐ small kitchen knife
- ☐ large serving spoon
- ☐ ladle
- ☐ salt and pepper shakers
- ☐ good can opener
- ☐ stainless steel utensils
- ☐ unbreakable dishes
- ☐ plastic containers with screw-on lids
- ☐ small broom (for cleaning the vehicle's interior)
- ☐ two shatterproof one-litre bottles (one for alcohol fuel, the other for lamp oil)
- ☐ storm lantern

BASIC PROVISIONS

You can eat well on what is available locally, but one of the advantages of an automobile is that you can bring along a minimum of nonperishable items to add variety to the menu. The items suggested here are often expensive or not available in certain countries. The quantities will depend on how long a trip is planned and the capacity of the vehicle. Here is a basic list that can be varied to suit individual tastes:

- ☐ dried soups

- ☐ canned cheese
- ☐ peanut butter
- ☐ jars of jam
- ☐ canned tuna in oil
- ☐ canned sardines in oil
- ☐ canned corned beef
- ☐ canned pâté de foie
- ☐ bouillon cubes
- ☐ canned tomato paste
- ☐ spaghetti
- ☐ macaroni
- ☐ tea bags
- ☐ coffee or instant coffee
- ☐ cocoa
- ☐ condensed milk in tubes
- ☐ mustard in tubes
- ☐ sugar
- ☐ salt
- ☐ pepper
- ☐ spices
- ☐ steel wool
- ☐ liquid dish detergent
- ☐ laundry soap
- ☐ toilet paper
- ☐ waterproof matches

Food items that have to be kept moisture-free can be stored in plastic screw-top containers or watertight freezer bags. All the provisions should be stored in a sheet-metal coffer that closes tightly so that you won't be troubled by roaches and ants.

SHIPPING THE VEHICLE BY SEA

Even a trip to Rio de Janeiro involves a sea-crossing, since there isn't yet a road connection between Panama and Colombia. Of course there are even more compelling reasons why you will have to go by ship with your vehicle if you plan a trip in Africa or Asia.

I advise you to travel along with it, which means finding a freighter that accepts passengers or a liner that ships vehicles.

Make *both* reservations as far ahead as possible. And be ready to pay at least as much for shipping the vehicle as for your own passage. You may be in for a financial shock.

Hold on carefully to the bill of lading issued to you by the shipping company, without which it will be hard to regain possession of your property once you reach port.

The company normally allows you to leave your gear in the vehicle during the crossing. Check this out beforehand.

Watch over the unloading of your vehicle at dockside and don't leave it until it has cleared customs, which can take many hours. If need be, and if permission is granted, spend the night in your vehicle.

SALE OR PURCHASE OF A VEHICLE ABROAD

Even though shipping costs are very high, I advise you to buy your vehicle in Canada. This gives you more time to choose it, make modifications, and equip it. It also makes it easier to get the indispensable Customs Driver's Permit.

You may perhaps be tempted to sell your vehicle at the end of the trip. It won't be easy, and lots of time will be lost in administrative hassles. You will have to pay out huge sums in taxes and customs duties, unless the sale is made to a diplomat or a duty-exempt foreign resident. At any rate, be sure that everything is cleared with customs and that this is confirmed in writing, without which you risk losing the guarantee given to your automobile club in Canada.

FORDING RIVERS

In Third World countries, you often have to ford rivers or wadis. Before you drive across one, check its depth and the nature of its bed. If there are people in the neighbourhood, ask them to show you the best place. But check anyway! One person should wade ahead of the vehicle to act as a guide.

Before leaving dry ground, let the motor cool down, let air out of the tires if the bottom is sandy, remove the fanbelt, use a tarpaulin under the hood to cover the motor, put a good-sized length of radiator tube at the end of the exhaust pipe and raise it as high as possible, . . . and pray!

Naturally, go as slowly as you can across the river. To keep the water from reaching the motor, don't make waves.

Once in the south of Mexico it happened that my car stalled in the middle of a river. Of course I hadn't taken the above-mentioned precautions.

Here are some extracts from my travel diary:

Disaster struck in the middle of the roaring Tehuantepec River, about three hundred metres wide and the deepest we have yet encountered. In mid-river we are navigating in water more than two feet deep. The motor sputters a few times, lets out a last groan, and then gives up the ghost. It's no use pushing. We have to wait for the unlikely arrival of help.

It's night, and the heavy skies have just burst open. We are drenched by a tropical storm—not that it matters, we've already had many unwanted baths trying to free the car. In the distance we think we can make out the lights of Tehuantepec, which is a source of comfort. After several hours an enormous truck comes to our aid, and with great difficulty tows us to the village.

Serious damage. No doubt the car is due for a long stay in the garage. All the more so since the sympathetic Mexican garage-men are particularly slow. Our mechanic invites us to stay with him for the duration of the repairs....

(*Autour des trois Amériques* [Montreal: Beauchemin, 1948])

It was to be four days before we continued on!

CROSSING THE DESERT

You don't venture into a desert of any size without making serious preparations. You have to study the maps, read the most recent accounts of travellers who have gone before, and talk with truck drivers who make regular runs on the route planned. If possible travel with two vehicles.

Gas stations are very few and far between in, for example, the Sahara, and the further you get from the last town the more expensive it gets. You should, then, take as many jerry-cans of gas as experts advise. I took eighteen of them during my last crossing of the Sahara, and that was none too many. I also had three jerry-cans of drinking water, even more important than gas if you have a breakdown or, worse still, the back luck to get lost. All of which, of course, has happened to me.

A four-wheel drive vehicle is ideal for desert tracks. Be scrupulous about following the advice given earlier about inflation of the tires.

In the last town before the desert, get two small aluminum ladders, or two lengths of chain-link fencing, or two flat surfaces. And a good shovel! Many times along the track you will get stuck in a sand dune that wasn't there the day before, or cross vast expanses of *fesh fesh*, a kind of fine powder in which you easily get bogged down.

The ritual then begins. With the shovel you take as much sand as possible away from around the wheels. You put two flat surfaces in front of the rear wheels, set the two front wheels in traction, and start the car moving without jolts. It doesn't always work, and you repeat the process as often as necessary. In the worst cases, you can use the two jacks to raise the rear of the vehicle. When nothing works, make a good cup of mint tea and wait for the (highly infrequent) passing by of a helpful truck or caravan.

Since a desert track can disappear in a sand storm, you can lose sight of it and get yourself lost. This is extremely dangerous, and many travellers have died of thirst. As soon as you feel that you are on the wrong track, have the good sense to go back until you find the *right* one. When you are really lost, the *only* thing to do is to stay with the vehicle and wait for help. With a good supply of water and food you can wait a long while, and help will come in due course, particularly if you have signed a breakdown-service contract with a trucking company, which unfortunately isn't available everywhere.

In the desert you should get underway at first light, while the sand is harder and the motor and tires won't heat up as much. Then rest during the heat of the day, and travel again from afternoon until nightfall.

CHAPTER 11

The World's Great Itineraries

When you leave for a long road journey, particularly in Asia or Africa, it is best to have many months ahead of you, six at least. A ten-month trip seems ideal to me, if only to justify the cost of equipment and sea travel. I've taken twelve- and even fourteen-month trips, but I admit that the last months seemed less worthwhile. Weariness builds up, curiosity films over, and . . . we begin to miss Canada.

For trips of less than three or four months, you should be satisfied with Mexico or Central America, or the Andean countries, or Brazil, or, if you must, North Africa.

Every continent offers a great variety of itineraries to the imagination. As examples, I'll give brief accounts of the ones I took during my trips to Africa, Asia, and Latin America. In some cases they are easier now, with better roads, than they were in the 1950s. Other itineraries I took cannot at present be followed exactly because ideological conflicts or wars have shut off several borders to travellers. But, Allah willing, this won't always be so.

LATIN AMERICA

On April 18, 1946, I left Montréal with three friends, Yvon Champagne, Pierre Gascon, and Marcel Girard, in a rusty wreck of a 1931 Chevrolet convertible coupé. Two of us at a time had to take turns sitting in the rumble seat, that is, exposed to the sun and rain. Because space was so cramped, we had to tow along a trailer filled with baggage.

What we had in mind was a leisurely trip through all the countries of North, Central, and South America. It was said at the time that this was the longest trip ever undertaken on the continent. I've never taken the trouble to check the accuracy of this statement, since our goal wasn't to set records. We were twenty years old and, as is normal at that age, we dreamed about adventure and discoveries. Along the way, I would send a weekly column to a Montréal newspaper to help pay for the trip, as I would do during my years of traveling in Africa and Asia.

We were to return to Canada fourteen months later after having gone through twenty-one countries, seventeen of them by car.

It took us more than two months to reach the Guatemalan border, mostly because we were in no hurry and stayed as long as possible in the towns and villages we liked, but also because the road became very bad after Oaxaca, in Mexico. We had to ford across many rivers and go by rail from Ixtepec to Tapachula, the road then being impassable.

In 1946 there was no way to go by road from Costa Rica to Nicaragua. We had to go by train from Rivas to the Pacific coast, a distance of twenty-one kilometres, and by barge from San Juan del Sur to Puerto Soley, in Costa Rica, a distance of twenty-three kilometres.

But that was only the beginning of our troubles. It took five strenuous days to go the few kilometres to the capital, San José, at an average speed of three kilometres an hour. Several times we had to hire a pair of oxen to help drag us over roads that the rainy season had turned into rivers of mud.

It became apparent that there was no road from San José to the Panamanian border, and we resigned ourselves to shipping the car and trailer to Panama City from the little port of Puntarenas. But the freighter wouldn't take on passengers, which led us into an unbelievable week-long trip to join up with the Chevrolet. We travelled by skiff from Puntarenas to Golfito, and from there to La Cuesta in a little wood-and-painted-canvas aircraft held together by string, on foot to the Panamanian border, by rail to David, by swaying bus to Divisa, and by truck to Panama City.

Even today, as then, the Pan American highway hasn't bridged the impenetrable, marshy jungle that lies between Panama and Colombia. Depending on their itineraries, motorists can go by ship from Panama City to Buenaventura, on the Pacific side, or from Colón to Cartagena (or Baranquilla) on the Caribbean. It was this latter route that we chose.

There is a wide variety of ships on either coast. To save money we chose the oldest and smallest coastal ship capable of taking on our car. It was a rough experience, as can be seen in a few paragraphs from my shipboard diary:

> Sky torrid. Waiting on Pier 5 for the seamen to decide to load our car and trailer on the deck of the *Marionetta*. Complicated piece of work. Lots of discussions, futile attempts, and swearing before the captain comes. After hours of canny manoeuvring, the moorings are finally cast free and the *Marionetta*, which has never seen such a weird animal on its deck, makes an uneasy departure from the port of Colón. The Chevrolet is tied down on the starboard, near the lifeboat, and causes the ship to list noticeably.
>
> The *Marionetta* skims through the night at top speed—ten knots. From the captain's side, on the helm, it seems to be the only thing afloat. Not a freighter, not a pirogue, crosses our path.
>
> But we aren't alone. The twenty-five passengers are divided into two classes: the ones who sleep on the deck and "these ladies and gentlemen of the first class," who are entitled to the single cabin. It is our hard luck to be so entitled.
>
> A mulatto woman weighing at least a hundred kilos with great exertion clambers up into the berth above mine and clambers back down from it for part of the night. The others, less weighty, are a poor man suffering from seasickness; an old, incessantly grumbling Indian woman; a small, shy gentleman; two mothers with two unhappy babies; and two other coughing, spitting, snoring passengers.
>
> At first we are delighted with the white sheets, but that just makes it easier to make out the swarming hundreds of mouse-size roaches. If these little creatures weren't enough to keep us awake, the mosquitos and ants would have done the trick alone. It's the mulatto woman who complains loudest: "Me, Señora Castro, in a place like this! What an insult!" And the whole compartment echoes her sentiments. The two babies vie with each other in wetting and throwing up. Because of a violent storm, the doors and portholes remain shut. The heat is hellish.
> (*Autour des trois Amériques* [Montreal: Beauchemin, 1948])

From Cartagena we headed towards Baranquilla, then towards Venezuela by the Maracaibo road, a faint track across the La Guajira desert, used at least by smugglers.

After pushing on to Caracas, we once again reached Colombia, this time via the Andes... which we were to cross six times before reaching Argentina. This is no small matter for a fifteen-year-old car dragging a heavy trailer. On a hundred steep slopes we had to detach the trailer, push the car to the top, then come back and pull the trailer up, again by leg-power.

We crossed Colombia without further incident, but that wasn't the case in Ecuador, where the road from Quito to Guayaquil was a Costa Rican-style nightmare. We had to take to the sea again to get from Guayaquil to Puerto Bolívar.

The only serious problem in Peru was after leaving Arequipa, where we came to the journey's highest peak, the Cumbre del Alto Toroya, at an altitude of over five thousand metres. From there to the Bolivian border the roads were indescribable. And we had to go from Viacha, in Bolivia, to Arica, in Chile, on a railway flatcar, sitting in our own car, blinded by cinders and steam from the locomotive.

There was a fine asphalt road down the endless, threadlike length of Chile and one just as fine from Santiago to Buenos Aires.

From Argentina you can go through Uruguay or bypass it and go straight into Brazil. We wanted to make the side-trip into Paraguay, but the the borders were sealed by a political upheaval.

Going from Buenos Aires to Sao Paulo took another month of hard going over horrible roads, with our car on the verge of giving its last gasp and our tires worn down to the threads and blowing out ten times a day. Because of the extreme shortage of cars in Brazil in 1947, we were able to sell it in Rio de Janeiro—for as much as it had cost back in Montréal!

There are many more roads now, and they are vastly better than they were at the time of my trip. You might say that motorists have too many roads to choose from in South America. They can dream up the quirkiest of itineraries and be sure before departure that the roads are good, thanks to information from embassies, consulates, and automobile clubs.

AFRICA

I made my first land journey in Africa from July 1948 to July 1949, when my friend Jacques Dupire and I travelled a distance further than around the world in twenty-five countries, at a time when virtually all of Africa was under the colonial yoke.

I say land rather than automobile journey because we had to abandon our vehicle in the middle of the Sahara and continue our trip by a wide variety of means—trucks, buses, trains and, on occasion, riverboats.

But the itinerary is still an interesting one and could have been done by car if we hadn't been foolhardy enough to leave Canada with a vehicle in poor repair, a panel truck whose rear and front axles had both been sprung, no doubt in an accident.

This was a serious mistake, excused by our slim finances and ignorance of mechanics. Not suspecting a thing, we dubbed the vehicle the *Alouette*.

We had already looked death in the face a few miles short of Halifax when a wheel came loose on a steep hill bordered by a precipice.

In Halifax we boarded the *Aquitania*, bound for Southampton. In those days you had to go to Britain to get a Customs Driver's Permit, the vital need for which had been impressed on me during my trip to South America.

There was a second breakdown between London and Dover, the beginning of a long series . . . .

Dunkirk, Paris, broken axle between Versailles and Houdan, Bordeaux, St.-Jean-de-Luz, Madrid, Gibraltar. Normally you cross the Straits of Gibraltar from Algeciras, in Spain, to Tangiers, Morocco, but we wanted to see Gibraltar.

The ship we took, the *Sevro*, was so small that at first you couldn't see how it could possibly carry our truck. The bumpers, in fact, stuck out over the bulkheads on both sides.

Tangiers, Rabat, Meknès, Fez, Oujda, the Algerian border, Oran, Algiers.

In Algiers it took us three weeks of feverish activity to get ready for the desert crossing and, among other things, find various parts that were prone to break down even on the good European roads. Spare parts for a 1938 Chevrolet were extremely few and far between. We finally got what we needed after a hard day's picking over of a junkyard full of the rotting hulks of old American military vehicles. We also had to meet with several dozen officials to get various documents: ration coupons for gas and bread, gray cards, pink permits, and blue certificates.

In addition to a good supply of spare parts, we brought along 120 litres of drinking water, 40 litres of motor oil, 400 litres of gas, not to speak of our provisions, including 10 kilos of dates.

We had all sorts of inside information before so much as entering the Sahara. We could recite the names of all the oases between Algiers and Nigeria by rote; we knew that there was a mechanic in one and gas and a telegraph station in another; we knew that the track had a ridged surface here and was buried in shifting sand there. We were ready.

Several great trails extend across the Sahara. The one we chose was the Tamanrasset, beyond doubt the most picturesque. Its real beginning is at Laghouat, gateway to the desert, that vast expanse where adventure still lies in wait for the traveller behind every dune.

I believe that it will be useful to quote long extracts from my log from Laghouat to El Golea, where I imagine the carcass of our truck still lies. Since the discovery of oil deposits, no doubt some Saharan trails have been improved and are safer. But even today the adventures I lived through are still there to be had on one trail or another.

October 29, 1948

Now easily reached from Algiers, Laghouat was long the Saharan station beyond which few Europeans ventured: further on was desolation, the unknown, danger.

Thousands of people are able to subsist on the strength of their courage and thanks to an endurance acquired over the centuries here in this boundless universe with nothing in it to attract life. In fact the desert is crossed by a great variety of nomads of different ethnic groups, while other sedentary inhabitants live at lost oases.

Leave Laghouat about ten o'clock. The trail is good at first and offers magnificent views of the oasis. Against a horizon of sand, the emerald green palm grove is as striking as a mirage. But it all disappears after a few kilometres. Now there is nothingness on all sides.

The desert doesn't look like the ones you see in the movies with white sand and graceful dunes. Near Laghouat there are still a few scattered plants, a kind of couch grass called *drinn*, and wild pistachio trees called *betouns*, whose leaves serve as forage for dromedaries.

We are crossing an area of *dayas*, enormous depressions where rainwater collects, a highly unusual phenomenon. Most often there is a total absence of life. Lunar landscapes, pyramidal hills, lots of sand, lots of pebbles.

The trail takes a turn for the worse. Holes, rocks, ridged surfaces. At Laghouat we'd been told: "There's only one way to get through it—go fifty kilometres with tires half-deflated."

Fantastic theory that we haven't yet reached the point of believing. We try it—it's hellish. The *Alouette* makes a terrible racket, the hood flies open, the chrome ornaments come loose, and we're constantly in mid-air between seat and roof. We drive on like this at fifty kilometres an hour for haunting kilometres, trusting in the unanimous opinion of Laghouat's most experienced drivers. Exhausted and sore, we finally take pity on the *Alouette* and slow down. But on this kind of terrain you either drive at fifty or at fifteen—anything in between is harder on the vehicle and us both. So what! We're in no hurry....

The trail gets ever bumpier, whipping us around like saplings, but only twice do we come close to being trapped in the sand before reaching Ghardaïa, the second oasis and sanctuary of the proud Mzabites.

October 30

Sunrise at about 5:30. Fill watertank and gastanks. Leave for El Golea on a track described to us in less than flattering terms.

But the still-cool air and the brilliant blue sky give us confidence. Three hundred and fifty kilometres of desert lie between us and the next oasis. There's no real danger of getting lost as long as we follow the Ariadne's thread of a trail through the labyrinth of dunes and wadis. Sometimes it seems to be a local road; it often disappears under the dunes or forks off in several directions, according to the whim of the truck-driver who went before us. First time stuck in sand. In record time we accelerate and change gear, to no avail. The sand acts as a powerful brake and brings us to a stop, a permanent one, it seems.

We learn our new trade under the leaden noontime sun.

First we have to use spade and shovel to exhume the wheels, buried down to the hubs. Then we lie on our backs under the *Alouette* and clear the differential by hand. The wind strikes up, blowing sand into the mouth, nose, ears, and eyes.

Finally we set the squares of chickenwire under the rear wheels. We start, move forward a few centimetres, and sink in again. Shovel, spade, and chickenwire—a few more centimetres. And we start all over...for hours.

Reaching solid ground again, no matter how bumpy, is a kind of deliverance.

All afternoon we are stuck time and again in the sand. From one o'clock until sundown, despite superhuman efforts, we don't move ahead more than a kilometre. And when darkness sneaks up on us, the *Alouette* is stuck in a hole so deep that we put off freeing it until the next day.

We put a can of wax beans on to heat over our little alcohol burner, set in a ring of stones. Suddenly there is a light on the horizon. It gets closer, and then there is noise. We can hear the slapping of pistons. Putt! Putt! The motor dies. Men's voices, sounds of shovelling. Finally we see the headlights of a powerful truck. Since we're blocking the track, and the sand on either side is softer still, the trucker comes to a stop. A Frenchman from Algiers, jolly and congenial. With the help of his pushing, panting, shouting men he succeeds in towing us to solid ground. And thanks to our pieces of chickenwire he gets across the dune without mishap.

October 31

At about nine the trip's first flat, which makes us lose an hour and a half and a good litre of sweat.

A few kilometres further comes the fatal dune. We sink in very deeply, squarely in the middle of it. Shovel, spade, chickenwire. Nothing doing this time. When we start up there is a sharp report, and, at the same time, the motor races crazily, in a void. Disaster! No doubt an axle is broken. Fine. We have a spare. But what if we're unlucky enough to have it turn out to be the driveshaft? Or the crown wheel? Or the ring gear?

We can only wait for a truck to come by.

Landscape: a dozen rocky promontories, dunes as far as the eye can see, oppressive sky, a wind that blinds us with sand and dries our throats.

Let's examine the situation. There's a truck between Ghardaïa and El Golea at least every two or three days. We have a two-day supply of bread and a two-week supply of canned provisions and dates. And water? Our tank holds one hundred and twenty litres, but we discover that it's leaking. And to make a bad situation worse, what we have has a terrible taste of gas and burnt rubber.

Time goes by quickly. We walk, read, sing, and are visited by a beautiful bird with a pointed beak and a long black tail.

We drink mint tea and enjoy the softness of a Saharan night. Not the least sound—even the wind is silent. But yes, we do hear something: "Plock! Plock! Plock!" Our water dribbling away into the insatiable sand.

November 1

We've been stuck here for twenty-four hours. Nothing, still nothing. Then two men come out of nowhere. Probably Berbers. The right arms go up: "Peace be with you!" They don't speak French but make us understand by energetic signs that a truck will be by.

Unconcerned about each other now, we go about our usual business, while the two Berbers heat up the water in a tiny teapot. We offer them dates, and they in turn serve us a delicious mint tea.

The expected truck finally arrives. The Arab driver agrees to get us out of our sandtrap but says he knows nothing about mechanics. "The mailman comes by tomorrow. He knows all about it." Fine. Tomorrow it's down to business.

November 2

The most beautiful part of the day is from seven until noon. We waste it chasing away the hundreds of flies that buzz around the *Alouette*. Either we've taken along the flies for the trip, or they were left behind by the two Berbers and the truck.

At noon the hum of a motor. In the desert quiet you hear the noise of the motor a half-hour before you see the vehicle. Finally an enormous tanker rig draws up, driven by an Alsatian. "I can't leave you on the track. Get yourselves ready, and, presto, I'll tow you to the *bordj*."

After twenty horrible kilometres (the truck doesn't let the worst surface slow it down) we arrive at the Hassi-Fhal *bordj*, a sort of little white fort under the charge of Roehlly, an old Sahara hand and veteran of the Foreign Legion.

We're safe now in a place with food and water.

November 3

Mechanics by necessity, we remove the rear axle and decide that the driveshaft has to be replaced. To be sure, though, we have to wait until a truck comes by with a driver who knows more about it than we do.

November 4

These days the track is swarming with trucks. As many as three a day come by! Soon we know the drivers, all of whom have been aware of our plight for a long while. News in the Sahara travels with astonishing speed over a mysterious wavelength, the Arab telephone. A driver coming up from the south Sahara tells us that we're already expected some thousands of kilometres away, and that all the details of our breakdown are already common currency in In-Salah, Tamanrasset, and In-Guezzan.

Spending three days broken down on the trail is enough to win the sympathy of the veterans of the desert. An Arab driver, Mr. Phal, offers us a box of delicious Deglat dates. Another gives us an hour of his time to help reinstall the truck's rear axle. The warmth of brotherhood among men of the desert makes me think of the similar bonds among seafarers.

November 5

All the parts are in place. The motor runs well, but the *Alouette* won't budge a centimetre. Hidden somewhere in the differential is a devil that has it in for us! We have to wait for another driver-mechanic to come by and shed light on this latest mystery.

No trucks since the day before yesterday. Friend Robert arrives at about four o'clock. He discovers that, oh yes, the driveshaft is cracked all right. But it can still be welded. There's a welder in Ghardaïa... where we were ten days before.

November 7

Together with a dozen Arabs, carrying the part to be welded in one hand and with the other hanging onto the cables holding fast twice as many sacks of wheat as this old truck should be carrying. So what! The driver knows the trail well and hardly ever takes more than five hours to get to Ghardaïa.

The trip took sixteen hours! Countless breakdowns due to running out of oil, gas, and water; electrical failure; flats; short circuits; and getting stuck in the sand. My Arab companions are admirably patient: "If we don't arrive today, we'll arrive tomorrow. *Inshallah!* God willing!"

The travellers get down from the truck when it looks as though the breakdown will last an hour or longer. They eat dates in silence, sleep wrapped in burnooses, go aside and pray to Allah.

We're totally bushed at about three in the morning when we reach Ghardaïa, where my new Arab friends invite me to sleep on the packed-earth floor of a hovel where, despite my weariness, I take part in the drawn-out tea ceremony around a little dromedary-dung fire.

November 8

There are two welders in Ghardaïa, one Christian and the other Jewish. It's just my luck that the first happens to have no acetylene and the second no oxygen. Neither one wants to give his enemy and rival the gas needed if either is to do any welding. My day is spent acting as a diplomatic messenger between Christian and Jew. Finally I have to call on a third party, a Christian who has some acetylene. Then the welding is put off until the next day. I go back and spend the night with my Arab friends, who shower me with little kindnesses. One gives me a little carbide lamp, another a course in mechanics, the third was designated to make tea at all hours.

November 9

The part was welded very early this morning, just in time for me to go back to the *bordj* with the mail truck. The metal is still burning hot when we leave.

For the third time I go over this wretched track. But the trip will be more pleasant with Lalmas, a very pure-blooded Kabyle. And after being shaken up for five hours, we see the rectangular white shape of the Hassi-Fhal *bordj*, in front of which sits the shiny red *Alouette*. It feels like a homecoming.

Roehlly fixes us a camel stew *aux fines herbes* that we eat while talking about El Golea. "You'll be there tomorrow," Roehlly assures us.

November 10

The whole modest population of the *bordj* is watching when the moment comes to put the driveshaft back into its flared tube. Not so fast! The welder in Ghardaïa added too much metal, and we absolutely have to have a big file. But try to find a file in mid-Sahara! "Two trucks are broken down at Kilometre 110," Roehlly tells us. "Englishmen. They're very well equipped, and you'll find all the tools you need. Walk straight over the mountain, bypassing the trail, and you'll save five kilometres."

Instinctively I prefer to take the trail, but Roehlly insists, and his instructions are so clear....On the horizon is a chain of mountains pierced by a crescent-shaped col—the English trucks are there.

I leave at ten in the morning with a flask of water, a can of sardines, a handful of dates, and two oranges. The breeze is cool, the pure breath of a fine desert day. Finally, what a pleasure it is to take this unforeseen jaunt! And, sure of not disturbing anyone, I sing at the top of my lungs:

> *Les plus belles maisons,*
> *C'est des prisons!*
> *Il faut l'espace!*
> *Il faut des horizons*
> *À ceux qui passent*
> *Et qui s'en vont!*

> The loveliest houses
> Are no better than jails.
> You have to have space.
> Those who pass by
> And those who go away
> Need to have horizons.

I'm expected back for lunch by Roehlly and my travelling companion.

Totally missing is the beckoning golden Sahara drilled into us by

Hollywood. The desert here is a death valley paved with gray pebbles or, supreme desolation, black ones.

Depressions, large rocks, *fesh fesh*—painfully slow walking. The mountain doesn't budge; the *bordj*, though, gets smaller by the second. A sugar-cube, you could say, set on a big yellowish tablecloth.

It's noon. I should have sighted the two trucks. But to get around the dunes you don't travel in a straight line, you go down the beds of dried up wadis. That does it, the *bordj* is out of sight. Now I see two crescent-shaped cols in the mountains, then three...six...ten....I think about turning back, but my steps leave no traces on the hard ground. Tough luck! There's always the mountain. Like Mohammed...

I walk fast, but I've stopped singing. I have a strange pinched feeling around the heart: "Don't be an idiot! You're about eight or ten kilometres away from the *bordj*. You'll be able to get your directions from up on the mountain. And the trail! Somewhere on the right is the good old trail where you don't get lost."

The word was uttered! But still I resist. I scold myself: "Lost? No kidding! You don't just get lost like that. You think you're in the movies or something? Come on! The hell with it! Show a little courage!"

Finally I come to the foot of the mountain. Enormous. From far off you would say it was a hill in a public garden. A sort of sawed-off cone falling apart under your eyes, lumps of sand-conglomerate continually breaking off at the top and rolling down to the base. After a hard climb I reach a tiny plateau. Like an islet in mid-ocean. I look for the *bordj*, the trucks, the trail.... Nothing. Dunes, pebbles, dunes....

Let's think it over. All evidence is that I don't know where I am—ten kilometres away from the *bordj*, no doubt, but in the direction of which dune? In the euphoria of the first hours I ate the two oranges and the dates, which leaves the can of sardines and three mouthfuls of water. And the sun? It's sinking.

When I left the *bordj*, the mountains were straight ahead and the trail ran to my right. Again the best thing is to turn back—easy to say!—edging to the left to meet up with the good old trail.

I run like a maniac, trailing a cloud of dust all the way down. "Now, now! Don't lose your cool!" Sand, big pebbles, *fesh fesh*.

"Hey, I recognize this hill!" But no, it's another one. All the hills look alike . . . .

The sun begins to look like a big orange rolling under the horizon. Too fast! This orange reminds me that I'm thirsty. "Imagining things! At bad moments in the desert you think you're thirsty. You're not thirsty! You're not thirsty!"

Night has fallen. Now I can't see where I'm going, and my feet twist on ground still cluttered with rocks. In the middle of a desert, a man feels insignificant and ludicrous.

At my feet there's a sudden splash of white, like a small fallen star. I stop, No, it can't be—a flower! A flower in mid-Sahara—a miracle! A seemingly stemless flower set on the sand like a waterlily on a pond.

For a moment I forget the only thing that counts—getting back to the trail. Thanks to a flower. And that brings back courage. It has to—I can't see where I'm going any more, my strength is gone, and my teeth are chattering from the dry cold.

Get a move on! Forward march! I walk like a robot.

I know that my feet are hurting, but I don't feel a thing. And I'm not alone any more. I hear familiar voices, see the faces of loved ones . . . .I'm dreaming, and think that I'd dream better lying down on the sand. "Don't give us that! You've got to keep moving!" cry out the friendly voices.

And without warning the *bordj* suddenly appears before my eyes, at the end of the night. I slap myself on the forehead to make sure I'm not dreaming. Still the *bordj* comes closer. Light shines from a window; Roehlly and my companion are expecting me. That does it. I'm convinced. And for several minutes I laugh hard enough to throw my jawbone out of joint. I empty my flask in a single pull. Ah, it feels good to be alive! It feels good to laugh! It feels good to find a little lost fort all in white.

When I arrive at the *bordj* I make only a simple statement, "Sorry, but I didn't bring back a file. Impossible to find those damned English trucks." And Roehlly, who knows the ins and outs of the dunes and wadis like the back of his hand, fails to understand: "But still it was so easy. . .the low part of the mountain. . .a two-hour walk at the very most." Not wanting to make him feel badly, I say nothing about the little flower and the sun that looked like an orange.

November 20

After a forced stop of three weeks at the little Hassi-Fhal *bordj*, we went back on the trail headed to El Golea, which we should reach this evening. If all goes well. *Inshallah!*

But our *Alouette* must still have its say—funny noises from the direction of the motor and the rear axle. The radiator leaks like a sieve, and the water isn't long in coming to a boil. So we stop, sniff the air, let it cool off, fill it up. This little game will soon use up our store of water.

Soon come the Great Erg dunes, a stunning sight and welcome contrast to the dull, pebble-strewn desert.

Another wretched episode is heralded by a fierce smell of burning rubber. We stop just in time. Another kilometre and the rear wheel would have come off—ball bearings ground down to powder, twisted half-axle. There's no doubt that the rear axle is totally out of alignment.

Kilometre 55. We've broken down an hour or two short of El Golea, the next oasis. And for how long? Luckily today is mail day, and our old trail-buddy Lalmas is due to arrive in the late afternoon.

We've run out of bread. Lalmas shouts to the Arabs crowded in his truck. Then there's a true multiplication of the loaves. Everyone brings us a hunk. We end up with a two-day supply.

November 21

The only truck of the day comes by at three o'clock. It's Robert, another old friend. He's heartbroken seeing us at a standstill. He'll try to get us ball bearings in El Golea so that we can get to the oasis under our own power. He leaves us all his cigarettes.

November 22

At daybreak we hear a truck go by on the trail. It's already long gone when we emerge from the *Alouette*, but we find a litre of olive oil left by the driver, whose name we'll never know.

What a marvelous human experience a breakdown in the Sahara is!

November 23

Terribly cold night. Our sleep is fitful due to the truck being stuck on a slope. My friend, sleeping on top of the water tank, rolls towards the door. As for me, I'm constantly about to fall off the trunk.

Out of bread. But while we're still in bed a truck arrives from El Golea with provisions sent by our friend Robert: a two-day supply of bread, oranges, dates.

Four days now at Kilometre 55, we continue to be the trail's pampered children. Everyone is worried about the "Canadian kids." People ask about us in Laghouat and Tamanrasset, that is, at a distance of fifteen hundred kilometres.

After a day's work, we succeed in taking down the rear axle and the driveshaft, which we'll bring to the oasis to be checked. Let's wait for the next truck.

November 24

At about ten there's the sound of a motor—Hadj Miki! Delighted to be of service, Hadj Miki, a local notable, urges me to hop aboard, pieces of scrap iron and all.

Sitting on top of a truckload of dates, I get badly shaken up and shiver all the way to El Golea. But once we arrive in this oasis of dreams, all the hardships of the trail are forgotten immediately. After a month in the desert, the sight of palm and orange groves and a plain kitchen garden makes me feel born anew. For the moment, unfortunately, I don't have time to frolic in the gardens. A slave of the machine, I have to analyze the rear axle's defects with the mechanics and solve the problem, if only it can be solved....

November 25

I leave El Golea with Hadj Miki in the hellish 3:00 A.M. cold and three hours later am back at Kilometre 55. There are some mechanical fun and games in store. The wind is blowing and sand seeps in everywhere, so that every part to go back in has to be wiped off with gas a hundred times. It's also so cold that your fingers are freezing—at noon the place is swarming with flies but night falls at five—we won't make it.

November 27

We're black with oil, grease, and dust. Let's face it, we aren't cut out to be mechanics. Provisions are running low. Water too, but at day's end the mailman comes and leaves us a little.

November 28

As we're about to leave, we realize that there's water in the gas filter. We empty it, siphon it out, and swallow our fill of gas.

The radiator is leaking on all sides. We don't go a kilometre before it boils up to the bursting point. We stop, let it cool down, fill it with water. Won't start—more water in the gas. No doubt the solution is to direct all this water to the radiator. When we finish emptying the gas lines, the radiator is empty. In the distance trots a dromedary at a steady, measured pace.

A kilometre of trail and it starts all over again. The battery is dead, we don't have a crank, the motor is flooded. Totally disgusted, we decide to have a quiet lunch and take a nap.

Again we make two or three kilometres' progress. The *Alouette* turns into a steam engine until the store of water is exhausted. But since it's our lucky day, there's another truck stalled shortly ahead. All trucks in the Sahara carry enormous vats of the precious fluid.

After taking on water, we move on. New kind of misfortune— the brakes fail. The proverbial straw! And more water in the carburetor. And the trail is so rough that the *Alouette* is in danger of being shaken to pieces. In brief, an unspeakable trip broken off eight kilometres short of the goal because, on one hand, there's not enough water, and, on the other, there's too much. On the skyline we can already make out the first palm groves of El Golea....

A meager snack and so to bed, leaving the solution for the next day. Hardly have we fallen asleep than the sound of a motor wakes us up. "On the trail at this hour...who could it be?" The motor stops besides us: "Hey, Canadians, already in bed?"

I recognize the congenial voice of our new friend, Joussen. He was worried by our delay in reaching El Golea and, with the thermometer down to 35°F (1.6° C), he came by motor scooter over a particularly dangerous stretch of the trail to bring us a hot meal.

We arrived just in time. The *Alouette* seems ready to expire. We drudged away like slaves from Kilometre 5 to the El Golea town square, where a rear wheel finally gave out. The same old story— worn out ball bearings, twisted and eroded half-axle. Aubertin, the local authority on mechanics, tells us what is evident even to us: our car is out of service and can't continue on. It's no use arguing with a hunk of metal; totally ruined by the rough Saharan track, that's what the *Alouette* has become. We leave it in a little courtyard shaded by big weeping palms. It will never leave this spot. At least we owe it five months of high adventure.

(*Autour de l'Afrique* [Montréal: Fides, 1950])

And that's what happens to incautious young people who make the mistake of taking on a continent like Africa with a car that's not up to scratch. Q.E.D. . . .

Nonetheless the trip went on, by land. We continued the desert-crossing from El Golea on one of the enormous diesel trucks of SATT (Société africaine des transports tropicaux) linking Algiers with Agades.

In-Salah, the Arak gorges, the Hoggar massif, Tamanrasset, meeting with the Tuareg king, In-Guezzam, goodbye Algeria, hello Niger. But the Sahara laughs at borders. It extends from Egypt to the Atlantic, eats away at Morocco, Algeria, Tunisia, Libya; its tentacles stretch south on one side to Khartoum and all the way to Sahel on the other.

Past Agades, plant life begins tentatively to get a toehold. Zinder, the border with Nigeria, then British, Noël to Kano. From there to Chad with an English captain emigrating from London to Southern Rhodesia, known since independence as Zimbabwe.

At Fort Lamy (now N'Djamena) we find a French merchant going to Cameroon. He has a convoy of three trucks and never travels without a cook. Bongor, the Ubangi-Shari border (now the Central African Republic after a spell as a short-lived empire), Cameroon, Yaoundé. Take a little train from Yaoundé to Douala, on the Atlantic coast.

It would have been simpler, of course, to go from Chad to Bangui and from there to Zaïre, then known as the Belgian Congo, but we wanted to pay homage to the famous Dr. Schweitzer. Going to Lambaréné meant crossing Cameroon and taking a freighter or coastal steamer from Douala to Libreville, then going up the Ogooué River by pirogue. In Douala we find out that Dr. Schweitzer has gone to France for a rest. We then decide to go to Pointe Noire, some three hundred miles to the south, on a modest freighter of His Britannic Majesty's merchant fleet.

Three days at sea. Pointe-Noire, Congo. Eighteen hours by train from Pointe-Noire to Brazzaville. Only the Congo River stands between us and Leopoldville, Belgian Congo (that is, Kinshasa, Zaïre).

We then go upriver on an old riverboat, the *Luxembourg*, that has been sailing on the Congo and Kasai for forty years... at a speed of six knots. We get off at Pont-Franque, end of the river segment.

By van to Mushenge to go and meet Lukengo, king of the Bakubas, who is said to have nine hundred wives. By rail to Elizabethville (Lubumbashi) and then to Northern Rhodesia (Zambia), Southern Rhodesia (Zimbabwe), Bechuanaland (Botswana), South Africa and Capetown, the southernmost point of our journey.

Another thirty-eight hours by rail from Capetown to Maseru, capital of Basutoland (Lesotho), a country that we wanted to explore in more depth.

Train to Johannesburg, Bulawayo, Victoria Falls; return then to Lusaka to make a detour via Nyasaland (Malawi), which will take two days on local buses.

Off to Tanganyika (Tanzania) by wheezy truck, Mbeya, Dadoma. Third class by bus to Arusha. To Nairobi on an Indian bus. Twenty-five hours by train from Nairobi to Soroti, in Uganda. By truck to Lira, Gulu, Nimule and finally Juba, in Sudan, where we take a barge headed for Kosti—nine days on the Nile.

From Kosti to Khartoum by rail, seven to the tiny third-class compartment. Twenty hours. Another train from Khartoum to Wadi Halfa, last oasis in Sudan, the green gateway to Egypt. A small river-steamer further down the Nile to Shellal, and by train from there to Cairo and then Port Said. We've looped the loop—on June 22 we board the British freighter *Chinese Prince* headed for Halifax.

Two and a half years later I was to even the score with the Sahara by taking a second eight-month African trip.

This time I left with a brand new vehicle, a four-wheel drive Willys Jeep Station Wagon, well equipped and properly set up for sleeping. Since I was now travelling with my young wife, Thérèse, not yet turned twenty, there was all the more need for a comfortable *Alouette*. There was no lack of adventures, but for the purposes of this chapter it's enough to describe the second African itinerary, still possible for today's motorists.

After arriving in Europe, at le Havre, we first had a long stay in Paris, essential in those days to get visas for the large number of African countries still under French domination.

We crossed the Mediterranean from Marseilles on the *Ville d'Oran* and arrived in Algiers on August 26, 1952.

Oran, Saida, Colomb-Béchar, Béni-Abbès, Moroccan border, Ksar-es-Souk, Ouarzazate, Marrakesh, Casablanca, Rabat, Mogador, Agadir.

Return to Algeria, our take-off point for crossing the Sahara, this time by the Bidon 5 trail, which goes from Colomb-Béchar to Gao, in French Sudan, now called Mali.

This time I go into the desert with full confidence. We have a fine vehicle, large reserves of gas (more than four hundred litres), and enough food for several weeks. We have, moreover, signed a breakdown service contract (required, incidentally, by the authorities) with the *Société africaine des transports tropicaux*. For thirty dollars and a cash deposit returnable in Gao, the SATT agrees to come to our aid if we have a breakdown on the trail. Since we're in the middle of the cold season and SATT trucks go regularly down the trails, there's no risk that we'll be left to our own devices in the Sahara for two or three days.

Again we pass through Béni-Abbès, the first oasis, go to Adrar, then to Reggan on the Algerian frontier. A distance of fifteen hundred kilometres stands between us and the next frontier post, at Gao.

We take on the Tanezrouft crossing, the most desolate part of the Sahara, called "the land of thirst and fear." You come out of it at Bidon 5, a dot on the map without which travellers would think twice before venturing into the Tanezrouft.

The tiny village of Tessalit, whose claim to fame is its wells—an indispensable waterhole for Moorish shepherds, Tuareg caravanmen and Saharan travellers. And five hundred kilometres further is Gao, the first population centre of any size since Colomb-Béchar and the end of the desert... that we crossed this time in a mere mishap-free nine days!

Gao, the border of Upper Volta (now Bourkina-Faso, which means "the homeland of honest men"), Ouagadougou, Bobo-Dioulasso, return to Mali, Bamako, Nioro, Kayes, from which, we find out, it has been five months since anyone has travelled on to Dakar. We have a fine all-terrain vehicle, so this year it will be the *Alouette* that opens the Bamako-Dakar road, passing through Nayes, Tambacounda, and Kaolack.

Pass through Kaolack and Tambacounda again on the way to Guinea, Guinean border, Labé, Mamou, Kankan, Ivory Coast border, Man, Bouake, Bondoukou.

Gold Coast (now Ghana) border, Yegi, Bolgatanga, Navrongo, Salaga, Kumasi, Accra, Togo border, Lomé, Dahomey (now Benin) border, Cotonou, Porto-Novo, Nigerian border, Lagos.

From Lagos, on the Atlantic coast, we decide to cross the whole of Africa from west to east to the Red Sea. Ibadan, Ifé, Asaba, across the Niger by ferry, Cameroon border, Banganté, Bafia, Bertang, Ubangi-Shari (Central African Republic), Berbérati, Bangui.

The Ubangi River separates the Central African Republic and Zaïre (then Belgian Congo). Zongo, Libenge, Lisalak, Bumba, Buta, Stanleyville (Kisangani), Beni, Ugandan border, Katwé, Lake Edward, M'Barara, Kampala, Entebbe, Kenyan border, Kisumu, Lake Victoria, Nairobi, Nanyuki, Meru, Wagir, the Ethiopian border, Moyale, Iavello, Algeremariam, Dilla, Shashamana, and after a very difficult drive across Ethiopia, the capital, Addis Ababa.

Last stage—Addis Ababa to Port Sudan via Waldia, Asmara, the capital of Eritrea, and one thousand kilometres of Sudanese desert—Kassala, Aroma, Amm'Adam, Derudeb, Suakin and Port Sudan, on the Red Sea. That's the end of the African odyssey. From here we'll sail on an old Arab freighter, *Al Amir Saud*, to Genoa, Italy. A bit of driving across Europe to le Havre and by ship to Québec City.

It took a few pages to outline this African itinerary, but five hundred were needed to tell about its endless adventures in *Nouvelle aventure en Afrique* (Montreal: Fides, 1953).

ASIA

My trip to Asia, a round-the-world tour by Jeep, took place between the two African journeys and lasted exactly a year, from June 24, 1950, to June 24, 1951.

In the course of these twelve months, my friend Jean Phaneuf and I travelled sixty-five thousand kilometres and passed through twenty-eight countries and colonies. Naturally we had to travel by sea for a good many of these kilometres. Sad to say, the part of our route that took us through Afghanistan, Iran, and no doubt Iraq, is barred nowadays. From Pakistan, for example, you would have to branch off towards Africa, go from Karachi to Djibouti and return to Europe via Cairo or even Tangiers.

Leaving it up to the individual traveller to imagine the necessary detours, I'd still like to sketch the route I took through Asia at the beginning of the 1950s, the essential part of which is still open to travellers. After leaving Montréal in a Jeep that was, unfortunately, rather old but very well set up, we first drove across the United States to San Francisco to sail on the *President Wilson* for Japan, with a stopover in Hawaii. Two weeks of absolute discomfort in a third-class cabin deep in the hold. We were the only whites, since this class was then reserved for non-whites. It took hours of long and laborious argument to get the shipping company to deviate from its racist policy.

The Korean War had just broken out. From day one, the South Koreans and their American allies were driven back to a slim toehold at the Taigu bridgehead. As a present for my paper, *Le Devoir* (which hadn't asked me to do a thing), I succeeded in getting accredited as a "United Nations War Correspondent" and going and risking my neck in Korea for a few days. After this episode, we made a quiet visit to Japan from Nagasaki in the south to Matsu-Shima in the north.

Another sea voyage from Yokohama to Hong Kong via Manila. In third-class, of course, with the Asians. After two weeks in Hong Kong and the inevitable side-trip to Macao, we were able to get a booking for ourselves and our Jeep on a French freighter bound for Saigon with stops at several ports in Tonkin, which was to become North Vietnam before amalgamating with South Vietnam into a single Vietnamese state.

From Saigon we finally took to the generally good road across Cambodia under military escort, the Indochinese War now well underway.

Naturally we wanted to go from Bangkok to India via Burma, but then as now the Burmese were reluctant to give visas except for brief stays in the Rangoon and Mandalay area. We had long sessions with Burma's military attaché to Thailand, who sketched out our route on detailed maps, but thought it highly unlikely that we would get necessary go-ahead.

"There are five thousand Chinese here," he explained. "They are sure to attack and, if they let you live, you can be sure that they will rob you of all you've got, jeep included. A little further on you will come to the rebels and the communists, who beyond any doubt will shoot at you."

At any rate, Rangoon turned us down, and we regretfully changed itineraries and headed for Singapore via Malaysia, itself fighting guerillas. Still, the road from Hua Hin to Haad Yai in Thailand was impassable, and we had to cover a seven-hundred-kilometre stretch with a four-day rail journey.

In Singapore we took to the sea again for the last time before Dunkirk, an eight-day sail over the Indian Ocean to Madras, India, on the ageing freighter *S.S. Jalagopal.*

There's no end of ways to drive from Madras to Pakistan, and what would be ideal would be to visit all the states in this fabulous India. The route we chose is as good as many others: Madras, Guntur, Ruriapet, Hyderabad, Wharda, Sewagram, Nagpur, Benares, Gorakhpur, Lucknow, Kampur, Agra, Delhi, the Pakistan border, Lahore, Peshawar.

From Pakistan we took the historic Khyber Pass to Afghanistan in what turned out to be the roughest stretch of the entire trip—very poor, often snowed-under roads, since we were in the middle of winter. The Jeep dragged along from one breakdown to the next. But what an extraordinary and seductive country! Kabul, Mukui, Kandahar, Girishk, Dilaram, Farah, Herat, sixty kilometres from the Soviet border....

Past the Iranian border there was a marked improvement in the road, and the weather was a little better. Yusufabad, Meshed, Teheran, Kazvin, Hamadan.

We had been suffering from the cold for nearly two months, in part because it was winter, and also because we had travelled at high altitudes from the Khyber Pass through Afghanistan and Iran. Now we were going to come back down to the Iraqi desert, the Mesopotamian plain, and the sea, going abruptly from winter to spring and then summer. Baghdad, Rutba, the Jordanian border, Amman, Palestine, Jerusalem (then half Palestinian and half Israeli), Bethlehem, Bethany, "border" between Palestine and Jordan, back to Amman, Syrian border, Damascus, Lebanon, Beirut, Tripoli, back to Syria, Homs, Aleppo, Turkish border, Antioch, Iskenderun, Ankara, the Bosphorus, Istanbul, that is, Europe.

The rest of the trip was a tourist's jaunt, almost always on asphalt roads, through Greece, Yugoslavia, Austria, Italy, Switzerland, France, and Great Britain, where we sailed from Liverpool to Québec City.

CHAPTER 12

Other Kinds of Transportation

LOCAL BUSES

An excellent way to see a country and get to know its people. In addition to run-of-the-mill buses, you will sometimes find deluxe coaches (everything being relative!), more comfortable, faster, and making fewer stops along the way. Deluxe coaches are better maintained and so safer and more expensive.

The usual kind of bus is almost always rundown, dirty, and uncomfortable. They stop on the smallest pretext and break down frequently. They are generally jampacked, each passenger bringing along piles of baggage, including bundles, wicker crates, guerbas, suitcases, sacks of rice, food, babies, live chickens, and other household or agricultural goods.

If you have the time, a trip across Malawi or Pakistan under these conditions won't soon be forgotten. After ten hours on the road, three flat tires, a landslide, and ten stops, a spirit of solidarity builds up among the passengers, and it can happen that you strike up lifelong friendships.

You don't have to bring chickens along but take at least some emergency provisions: fruit, nuts, cookies, a good canteen of drinking water, and toilet paper.

Keep a close watch on your travel bag and your money, not forgetting about your suitcase perched on top of the bus. When stops are made to let someone on or off, take advantage of the opportunity to make sure that your suitcase isn't about to fall off, or that some misguided person isn't helping it do so!

Impatient and finicky people and those short of a sense of humour should shun this kind of trip. Others will have a great time and learn a great deal.

TRAINS

In Africa. A very few Third World countries, Libya and Rwanda for example, have no railroads at all. Some others have only a single narrow-gauge line between the capital and another major city or a large capital city in a neighbouring country. This is the case with the rail link between Bamako, Mali's capital, and the Senegalese capital city of Dakar, which is Mali's main outlet to the sea (a twenty-seven-hour trip when all goes well). In neighboring Mauritania, on the other hand, the single railroad line is six hundred kilometres long and used to ship ore from Zouerate, in mid-desert, to the small Atlantic port of Nouadhibou.

You can't make an east-west crossing of the whole of Africa by train, but from north to south you can take the train all the way except for a few hundred kilometres between Sudan and Uganda.

In Latin America trains function well enough, and some lines through the Andes provide the passenger with spectacular views and wild thrills. Train buffs who go to Peru shouldn't miss the trip between Lima and Oroya and from there to Huancayo and Huancavelica. This line is said to be the highest in the world, hugging the mountainside at an altitude of forty-eight hundred metres. Don't try it if you can't take the thin air at these heights.

In Asia. If it weren't for various conflicts along the way, you could take the train from Calais, in France, all the way to the Pacific Ocean. All of Europe and Asia could be crossed.

Trains go everywhere in India thanks to the fine Indian Railways system, the world's largest—thirty-eight thousand miles (sixty-one thousand kilometres) of track plus seven thousand stations, eleven thousand locomotives, and ten million passengers *a day*.

On more important routes, there is a choice of classes from the air-conditioned coach and bedroom to the wooden benches of second-class. Between these two extremes are opportunities for comfortable, cheap travel. Trains are part of the Indian way of life, and they are an excellent means of getting to know the country.

Rail travel is just as pleasant in China, especially in first-class, which should come as no surprise, even in a society that is supposed to be classless.

In Asia as elsewhere bring your food along with you unless you are travelling first-class and there is a dining car. At any rate, you run no risk of dying of starvation. In the Third World, trains are met at small stations by swarms of vendors who make a dash for the windows and offer tacos, fritters, kebabs, ice cream, candies, and fruit. Since you will turn down all these good things except for soda pop and fruit that you can peel, it is wiser to rely on your own supply.

Don't forget the flask of drinking water and the roll of toilet paper, without which the trip can be a miserable one.

And of course be on the lookout for thieves, particularly when the train pulls into a station. Hardly has it come to a stop before there will be a swarming horde of vendors and all the relatives of people getting on or off.

RIVERBOATS

From time immemorial the rivers and lakes of the Third World have served as communications arteries.

Some famous routes will long continue to bring joy to the hearts of travellers who wish to get out of the towns and go into the heart of the country. Who hasn't dreamed of going up the Amazon in a Brazilian riverboat from Belém to Manáos? Or going from Bamako to Timbuktu on the Niger? Or taking a long easy trip on the Ganges or the Yangtze Kiang, the Blue River?

The more daring will sail the Senegal or Gambia Rivers on a pirogue, the Yellow River on a sampan, and cross Lake Titicaca on one of those charming little boats of rush.

Extraordinary adventures are there to be had out in the current. Only remember not to swim in fresh water or even dip your fingertips in it. The piranhas and crocodiles are less of a danger than the bilharzia, whose larvae enter through the skin's pores and infect you with bilharziasis, a debilitating disease suffered by more than a hundred million people in the Third World.

FREIGHTERS

Modern freighters bear little resemblance to the old tubs of the novels of yesteryear. They're fast (up to twenty-five knots), clean, and generally know where they are going. But even today there is nothing to stop a freighter headed for Osaka, Hong Kong, and

Singapore from forgetting about Hong Kong and making a detour to Taiwan if that is the latest order from the shipping company.

If you choose to travel by freighter, don't have too exact a destination or be in too much of a hurry. You may go on a voyage for twenty-six days and learn on the way that it will take thirty-two. That won't cost more, but if you have an important appointment (or seasickness!) the six extra days can seem to drag on.

A constantly shrinking number of freighters accept passengers, but there remain a certain number that generally have twelve passenger cabins, well-placed amidships. They cost much less and are sometimes roomier than first-class cabins on a cruise ship.

You have to like the quiet life, reading or bridge, since there are hardly any diversions on board a freighter. No pool, no night club, no movies, and no shops. But if you dream about relaxing or writing a book, you will get a boundless taste of life at sea. You can, however, visit a port from time to time without having to undergo the hastiness of airports or take the trouble of registering at a hotel, since you come back on board at night. Don't forget to get all the needed visas, or you will admire the city from the ship's rail.

Since passengers eat with the officers, the food is often excellent, particularly on French or Norwegian vessels, less so on British or Greek ones. You may meet interesting people on board since traditional tourists hardly ever choose to go by freighter. In good weather you can jog or go for a walk, breathe in the sea air, or sunbathe.

In addition to the minor disadvantages mentioned above, remember that there won't be a doctor on board. If someone falls seriously ill, the captain will try to have him transferred to a ship with a doctor on board or take the first opportunity to land him at a port or hospital. People in poor health or of very advanced age shouldn't take this kind of chance. For that matter, many lines won't take on passengers aged sixty-five or more, or will do so only on receipt of a medical certificate ensuring that they are in good health and can travel without problems.

Your travel agent should be able to tell you about the routes, fares, and departure times of freighters that accept passengers. Be advised, however, that you will have to sail from an American port. Only one line (Yugoslav) has freighters leaving Montréal headed for the Mediterranean.

In all but exceptional cases, you should make it a cruise, that is return to your port of departure, or take an air-sea cruise, including air travel for part of the trip.

Specialist agencies, of course, are better informed. Here are some of them:

Freighter Cruise Service, 5925 Monkland Ave., Room 103, Montréal, Qué. H4A 1G7. Telephone: (514)233-8496.

World Wide Travel Service, 318 Wilson Ave., Downsview, Ont. M3H 1S8. Telephone: (416)635-5661.

Cruise People Ltd., 1752 Victoria Park, Scarborough, Ont. M1R 1R4. Telephone: (416)759-6606.

Thomas Cook Overseas Ltd., 416 Seymour St., Vancouver, B.C. V6B 3H1. Telephone: (604)688-0231.

OCEAN LINERS

There are now hardly any of those great, proud ocean liners that used to take us to the "old countries" in high comfort. You hardly noticed the time lag and felt fresh and fit at the other side of the world.

On the way to Africa and Asia for my automobile journeys, I had to cross the Atlantic five times on board the old Cunard liners, the Jeep on the bridge. Tourist class of course, but it was pleasant. I crossed the Pacific once on a handsome ship of the President Line—in third-class at the bottom of the hold. That was less fun....

With the arrival of the big transatlantic jets, it was to be expected that passengers would prefer the plane, which is so much quicker and cheaper. And so passenger liners in fine condition were shunted aside or converted into cruise ships, a kind of travel that has become increasingly popular, particularly among people ripe in years... and ripe in wealth.

In 1986, members of the Cruise Line International Association alone account for eighty-five cruise ships belonging to twenty-three different companies. They carry one and a half million passengers a year.

From short cruises to the Caribbean or off the west coast of Mexico to round-the-world tours, there is an endless variety of cruises, the most interesting of them addressed to specialized interests: archaeology buffs who go to the Greek islands and Egypt, or naturalists who admire the tortoises, seals, and penguins of the Galapagos. Also available are air-sea trips, in which you take a cruise ship to the port of your choice and return by air.

One feature of cruises is their very high cost. A cruise on even a very ordinary ship will set you back $150 a day. If you choose a deluxe cruise be prepared to pay at least $250 a day, and your cabin will be tiny.

And the price isn't all-inclusive. It will cost more if you take the excursions suggested at each port of call, or if you spend a lot of time at the bar or casino. There's also the five or six dollars a day in tips to the chambermaid or waiter.

In short, if you like cruises, don't make the mistake of being poor.

Life on a cruise ship is loafing in luxury, satisfying one's gluttony (five meals a day), sports, gambling, shopping, movies, concerts, night clubs, sometimes pleasant encounters, and an occasional rather hurried visit to a seaport.

Since I'm obviously not an expert on the matter I can only advise you to consult your travel agent, who will be delighted to talk over a three-to-five-thousand-dollar cruise. I can also recommend a good guide: *Fielding's Worldwide Guide to Cruises*, by Antoinette Deland (available from William Morrow and Company, Inc., 105 Madison Ave., New York, N.Y., U.S.A. 10016). This 350–page book will tell you all you want to know about cruises and then some: practical advice, a list of routes, and descriptions of principal ports and a hundred ships of forty-four different lines.

SAILING VESSELS

My interest has always been to see countries from the inside, cross them from border to border, and overcome their deserts and mountains, so I've never been attracted to sailing craft. But I admire and secretly envy the adventurers who, alone or with companions, set out to discover wonderful islands in the Pacific or Caribbean or circumnavigate the globe in a vessel fifteen metres long.

Since they spend vastly more time on the ocean than in port, I gather that they prefer the sea to the rest of the world. I can understand that, but that's not how it is with me . . . and to top it off, I don't even have my sea legs!

Despite all this, much of the information in this book should be of help to travellers setting sail for the tropics.

HITCHHIKING

Young travellers who have practised this sport in North America, Europe, and even Australia and New Zealand shouldn't assume that it will be as easy in the Third World. Traffic on African roads is spread very thin except for the always-overloaded trucks. There is more traffic in Latin America and Asia, but the cars you meet on the road are often full.

Apart from a few countries with large numbers of young foreign visitors on the roads, there is hardly any hitchhiking as it is understood in Canada. The owner of a truck, van, or car has to make a living from it; often it is his entire capital. He will find it hard to understand why a young Canadian, someone from a wealthy country, expects a poor man to give him a free ride. If a driver stops on your signal, he will almost always ask for a sum of money to drive you from one place to another while, as often as not, you sit perched on top of a load of sugar cane or sacks of rice. You can bargain, and the price is never very high.

The easiest way is to meet the truck drivers at their gathering places: the market square, gas station, ferry dock, or border post. Then you can take your time about bargaining, and compare prices and the relative comfort of the trucks. (Pick sacks of rice over sugar, which attracts flies.)

A hitchhiker in the Third World then should take it for granted that, with a few exceptions, he will have to pay his way and sometimes, on infrequently travelled roads, resign himself to taking the bus. He will have to walk many kilometres under a blistering sun in Nigeria or biting cold on the high plateaus of the Andes. He will have to bring the proper clothes, while cutting down the contents of his knapsack to a minimum. You don't walk far carrying more than fifteen kilos.

The basic rules for hitchhiking are the same in the Third World as everywhere else. A boy and girl travelling together inspire confidence; be clean and neatly dressed; never get into a vehicle if the driver seems to be intoxicated or get out as soon as you can; make sure that you won't be dropped off in some out-of-the-way spot.

Despite the drawbacks, particularly in the poorest Third World countries, hitchhiking has certain advantages and is one of the best money-savers. You can meet a very wide range of people and share with them the adventures you will certainly have on any long journey by truck through the desert, bush, or jungle. And you will have a chance to work on the local language.

BICYCLE

I know. There are unsung heroes who have gone around the world by bicycle, pushing their mount over sand dunes, dragging it along muddy roads, living for months, even years, in material conditions made even rougher by a cyclist's inability to bring along much of anything.

I advise against this kind of an expedition, which is more of a feat of endurance than a journey. Except for short trips in countries with good roads, bicyclists should be satisfied with renting their favourite vehicle in a town and setting out to explore nearby villages, places undiscovered by the usual tourist.

MOTORCYCLE

Here's a machine that's much better suited to the Third World. With it you can bring along light camping gear and take roads and trails inaccessible even to all-terrain vehicles. And if there are still a few spots untouched by tourists, it's the motorcyclist who has the best chance of discovering them.

CAMEL

Sometimes the back of a mule, horse, or even elephant is the best way to get to a little temple deep in the jungle or ruins perched on a mountaintop. But for covering long distances in the desert or on the high plateaus of Afghanistan, there's nothing like the camel or, in Africa, his one-humped kin, the dromedary.

Large numbers of intrepid travellers have crossed the Sahara on camelback by joining a caravan leaving, for example, from Laghouat, south of Algiers, and taking the Hoggar Trail to Gao. What you need is all-purpose endurance, lots of patience, and a love of eating dates. But what an adventure it must be! During my crossings of the desert by jeep, the sight of those long, silent caravans passing in the night set me to dreaming!

Only a few years back I happened to be in Tunis and was hit by a sudden attack of nostalgia for the Sahara. Without thinking too much about it, I rented a car (one time does not a habit make!) and drove as far south as you can get, that is, to desert's edge, at Douz.

I signed in at the only hostelry, a converted barracks, found a French-speaking guide, and with him made contact with the corner camel drivers. Without bargaining hard, I was able to hire three dromedaries and three camel drivers for a handful of dinars, about twenty dollars if I remember correctly.

The caravan's departure was set for five in the afternoon, when the sun's heat begins to ease.

"Where do you want to go?" the head camel driver asked me.

"Due south! When we're tired, we'll stop and sleep and then come back tomorrow morning."

Wearing a cap veiled in back, I mounted the first dromedary. My translator got on the second, and the third carried my baggage—a woolen blanket, sheets, and even a pillow borrowed from the Douz innkeeper. The three camel drivers went on foot, leading their beasts over the rocky ground.

Night fell, the air grew cool, and the moon shed a grey-blue light on the rocks and dunes. For hours we let ourselves be exalted by the stillness and rocked by our mounts. Now and again the lead camel driver burst out singing some heart-rending Arab lament and was answered by what sounded like harmonious groaning from the other two.

A few hours out of Douz, a few hundred kilometres from Tunis, I was suddenly Lawrence of Arabia heading for Aqaba.

At about midnight I gave the sign, and the three dromedaries knelt down, roaring. The camel-drivers had brought along a *guerba* full of water, a little black tea and dried mint, some lumps of sugar, and a few twigs. They lit a fire and unhurriedly brewed some mint tea to be drunk out of tiny glasses.

We slept soundly under the stars in the cool of the Sahara night, but got up early, knowing the morning sun would be quick to reassert its strength.

"Due north!"

We arrived back in Douz a few hours later—five men representing opposite sides of the globe who had become more brotherly than the day before.

CHAPTER 13

Respect for Other Cultures

Anyone staying in a foreign country, particularly one in the Third World, experiences a greater or lesser degree of culture shock. Sometimes it is so severe that the traveller would like to take the next plane home.

This phenomenon has been under study for some time by psychologists and sociologists. It is sometimes defined as a deep unease or an anxiety attack due to the sudden disappearance of all the signs and symbols specific to the society familiar to us since birth.

A similar shock is experienced on returning home from a stay of any length in a foreign society into which we have begun to integrate ourselves.

Travellers familiar with the three characteristic phases of the inevitable culture shock will make a quicker recovery from it.

First comes the honeymoon phase, in which the traveller is thrilled at being plunged into a new culture.

The second phase is harder to get through, with the visitor confused and upset and unable to take any more clashes between his values and radically different ones. This could lead to withdrawal and depression or, on the contrary, open aggressiveness.

The third phase brings peace, reconciliation to a new way of life, and the will to understand the foreign culture and, to a degree, become part of it for a few weeks, months, or years.

The forewarned traveller, then, will be able to confront culture shock without too many problems. The few bits of advice I've put together in this chapter will help him feel comfortable with himself as quickly as possible.

THE LANGUAGE PROBLEM

Not everyone has a gift for languages, but few find it impossible to learn a minimum number of basic words, numbers, polite formulas, and some key phrases even in a difficult language. It is also true that the use of certain European languages is widespread in the Third World.

There's no doubt that *English* is most widely used as a second language. The official language of many countries, it plays a major rôle in a great many others, as, for example, in India, where without English many Indians would have trouble understanding each other. There are forty-eight English-language countries, forty-two of them in the Third World.

In a general way and certainly in tourist centres, you can do quite well with English in former British colonies. In Indonesia and other former colonies of the Netherlands, the Dutch language, once imposed by law, has been dropped in favour of English. Let's face it, the language of Shakespeare has become the world's favourite second language.

In former French colonies, where the people often have to cope with a bewildering variety of dialects, *French* is at least the second language when it isn't the official one. That's how it is in twenty African countries, not to speak of Madagascar, many islands in the Pacific and the Caribbean, including Haiti, and even though it is losing ground, French is still spoken in Lebanon, in what used to be Indochina and is now Vietnam, Laos, and Cambodia, or Kampuchea. There are twenty-nine French-speaking countries, twenty-three of them in the Third World.

Spanish is the third most useful language but foremost in all of Latin America except Brazil, where Portuguese is spoken.

Someone fortunate enough to know English, French, and Spanish can travel just about anywhere in the world and be sure of being understood in the big cities.

Despite all this, before leaving on a trip take the trouble to learn at least the rudiments of the language spoken in the country of destination. It will smooth the way for human contacts and intellectual exchanges and make your trip a great deal more pleasant. People will be delighted at your efforts to communicate in their language, and they will open their doors and hearts more readily.

If you plan to stay a long time in, for example, one of the French-speaking African countries, don't forget that hardly ten per cent of the people know French and that this élite is concentrated in the cities. It's no different in the so-called English-speaking countries. In the Tanzanian interior, Swahili is more useful than English, and Diola more than French in a good part of Mali.

Get information from embassies and consulates before departure, and get together with students from the countries you plan to visit. They will charge you very little for lessons in Arabic, Sinhalese, or Tagalog and, as a bonus, will start you in on the non-verbal language.

You should nonetheless bear in mind that human beings can always manage to understand each other, even if they don't speak the same language. All that is necessary is a real desire to do so. I've had interminable conversations with unilingual Tuaregs, Quechua-speaking Bolivians, and Burmese, the name of whose dialect escapes me. It's hard work, you laugh a lot, and you make lots of drawings in the sand. And you end up by saying a whole lot of things.

RELIGION

While there as been a considerable falling away from religious practice in industrialized countries, it is still intense just about everywhere in the Third World.

Christianity. The vast majority of Latin Americans are Roman Catholic, while a certain number adhere to other Christian denominations. Religious celebrations, sometimes influenced by the ancient Amerindian religions, are spectacular and can go on for several days. Find out the date of the next feast day when you arrive in a Latin American country. You may live through something extraordinary in some small village only kilometres away from the capital. Foreigners who behave and dress suitably receive a courteous welcome. In churches, women should cover their heads with a mantilla or scarf.

Christianity is the dominant religion in some countries in Black Africa, in at least one Asian country, in the Philippines, and in many Pacific and Caribbean islands. It is the religion of a billion human beings.

Hinduism or Brahmanism is the principal religion of India, a country of many faiths, the kingdom of gurus, astrologers, yoga, and ashrams. No doubt that is why people in search of the absolute and young westerners disgusted with our materialistic societies often turn to India. These "pilgrimages to the sources" are often disappointing to superficial and ill-prepared visitors, but they have a profound influence on others.

A visit to an ashram can be highly stimulating. On my first trip to India, I stayed at the Sewagram ashram, famous because Gandhi lived there from 1936 to 1946 (except for some time spent in British jails). The ashram's father, the bapu, was still Aryanayakam, a Gandhi disciple to whom the Mahatma had confided his plans for the reform of education.

My intention was to spend a day at the ashram, but I was laid low by fever and forced to stay for twelve of the most memorable days of my life.

I was cared for with infinite patience and great kindness, and Aryanayakam wouldn't let me leave until he was sure that I was completely better. He put me in the care of a young Hindu my age, Nana, who bore a strange resemblance to the Saint Louis de Gonzaga of my college days. Nana sat by my side in the infirmary hut, and when he wasn't busy fixing me a juice or potion, washing me or giving me a sponge bath, he prayed in a lowered voice or chanted verses from the Gita, one of the sacred Hindu books.

Nana came from a wealthy family in Assam, in the north of India. But he shunned the businesses that made his people wealthy and, forsaking even his fine clothes, had chosen to wear the ashram's plain *kadi*—a shirt, billowing trousers, and jacket that he had spun and woven himself after having sown and harvested the cotton in accord with Gandhi's teachings as they were still applied at Sewagram.

Like the other members of the ashram, he divided his time between prayer, household chores, tending the fields, and caring for the sick.

I'll never forget our final goodbyes. Here are the notes I took down at the time:

Nana is waiting for my friend and me at the door of his little cabin—a single tiny room with just enough space for an Indian bed, a worktable, and a wardrobe; a Carthusian monk's cell, you might say.

He greets us with hands joined over the breast, more St. Louis de Gonzaga than ever....Wisps of blue smoke from the incense he's burning in our honour curl around his handsome face. He's radiant with the joy of giving us pleasure and has us sit on his bed, in front of which he has placed a little table adorned with the stick of incense and four flowers—two yellow and two blue. Knowing Nana, we are aware that he grew them himself and has just cut them to offer to us.

Still smiling but not saying much, he brings us a platter of fruit— mandarins, guavas, and dates. Usually his cupboard is bare, but for his friends who have to leave he's found milk and, an unheard of thing, some Ovaltine. We sip the chocolate-flavoured drink of our childhood and eat fruit in front of Nana, who eats nothing, says nothing, but is happy. We are happy too, on the edge of tears. What an extraordinary feeling it is to meet a man who calls you brother at the far end of the world.

With all the warmth at my command, I thank him again for having cared for me and kept vigil over me. "You would have done the same for me if I were sick," he answers.

Ah, dear Nana, how I'd like to be sure of that!

As elsewhere, all is not sweetness and light among the Hindus. It's hard to understand why the caste system has lasted until now, shaken hardly at all by Gandhi's fervent denunciations. Tolerance has to be stretched to the breaking point to accept cows being considered sacred in a country that is always on the edge of famine. Everything ends up explained, though, if you take the trouble to open heart and mind to values that may be the opposite of ours but are valid all the same.

Buddhism, a philosophic and religious doctrine of Indian origin, has more than half a billion adherents. This reformed Hinduism is professed in Tibet, Sri Lanka, Burma, Thailand, Bali, China, Japan, and other places.

The basic message of Buddha's deeply pacifist and moral sayings is that suffering is essentially caused by the desires of man, who should follow the "middle way" on his own, without help from any god, to attain nirvana, that is, illumination, a state of supreme serenity.

And it is true that in Buddhist countries you have a feeling of serenity, harmony, safety, peace. Buddha's philosophy doesn't call for a blind acceptance of dogma; rites are kept to a minimum. But religion is a part of every Buddhist's life, and, for example, in

Thailand and Burma every young man of twenty or more must become a monk for a greater or lesser period. A certain number of them will live out their days as *bonzes*, renouncing life's pleasures.

Still Buddhism isn't a sad religion. Religious celebrations are on a grand scale, colourful, bursting with mystic joy, always alive with dance and music.

If you are in Sri Lanka during July and August, don't miss the *Esala Perahera*, the world's most dazzling religious celebration. Find out the dates of the large number of celebrations spread throughout the year in honour not only of Buddha but also of Jesus and Mohammed.

Islam, for its part, is the dominant religion in vast reaches of the Third World. The Koran has spread like wildfire from Arabia to the heart of Black Africa and, to the west, through Indonesia to come more or less to a halt on the island of Mindanao, in the south of the Philippine archipelago. Today there are more than 700 million Muslims in the world.

Non-Muslims are always deeply impressed by the vibrant faith characteristic of Mohammed's followers. Five times a day the muezzins call them to prayer from atop the minarets. Wherever they may be, the faithful unroll their little rugs or, if they are poor, their straw mats. They kneel facing Mecca, and after the ritual ablutions call on Allah while kissing the ground repeatedly. In some large cities such as Jeddah the merchants roll down their steel shutters, time comes to a stop, and the whole city prays. Like Quebec in the old days on the sounding of the Angelus....

A good Muslim answers the muezzin's cries but also fasts and gives alms and, if possible, once in his lifetime he will make a pilgrimage to Mecca, which guarantees that he will go to Allah's heaven and gives him the right to the title of *Hadj* until the end of his days.

Every year Muslims observe a fast during the month of Ramadan, during which they abstain completely from food, drink, and tobacco from dawn to sunset. In the most religious countries, even foreigners are expected to show their respect for Ramadan by the same kind of abstaining, in public at least. At hotels of any size, room service will provide meals, but you should have something put away for a snack. Travellers who don't take this recommendation to heart could give offence to strictly observing Muslims.

You should try then not to schedule trips involving business or meetings with officials during the last days of Ramadan. As with most religious feasts, the beginning date of Ramadan varies from year to year. Check with the embassies.

Every time you meet a Muslim he shakes your hand, holding on to it longer than we do in Canada. *Never* offer the left hand.

Women are kept apart in many Muslim countries and are never the object of comment. Never ask an Arab how his wife is... all the less so in that the Koran allows him to have four of them. On the other hand, suitably dressed women are more likely to be accepted in a group of men.

The Koran forbids any consumption of pork or alcohol. In certain strict countries, such as Saudi Arabia, customs will seize the bottle of whiskey you very unwisely brought in and will often make you pay a fine. Theoretically it is impossible to find a drop of reliable alcohol except, of course, in the embassies, which are foreign territory.

As you get further from Mecca in the direction of Equatorial Africa or Southeast Asia, Muslims become less strict about alcohol. Nonetheless they always feel a little guilty about drinking. Every time a Javanese friend of mine shared a beer with me, he would say, "Ah, I'm a very bad Muslim, you know!" When a subordinate or, even worse, a superior was present, he would make a show of ordering an orange juice. It would have been a blunder to offer him a beer.

There are also 300 million Confucianists in the world, 60 million Shintoists, 30 million Taoists, 6 million Sikhs. And ??

NON-VERBAL LANGUAGE

It is unforgivable to visit a city, its museums, parks, and shops, without having established human contact with its people, who are, after all, the heart and soul of their culture. Some people have the gift, which I envy, of easy communication with anyone. Others can contact organizations of which they are members (perhaps the YMCA, a chamber of commerce, or an auto club) or go to tourist offices that will put them in contact with local people who would like to meet foreign visitors.

At any rate, Canadians should change their attitudes, behave with more tact, and be wary of non-verbal language, which varies from place to place. North Americans, for example, say OK by making a circle with the thumb and index finger. In Brazil and other parts of

Latin America this gesture has a meaning that is vulgar in the extreme. Latin American men exchange *abrazos*, a strenuous hugging reserved for friends. Women who are good friends kiss each other on both cheeks.

The greeting in India and Buddhist countries is joined hands on the chest and a light bow of the head. You should always avoid being familiar, making crude jokes, backslapping, sloppy gestures, all of which are shocking to an Oriental.

Contrary to the Canadian habit, never be direct in your questions, remarks, and above all criticism, if some has to be made. Neither should you expect to get direct answers. Whatever may happen, keep smiling, or at least remain impassive. You lose face if you raise your voice or show anger. The response is quiet mockery and unspoken contempt.

Everywhere in the world you should show the greatest respect around religious and funeral ceremonies. It would, for example, be totally out of place to take photographs of the bodies cremated on the *ghats* at Benares (Vârânasi) or elsewhere.

With few exceptions, foreigners can visit pagodas, mosques, and Hindu temples. The smallest trace of flippancy at such places is hurtful to believers, even insulting, while they are touched by any sign of reverence or simple courtesy. Ideally a visitor should be accompanied by a local resident.

You always have to remove shoes and sometimes even socks before entering a religious edifice. I have vivid memories of visits to certain temples where I had to go barefoot over the burning hot marble of interior courtyards.

In Southeast Asia you should try not to make gestures with your foot, considered the most vulgar part of the anatomy. Never use it to open a door, point something out or, even worse, point towards someone when, for example, you are sitting with legs crossed. If you must cross your legs, do it so that no one can see the soles of your shoes, which is considered an insult in several countries, including Thailand and Taiwan. If someone, even a child, is lying on the ground, go around rather than step over him or her.

By contrast, the upper part of the body is considered noble and the head sacred. That is why it would be an insult to run a hand through the hair or give a friendly little tap on the cheek of even a child.

Gestures have so many different meanings in various countries and localities that it is impossible to understand them all. Make queries locally, act reserved and modest, and count on the boundless tolerance of Third World people for foreigners of good will.

HOSPITALITY

One of the joys of Third World travel is the generous hospitality you are offered by the poorest among them, especially the very poorest.

I've lived through unforgettable times with Syrian Bedouin who gave me shelter in their black tents poised like huge bats on the sand. One was a notorious bandit, wanted for many murders. There was no risk in being his guest except perhaps of eating too many of the delicacies served along with the copious glasses of tea.

The hospitality of Muslims, and Arabs in particular, is as exquisite as it is legendary.

Latin Americans have great *joie de vivre* and love food and drink. If they take a liking to you, they will bring you home and lavish kindness on you. The humblest *campesino* in the Andes will offer you a coffee and a *galleta*.

Better-off families will sometimes invite you to a traditional family dinner, always congenial. As in Canada, be sure to bring your hostess flowers or a box of candy. Don't turn down any of the dishes offered, and don't hesitate to give the cook your heartfelt compliments.

Latin Americans are not punctual and don't think it impolite to arrive very late for a dinner or even a business meeting. They nonetheless expect Canadians to be on time, or almost.

Black Africans, particularly in the villages, are rather reserved at first but little by little become warm and friendly. When I travelled the African trails by Jeep and stopped to camp at the edge of a village, my first visitors would be children, who would gather in a circle around the car. After some time the women, shyer, would make their approach, more readily still when I was travelling with my wife. Although villages in the bush now and again saw white men come and go, white women were much rarer. Later the men of the village would come and join the others with the chief at their front bearing a gift of one or two eggs in his palm.

Sometimes I wished that these group visits didn't last so long, particularly at dinner or toilet times. But don't forget that a couple of

Whites setting up their field kitchen is an extraordinary sight in a Gabonese village...as would be the sight of a couple of Blacks quietly pounding their maize on the outskirts of Yellowknife.

In the course of a trip, you will sometimes be invited to share a family meal or at least have some coffee, tea, coconut milk, or palm wine. Even though it may involve some health risks, you can't always say no. Use a digestive problem as an excuse not to eat at least raw vegetables or curdled milk, but show your appreciation of the *couscous* or mutton kebab. There's no risk in tea or coffee, but the cups may be only relatively clean. Present your hosts with a small gift in return for their hospitality. In the countries of Southeast Asia, with their refined cuisines, a point is made of stuffing you from morning to night. On a more or less official visit to a village in the Philippines I had to get through five meals a day, the main one featuring a whole pig. I tried to cheat a little but soon came to understand that I had to taste every dish bar none.

A third of the human race eats with chopsticks; another third with the hands. Our knives, forks, and spoons put us in the minority.

If you intend to visit China or Vietnam, use our excellent Chinese and Vietnamese restaurants as a pre-departure training ground in the use of chopsticks.

Here's a method that's simple and infallible:

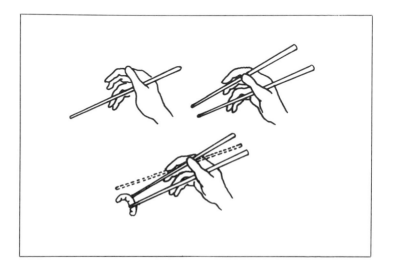

1. Hold the first chopstick rigid in the palm between thumb and index finger, steadying it against the ring finger.
2. Hold the second chopstick between upper part of thumb and index finger, steadying it on the second finger.
3. To pick up the food, move the second chopstick up and down with the index and second fingers.

With a little practice, you will wow the back rows by snatching up peas one at a time! But note that the wise men of China bring the bowls up to chin level to cut down the risk of droppage.

It's easier to get used to eating with the hands, following the custom of Africa and a large part of Asia, where everyone helps themselves from a communal platter. Always use the right hand, the left being reserved for other uses relating to personal hygiene. You will appreciate the importance of extending the right hand and never eating left-handed when you note the faucet or little pail of water next to the toilet... on the left.

A servant will come before meals and pour water on your hands for the necessary ablutions. Better off people will even offer you soap and a towel.

Although women eat separately among African and Asian Muslims, a foreign woman can take her place with the men. Before making judgements, remember that in Canada women are still not allowed in certain private clubs.

CLOTHES

Why let some whim about dress make you risk offending men and women who are endlessly kind about making us welcome in their homelands? These people aren't any less intelligent just because they have held on to standards of modesty that not so many years back were prevalent here as well. Have we forgotten our grandmothers' times or, still more recent, the time when Montréal police handed out paper boleros to American tourists who went down St. Catherine Street bare-shouldered? Anyone who refused to wear this ridiculous garment took the risk of being fined.

Elsewhere I've pointed out the obvious advantages in tropical countries of wearing roomy cotton clothes, lightweight pants, or mid-calf length skirts, and longsleeved shirts for protection against mosquitoes and malaria.

This kind of clothing is vastly more comfortable and won't shock local people as skintight jeans or shorts would. Perhaps you won't be made to feel it, but a judgement will be made on your personality and many doors will remain shut.

As I have said before, the general rule is that women should avoid bikinis and two-piece bathings suits and men skimpy trunks. Even in resort areas it's sometimes against the law to go around bare-torsoed, and often it is forbidden in hotels.

It's a mistake for men to have long hair and beards. Not only is it unhealthy in the tropics, but in countries that suffered through an invasion of more or less drugged hippies, there remains an aversion to people who look like them. Young travellers then should avoid sloppy, torn, or dirty clothes as well as T-shirts with slogans that are vulgar or could seem to be. Even a very passable young man with jeans and long hair would have a harder time being accepted in many countries, including those of Southeast Asia. Why deprive yourself of interesting contacts, complicate things at border posts, or even get yourself pointed at, when it's so easy to have the hair and beard cut, even though you plan to let them grow back when you return to Canada? If it's still the style...

THE STREET

Some people tend to get familiar with chance acquaintances too soon. They are amazed then when these people try to take over. You should be open to other people while holding on to your right to solitude or privacy.

It won't take long on the streets of Dakar, for example, before you will be approached by friendly, smiling young men who will tell you: "Oh, you're Canadians? I really like Canadians and Canada. I'd like to be your friend." The only aim of all this kindness, sad to say, is usually to extract some CFA francs from you on the pretext of a sick mother, an offer to act as a guide, or to sell you some worthless necklaces at stiff prices.

An odd little book published by Senegalese sociologist Isidore Mbaye Dieng consists of freely given interviews with people in frequent contact with tourists—waiters, taxi drivers, beggars, and prostitutes. Here's what a street vendor, or *bana bana* as they're called in Senegal, had to say:

For a *bana bana* a tourist is a customer who's easily fooled without suspecting a thing. They have the money and the wish to buy our goods, but they have no idea what these goods are worth....They spend foolishly. Last week I sold a gold-plated silver chain to a Swiss tourist for seven thousand francs; I would have sold it to a Senegalese for six hundred francs. But because he's a foreigner with money, you have to take him for as much as you can. The *toubabs* are rich. You have to make the most of their money since they come only to spend it and then leave. So the *bana bana* business is getting harder all the time, and the authorities are cracking down on the *bana bana*. There are often police sweeps downtown.

You have to be firm about staving off the onslaughts of parasites of this ilk, who can be found in large towns all over the Third World.

Firm, but not overtly angry. It does no good to shout at them even if they are doggedly pestering you. They will end by tiring of it. If need be you can go into a café, where usually you won't be followed. The same tactics can be used to shake off the crowds of prostitutes found in the capital cities of all poor countries.

If all else fails you can stroll towards the nearest police officer or police station. You won't be followed.

In all parts of the world, travellers tend to act as they do at home. For example, they'll put an arm around a waist or kiss in public, which is unthinkable in most Third World countries. Such gestures are inconsequential in Canada, but they scandalize Muslims and shock most Asians. Women should be particularly careful in this regard if they don't want to bring on the contempt of women and invite unwanted attention from men.

On the other hand, it shouldn't surprise you too much in Arab countries to see two men walking together with little fingers entwined. It's the custom, just as the Latin American custom is for men to hug each other.

In some very poor countries, there are swarms of beggars. Lepers thrust their eaten-away limbs at you, women their blind children, cripples their stumps. In the large cities of India the sight is unbearable, and some sensitive people, lacking the compassion of a Mother Teresa, are totally unable to bear it.

It's obvious that cases of extreme misery are due to underdevelopment in very densely populated regions. They should make us sick at heart rather than at stomach and be a reminder that the human family is one and that rich and contented members are duty-bound to share with the more deprived.

Many consciences have been jolted awake by a simple visit to Bombay and Calcutta. The beggars and disabled then have a rôle to play.

It's sure that no problem as vast as misery in the Third World can be solved by giving alms to a paralyzed person who will continue in that state until his fast-approaching death. But why use this as a pretext not to give a centavo, rupee, or dirham to a poor person who asks for it in the name of the God common to us all? The easy solution, the least troublesome and most humane, is to always have a good supply of coins at hand and unobtrusively hand them out to anyone who asks. You will feel a little better about yourself, and at the end of three weeks you will be out less than the price of a breakfast at the Hilton.

Most of the remarks above apply only to the large cities, and you will find even poor countries in which disabled people are cared for in institutions so that there are no beggars.

In small towns and especially in villages, the problem of young parasites and beggars simply doesn't exist. A Third World village is a large family in which everyone is poor but no one begs.

You will often have to line up at banks, airline counters, telegraph offices, and immigration checkpoints. Take it in good stride, reminding yourself that at that moment tens of millions of people are lined up somewhere in the world... including Eastern Europe.

Wear a hat in full sun and, if the street sights aren't enough to keep you amused, bring along a paperback or better still a city guidebook. That will bring a laugh to your neighbours in the lineup, and you will learn things that won't be found in any guidebook.

Sometimes the local culture doesn't include disciplined behaviour in lineups; you find yourself stacked twenty-five deep at the wicket, and the shoving is undisguised. This is a more touchy situation, but don't lose your nerve and, without shoving anyone, try not to let anyone steal your place. A smile will get you through a dense, jumpy crowd quicker than surliness and nasty remarks.

PURCHASES

Along with the crowds of street vendors waiting for you at the doors of the hotel and harassing you along the sidewalks, all sorts of merchants will try to get you into their shops. Once again it does no good to lose your patience, and what's more, you may occasionally want to take a closer look at a lovely batik tablecloth, a Javanese mask, or a Cameroonian statuette.

It can happen that a taxi driver or guide will try to get you to visit his uncle's shop, where you will get the discount for friends. These people usually work on commission for dozens of "uncles" scattered around the town.

A word of advice: never buy the first day. When you see something you like, take down the price and address and then try to find the best spot in town to buy that kind of thing. There's always a shop, sometimes government-owned, that has the best pieces of craftsmanship. Get advice from embassy people or foreign residents, who often are more knowledgeable about such things than natives.

Everything costs more in these shops and especially in the ones in large hotels, but the quality is superior. Why bargain when you have been offered a gorgeous batik shirt for less than $10?

But in the course of your strolls, you will run across magnificent woolen ponchos and tapestries with Incan designs in the smallest Ecuadorean *pueblo* or at the outdoor markets on the high Bolivian plateaus; magnificent wood carvings everywhere in Bali; and more or less ancient masks in remote corners of Zaïre. At such times you have to bargain because bargaining is a game that it would be ungracious not to join. And why pay ten times the going price?

What I cannot understand, though, is the relentlessness of some tourists who won't buy a thing without squeezing a last peso from a vendor dressed in rags.

PHOTOGRAPHS

I did some photography during my first trips. I even shot two hour-long films in 16 mm at twenty-four frames a second so that a sound track could be dubbed on.

I had to. The photos and films were used to illustrate the articles, books, and lectures that paid for the trips. But since then I've made it a principle to take absolutely no photos on my trips to the Third World. In thirty years I have never got back the nerve to point a camera at people, often in rags, sitting in front of their wretched hovels.

People who must use their cameras should at least show extreme tact and ask permission before taking a picture of a woman breast-feeding her infant or even an old Arab in a turban peacefully smoking his pipe in front of his shop. Some African people who have been especially harassed by foreign photographers sometimes charge a small sum of money.

I always feel like asking some photography enthusiasts, "How would you like it if your family were at your cottage peacefully stretched out in bathing suits when suddenly a mob of Ethiopian tourists dropped by and started shoving each other to get pictures?"

Still, a Polaroid-type camera can be used to bring pleasure to people not used to seeing pictures of themselves. It can be a good instrument for making friends or for leaving a personal memento with people who have helped you.

Of course, we all know travellers who take so many photos that I wonder if they ever take time out to peek at the landscape. When they come back home they boast about having taken two hundred slides of their trip to Egypt. But they practically never look at them afterwards. Unless, of course, they are among the fiends who subject innocent victims to painful and long-drawn-out slide-viewing sessions.

Some countries, including Mali, Cameroon, Libya, and Somalia, make you get a photography licence from the police, for which, in good logic, you need two passport photos. With or without a licence, don't take pictures of anything that could by any stretch of the imagination be considered a military target: bridges, train stations, hydro stations, airports, barracks, or other "strategic" structures. Finally, for very understandable reasons of self-respect, people in poor countries don't like to have pictures taken of beggars, disabled people, and shantytowns.

CLEANLINESS

The hygiene found in Canada and most of the industrialized world is the end product of education and economic development and is a recent acquisition. Our grandmothers took fewer baths than we do, and poor people used to use uncomfortable outdoor privies of doubtful cleanliness.

During my first visit to the City of Lights, I was amazed to see that most Parisians had no bathtubs and washed instead at the public baths. The toilets in cafés and restaurants were primitive in the extreme and often incredibly filthy. Obviously things have changed since then.

Generally speaking, Third World people wash as often as Europeans and a good number of North Americans. They deserve all the more credit in that water is scarce and soap a luxury. It always amazes me in shantytowns without sewers, water, or electricity when I see well-scrubbed and impeccably dressed men, women, and children emerge from some hovel. In Latin America you see whole families happily soaping each other up at a riverside, since there is no water in the village; peasants in India sprinkle themselves with water as often as possible; the faithful in Muslim countries follow the Prophet's dictates and perform their ablutions five times a day.

This said, it remains true that what plumbing there is in the Third World leaves a great deal to be desired. This is an economic problem rather than a cultural one. As soon as an undeveloped country has made important economic progress, it has no need to look up to us, as can be seen in Singapore.

But elsewhere the state of toilets in public places and small hotels can make you shudder. You will hardly ever find any toilet paper, which is why you should always have your own supply on hand. The toilet, if that's what you want to call it, is often nothing more than a hole in a slab of concrete. In many villages you answer the call in the open air like everyone else. In Indonesia you squat by the bank of a stream or small irrigation canal that has been flowing towards the rice paddies for centuries.

POLITICS

A large number of Third World countries live under very harsh military governments or equally unrelenting civilian dictatorships. It is natural for us to be shocked by this, but we have to take into account the historical circumstances leading up to these régimes and not forget the past or present responsibility of Western colonialists or neo-colonialists. Before passing judgement let's bear in mind that it was only a few years ago that some highly civilized countries such as Greece, Portugal, and Spain were totalitarian states, not to mention the Eastern European countries that are still.

Try to understand the political problems of the countries visited but avoid discussing them with any natives who are not old friends. Admitting that they agree with your criticisms would be an embarrassment for them and sometimes may involve a risk of going to jail. Others might be backers of the government and will react badly to your remarks. They could denounce you to the police as an enemy of the state.

People in the Third World are justly proud of their political independence. In most cases independence is of recent date, and often there was a very high cost in human life. An "old" country such as India became independent only in 1947, while Algeria "was France" until 1962.

For decades or centuries a great many nations were humiliated and exploited by the Western Powers. The most astonishing thing is still how little they resent their former colonial overlords and Whites in general. The Africans and Asians you meet don't necessarily know that Canada has no history of colonizing other countries and has been a victim rather than an accomplice of the imperialism and neocolonialism of the multinationals.

That's why we should handle subjects like this with the greatest tact and withhold judgement on the political systems. And what right do we have to criticize a country that has given us the privilege of exploring it? How would your neighbour take it if he invited you over and you used the occasion to point out that his house is decorated in bad taste, his children are ill bred, and his political opinions seem stupid?

Obviously you shouldn't give up your political opinions or, above all, your convictions about human rights, but if you want to meddle in a country's politics you have to *earn the right* by getting to know them in depth, which few travellers have time to do.

Again out of respect for your hosts, but also to avoid trouble with customs, make sure that your baggage doesn't contain any newspapers, magazines, or books criticizing their country's politics or ideology or praising their enemies'. When you came to Egypt in the 1950s, all printed material in your baggage had to be handed over to the censors. You got a parcel the next day, but often there were things missing. One Catholic priest was surprised to find that all references to Jews and Israel in his breviary had been crossed out in black ink.

Times have changed, but I would certainly try not to arrive in

Libya with a biography of Golda Meir or in Malaysia with a magazine criticizing its treatment of its citizens of Chinese origin.

Get detailed information before you leave Canada for a country in turmoil. Don't rely too much on travel agencies and even less on the embassies and consulates of the countries in question, which tend to underplay the situation. Rather write to the department of External Affairs of Canada, Ottawa, Ont. K1A 0G2. Telephone: (613)992-3705. Abroad, inquire at Canadian embassies or consulates.

You should, at any rate, advise the Canadian embassy of your presence when you arrive in a foreign country and keep them advised of changes of address and departure date.

Political demonstrations, including student protests, should be avoided even in countries at peace.

CONCLUSION

In a word, don't pass judgement on other societies, forms of government, or cultures even though some things about them are troubling at first glance. Since first impressions are often mistaken, we should start in by concentrating on things we find touching or marvelous.

Everywhere in the Third World we find values unknown to and lacking in us or that Western societies have long since lost: a keen sense of hospitality; a spirit of helping within families extended to include the least of grandnephews; respect for one's word of honour; the virtues of patience; high spirits and *joie de vivre*; a knack for being happy amidst deprivation; respect for old people, children, the disabled, beggars; worship of the past; a sense of the sacred.

Yes, we have a great deal to learn from our brothers and sisters in the Third World.

CHAPTER 14

Returning Home

At the end of a long trip, we can lash ourselves into a homecoming frenzy. Mentally we are in Canada thinking about the people we will soon see again and the problems soon to be faced. Try not to fall into this state of mind, which will prevent you from enjoying your last moments in a country you may never see again.

You should, nonetheless, give some thought to your trip home and get ready for it. Here's a highly practical memo that should help and be just as useful along the way when you leave one country for another:

> *Ticket reconfirmation.* Even if you rightly reconfirmed your airline ticket the day you arrived in the country, it is wise to go again to the airline office seventy-two hours before departure and re-reconfirm.
>
> *Exit visa.* In countries where one is needed, get it several days in advance.
>
> *Local money.* In the last few days, exchange your dollars only in very small amounts, as needed. That way you won't have to exchange your leftover local money back into dollars, which is often time-consuming and sometimes impossible. Put aside the exact amount in pesos or dinars that you'll need to cover final expenses:
>
> > ☐ tips for the chambermaid and the bellboy who carries your luggage down to the hotel lobby as well as the one who brings it from the lobby to the taxi
> >
> > ☐ cost of a taxi to the airport
> >
> > ☐ tip for the airport porter
> >
> > ☐ airport tax, which varies between five and fifteen dollars

and must be paid in local currency or, if need be, in American dollars

☐ a few pesos to buy a newspaper or pay for a last coffee while waiting for the often-delayed plane. If it isn't late, try to exchange your few remaining bills, with which it's better to buy an ebony curio than take a flat loss.

Dollars. Always have some American dollars in bills, which often come in handy during stopovers. If the flight is headed for Canada, switch some Canadian dollars from the moneybelt to your wallet to pay for the taxi or limo ride home.

Hotel bill. Settle it the night before if you are leaving on an early morning flight. Pay the difference in travellers' cheques if you are short of local money. Some American one-dollar bills will be very handy for reaching the exact amount.

Wake-up. Ask the front desk to give you a call if you are leaving early in the morning. But don't count too much on them and rely mostly on your alarm clock. Try to get to bed early to minimize travel fatigue.

Baggage. For morning departures, make up your bag the night before; it always takes longer than you expect . . . and the next morning you will be glad to get an extra half-hour's sleep. Always keep your travel bag with you in the hotel lobby and at the airport, and never take your eyes off the rest of your baggage.

The taxi. Very often there are a dozen at the doors of the hotel. Other times taxis are extremely scarce, particularly in the early hours of the morning. Reserve one the day before, not forgetting to negotiate the fare. If you have used the same taxi throughout your stay, which isn't a bad idea, you will be friends with the driver, and he won't turn on you the last day . . . hoping no doubt to get a generous farewell tip.

The airport. Be sure to get there at least an hour before the time suggested by the airline. If you forget why, re-read the recommendations in Chapter 9.

CANADA CUSTOMS

Before your plane touches down in Canada, the flight attendant will hand you a customs form in which you must mark down the value in Canadian dollars of all purchases made and gifts received abroad.

The same should be done for items sent by plane or ship that will arrive after you get home.

In the course of a trip you have the right to send gifts valued at less than forty dollars to Canada except for alcoholic beverages, tobacco, and other restricted items. Gifts sent from abroad are not part of your personal exemption. Gifts you bring with you, however, are added to your personal exemption.

If, as I recommend, you've kept the receipts for your purchases, it will be easy to list them and arrive at the value in Canadian dollars. (Is your pocket calculator handy?)

Actually you can bring back all you want from abroad (except for the restricted items discussed later). If you go over the amount of your personal exemption you need only pay the taxes and duty on the excess. In some cases that can still be advantageous.

Some time ago I bought a beautiful piece of lacquered Chinese furniture in Singapore. It was a cumbersome piece, and I had it sent by ship. Three months later customs advised me that a big wooden crate had arrived. If I remember correctly, the piece of furniture had cost me about two hundred dollars and at that point in the calendar year I had the right to import only about one hundred dollars worth of merchandise duty-free, so I had to pay duty on the difference. (I'd kept the receipt, of course, which made it possible to convince customs of the bargain I had made.) Adding up the purchase price, shipping costs, and customs duties, I realized that a similar piece would have cost me three times as much in Canada.

Every Canadian resident (including small children) has a right to a personal exemption and can bring in duty-free items not exceeding a certain amount. Parents or guardians make the declaration for a child, it being understood, of course, that the items are for the exclusive use of the child. This at least rules out cigarettes and cognac.

Here's a summary of the regulations, which the government changes from time to time:

After an absence of twenty-four hours or more you can bring in items worth a total of not over $20 (except for tobacco or alcohol) at any time. Customs requires only a verbal declaration.

After an absence of forty-eight hours or more, once a calendar quarter, you can bring in items worth a total of not more than

$100. Since a written declaration may be required, it's best to do it at leisure on the plane.

After an absence of seven days or more, once a calendar year, you can bring in items worth a total of not more than $300. A written declaration is required by customs.

Provided that it's on different trips, however, you can claim an annual exemption ($300) and a quarterly exemption ($100) in the same quarter.

But on each trip, whether your exemption is for $100 or $300, you get exemption from duty on only two hundred cigarettes *or* fifty cigars *and* 0.910 kg (two lbs.) of tobacco. You also have to be at least sixteen years old.

The same applies to alcohol. If you are of age in the Canadian province in which you arrive (eighteen in Manitoba, Alberta, Quebec, and Prince Edward Island; nineteen in other provinces) you can bring in 1.14 litres (40 oz.) of wine or spirits *or* twenty-four 355 ml. (12 oz.) cans or bottles of beer (or the equivalent in large bottles).

If you left Canada with expensive cameras or very valuable jewelry (which would be a mistake), you will have been sure to register them with customs at the airport *before* departure. They give you a certificate that will prevent problems if the customs officer asks for proof that this Nikon wasn't bought in Singapore or that diamond in Zaïre.

Strictly forbidden are such items as automatic or easily concealable weapons, explosives, fireworks, plants, seeds, food items, and living or stuffed animals of endangered species as well as parts of such animals, as, for example, elephant ivory.

Since this list isn't very detailed and can be changed the day that they put goldfish on the endangered species list, in doubtful cases it is better to ask your district customs office (see Appendix D) or at least get a copy of the latest edition of *I Declare*, a brochure published by the Department of External Affairs. Free copies are available at district customs and passport offices, travel agencies, airports and, abroad, at Canadian embassies. You can also write to the Public Relations Branch, Customs and Excise, Revenue Canada, Connaught Building, Ottawa, Ont. K1A 0L5.

Finally, any item undeclared or falsely appraised, as well as any restricted item, will be confiscated and may lead to severe fines and, if it is a can of talcum powder that contains another kind of powder, will surely land you in jail.

WELCOME HOME!

After the long hours of plane and airport, you finally have the pleasure of coming home to your own country. You will be amazed at how many little things you will appreciate that you never noticed before. Even a March snow squall will be a pleasure to behold . . . for a few minutes.

At home you will be back among your loved ones, familiar smells, a big stack of mail, your own bathroom, and the philodendron that missed you almost to death. Your first impulse will be to call your friends, even to invite over people who want to know all about your trip and are eager to give you the news that you are sure to have missed while you were away. There's not much about Canada in the Singapore *Straits Times* or *La Prensa* of Buenos Aires.

Naturally it is wiser to put off this warm reunion until the next day, along with all the other urgent things you feel like doing. The wisest course is to rest the first day, particularly if you have gone through five or six time zones.

After a day or two of euphoria you may experience homecoming shock, which will make you abruptly more detached, sometimes a little gloomy, and even aggressive. It's -20°C (-4°F), all the bills have to be paid, and Monday it's back to the office. This is a normal reaction, and everything should be back to normal in a few days. But don't make any important decisions before you have got back your physical and mental equilibrium.

If you have been in more or less unhealthy countries, all you need do is see a doctor specializing in tropical medicine. Even if you followed all the recommendations in Chapter 8, you may have picked up some puny virus or modest parasite or even intestinal amoebas. In all but a very few cases, the specialist will soon get them out of your system. Again, he should be consulted as soon as possible after your return, even if you feel in good form. Depending on which countries you visited and what kind of traveller you are, he will recommend tests of the blood, urine, and stools. Or he will prescribe a simple ointment for athlete's foot.

Finally, don't forget above all to take your two chloroquines every Sunday (*and* your Fansidar, as the case may be) for at least eight weeks. Travellers who didn't bother to do so have been unpleas-antly surprised by being laid low by an attack of malaria a month after their return to Canada.

One sure thing is that if you made a long and fruitful trip to the Third World, you will have undergone profound change. Henceforth you'll be more patient, tolerant, open-minded, and warm-hearted. With your enlarged outlook on the world you'll become more sensitive to the problems of developing countries and more aware of the responsibilities incumbent on our country and each of its citi-zens.

And before long you'll be dreaming of the next trip...

APPENDICES

A

DIPLOMATIC REPRESENTATIVES OF THIRD WORLD COUNTRIES IN CANADA

1. This list has been arranged in alphabetical order using the common name of each country followed by its sometimes very different official name, by which its embassy is called. Somalia, for example, is officially the *Somali Democratic Republic*, Oman the *Sultanate of Oman*, and Mongolia the *Mongolian People's Republic*.

2. The High Commissions (as embassies between Commonwealth countries are designated) and embassies are in Ottawa. Some countries also have consulates or are represented by honorary consuls in other cities. An example is Honduras, which has its consulate in Montréal, honorary consuls in Québec City and Vancouver, and an honorary consul general in Toronto.

3. Some countries not of the Third World, such as Japan and Australia, are included in the list because travellers getting around in the Third World often pass through them.

ALGERIA
(Embassy of the People's Democratic Republic of Algeria)

Embassy:

435 Daly Ave.
Ottawa, Ont. K1N 6H3
Tel.: (613)232-9453

ANTIGUA AND BARBUDA
(High Commission for Antigua and Barbuda)

High Commission:

112 Kent St., Suite 1701
Place de Ville, Tower B
Ottawa, Ont. K1P 5P2
Tel.: (613)236-8952

Consulate:

60 St. Clair Ave. E., Suite 205
Toronto, Ont. M4T 1N5
Tel.: (416)961-3143

ARGENTINA
(Embassy of the Argentine Republic)

Embassy:

Royal Bank Center
90 Sparks St., Suite 620
Ottawa, Ont. K1P 5B4
Tel.: (613)236-2351, 236-2354

Consulate:

1010 St. Catherine St. W.,
Suite 737
Montréal, Qué. H3B 1G1
Tel.: (514)866-3819

AUSTRALIA
(Australian High Commission)

High Commission:

130 Slater St., 13th Floor
Ottawa, Ont. K1P 6H2
Tel.: (613)236-0841

Consulates:

2324 Commerce Court W.
P. O. Box 69
Toronto, Ont. M5L 1B9
Tel.: (416) 367-0783

1066 W. Hastings St.
Suite 800
Oceanic Plaza
P.O.Box 12519
Vancouver, B.C. V6E 3X1
Tel.: (604)684-1177

THE BAHAMAS
(High Commission for the Commonwealth of the Bahamas)

High Commission:

150 Kent St., Suite 301
Ottawa, Ont. K1P 5P4
Tel.: (613)232-1724

BAHRAIN
(Embassy of the State of Bahrain)

Embassy:

3502 Int'l Drive N.W.
Washington, D.C.
USA 20008
Tel.: (202)342-0741

Consulate:

1869 Dorchester Blvd. W.
Montréal, Qué. H3R 1R4
Tel.: (514)931-7444

BANGLADESH
(High Commission for the People's Republic of Bangladesh)

High Commission:

85 Range Rd., Suite 402
Ottawa, Ont. K1N 8J6
Tel.: (613)236-0138, 236-0139

BARBADOS
(High Commission for Barbados)

High Commission:

151 Slater St., Suite 700
Ottawa, Ont. K1P 5H3
Tel.: (613)236-9517, 236-9518,
236-0014

BELIZE
(The High Commission for Belize)

High Commission:

1575 Eye St. N.W.
Suite 695
Washington, D.C.
USA 20005
Tel.: (202)289-1416

BENIN
(Embassy of the People's Republic of Benin)

Embassy:

58 Glebe Ave.
Ottawa, Ont. K1S 2C3
Tel.: (613)237-7366

Consulate:

429 Viger Ave.
Montréal, Qué. H2L 2N9
Tel.: (514)849-3695, 769-6088

BOLIVIA
(Embassy of Bolivia)

Embassy:

77 Metcalfe St., Suite 904
Ottawa, Ont. K1P 5L6
Tel.: (613)236-8237

Consulates:

11231 Jasper Ave.
Edmonton, Alta. T5K 0L5
Tel.: (403)488-1525

1242 Peel St., Suite 201
Montréal, Qué. H3B 2T6
Tel.: (514)861-4802, 934-0479

104 Mill Road
Etobicoke, Ont. M9C 1X8
Tel.: (416)622-2080

United Kingdom Building
409 Granville St., Suite 1157
Vancouver, B.C. V6C 1T2
Tel.: (604)685-8121

BOTSWANA
(High Commission for the Republic of Botswana)

High Commission:

c/o Embassy of the Republic of Botswana
Van Ness Centre
4301 Connecticut Ave. NW, Suite 404
Washington, D.C.
USA 20008
Tel.: (202)244-4990

BRAZIL
(Embassy of the Federative Republic of Brazil)

Embassy:

255 Albert St., Suite 900
Ottawa, Ont. K1P 6A9
Tel.: (613)237-1090

Consulates:

3630 Kempt Rd.
P.O. Box 8870, Stn. A
Halifax, N.S. B3K 5M5

1 Place Ville-Marie, Suite 1505
Montréal, Qué. H3B 2B5
Tel.: (514)866-3313

Box 4246, Postal Stn. A
St. John's, Nfld. A1B 3N9
Tel.: (709)726-0718

130 Bloor St. W., Suite 616
Toronto, Ont. M5S 1N5
Tel.: (416)921-4534

Royal Center
1035 West Georgia St.
Suite 1700, P.O. Box 11.152
Vancouver, B.C. V6E 3T3
Tel.: (604)687-4589

BRITAIN
(British High Commission)

High Commission:

80 Elgin Street
Ottawa, Ont. K1P 5K7
Tel.: (613)237-1530

Consulates:

Three McCauley Plaza
10025 Jasper Ave., Suite 1404
Edmonton, Alta. T5J 1S6
Tel.: (403)428-0375

1645 Granville St., 10th Floor
Halifax, N.S. B3J 1R6
Tel.: (902)422-7488

635 Dorchester Blvd. W.
Montréal, Qué. H3B 1R6
Tel.: (514)866-5863

777 Bay St., Suite 1910
College Park
Toronto, Ont. M5G 2G2
Tel.: (416)593-1290

1111 Melville St., Suite 800
Vancouver, B.C. V6E 3V6
Tel.: (604)683-4421

c/o Hignell Printing Ltd.
488 Burnell St.
Winnipeg, Man. R3G 2B4
Tel.: (204)783-7237

BURKINA FASO
(Embassy of the Burkina Faso)

Consulates:

200 Adelaide St. W.
Toronto, Ont. M5H 1W4
Tel.: (416)591-1697

81 St. Pierre St.
Box 158, Postal Stn. B
Québec, Qué. G1K 7A6
Tel.: (418)688-1153

BURMA
(Embassy of the Socialist Republic of the Union of Burma)

Embassy:

2300 S. Street N.W.
Washington, D.C.
USA 20008
Tel.: (202)332-9044, 332-9045, 332-9046

BURUNDI
(Embassy of the Republic of Burundi)

Embassy:

151 Slater St., Suite 800
Ottawa, Ont. K1P 5H3
Tel.: (613)236-8483, 236-8489

CAMEROON
(Embassy of the Republic of
Cameroon)

Embassy:

170 Clemow Ave.
Ottawa, Ont. K1S 2B4
Tel.: (613)236-1522

CAPE VERDE
(Embassy of the Republic of Cape
Verde)

Embassy:

3415 Massachusetts Ave. N.W.
Washington, D.C.
USA 20007
Tel.: (202)965-6820

CENTRAL AFRICAN REPUBLIC
(Embassy of the Central African
Republic)

Embassy:

1618-22nd St. N.W.
Washington, D.C.
USA 20008
Tel.: (202)483-7800

Consulate:

465 St. Jean St., Suite 800
Montréal, Qué. H2Y 2R6
Tel.: (514)849-8381

CHAD
(Embassy of the Republic of Chad)

Embassy:

2002 R St. N.W.
Washington, D.C.
USA 20006
Tel.: (202)462-4009

CHILE
(Embassy of Chile)

Embassy:

56 Sparks St., Suite 801
Ottawa, Ont. K1P 5A9
Tel.: (613)235-4402, 235-9940

Consulates:

1010 St. Catherine St. W.
Suite 731
Montréal, Qué. H3B 3R7
Tel.: (514)861-5669

330 Bay St., Suite 1205
Toronto, Ont. M5H 2S8
Tel.: (416)366-9570

305-1124 Lonsdale Ave.
North Vancouver,
Vancouver, B.C. V7M 2H1
Tel.: (604)985-6211

CHINA
(Embassy of the People's Republic of
China)

Embassy:

511-515 St. Patrick St.
Ottawa, Ont. K1N 5H3
Tel.: (613)234-2706

Consulates:

620 Church St.
Toronto, Ont. M4Y 2G2
Tel.: (416)964-7575, 964-7260

3338 Granville St.
Vancouver, B.C. V6H 3K3
Tel.: (604)736-6784, 736-6785

COLOMBIA
(Embassy of Colombia)

Embassy:

150 Kent St., Suite 404
Ottawa, Ont. K1P 5P4
Tel.: (613)230-3760

Consulates:

1010 Sherbrooke St. W., Suite 420
Montréal, Qué. H3A 2R7
Tel.: (514)849-4852

9–11 Hazelton Ave., Third Floor
Toronto, Ont. M5R 2E1
Tel.: (416)922-0140

4202 Musqueam Dr.
Vancouver, B.C. V6N 3R7
Tel.: (604)261-8211

THE CONGO
(Embassy of the People's Republic of
the Congo)

Embassy:

c/o Permanent Mission of the Congo
to the United Nations
14 East 65th St.
New York, N.Y.
USA 10021
Tel.: (212)744-7840, 744-7841,
744-7842

COSTA RICA
(Embassy of Costa Rica)

Embassy:

150 Argyle St., Suite 114
Ottawa, Ont. K2P 1B7
Tel.: (613)234-5762

Consulates:

1155 Dorchester Blvd. W.
No. 1517
Montréal, Qué. H3B 2L3
Tel.: (514)866-8159, 866-0442

1 Nicolas St., Suite 1510
Ottawa, Ont. K1N 7B7
Tel.: (613)234-5762

75 The Donway West, No. 507
Don Mills, Ont. M3C 2E9
Tel.: (416)449-8333

1550 Alberni St., Suite 603
Vancouver, B.C. V6G 1A5
Tel.: (604)682-3865

CUBA
(Embassy of the Republic of Cuba)

Embassy:

388 Main St.
Ottawa, Ont. K1S 1E3
Tel.: (613)563-0141

Consulates:

1415 des Pins Ave. W.
Montréal, Qué. H3G 2B2
Tel.: (514)843-8897

372 Bay St., Suite 406
Toronto, Ont. M5H 2W9
Tel.: (416)362-3622

DOMINICA
(High Commission for the
Commonwealth of Dominica)

High Commission:

112 Kent St., Suite 1701
Place de Ville, Tower B
Ottawa, Ont. K1P 5P2
Tel.: (613)236-8952

DOMINICAN REPUBLIC
(Embassy of the Dominican Republic)

Embassy:

260 Metcalfe St., Suite 5D
Ottawa, Ont. K2P 1R6
Tel.: (613)234-0363

Consulates:

1464 Crescent St.
Montréal, Qué. H3A 2B6
Tel.: (514)843-6525

170 Grande Allée W.
Québec, Qué. G1R 2G9
Tel.: (418)694-9613

59 Broad
St. John, N.B. E2L 1Y3

10 Forest Ave.
St. John's, Nfld.

808–1445 Marpole Ave.
Vancouver, B.C. V6H 1S5
Tel.: (604)738-1414

ECUADOR
(Embassy of Ecuador)

Embassy:

150 Kent St., Suite 407
Ottawa, Ont. K1P 5P4
Tel.: (613)238-5032

Consulates:

1500 Stanley St., Suite 226
Montréal, Qué. H3A 1R3
Tel.: (514)849-0200

151 Bloor Street W., Suite 670
Toronto, Ont. M5S 1S4
Tel.: (416)968-2077

777 Hornby Street, Suite 920
Vancouver, B.C. V6Z 1S4
Tel.: (604)689-0481, 689-0482

EGYPT
(Embassy of the Arab Republic of
Egypt)

Embassy:

454 Laurier Ave. E.
Ottawa, Ont. K1N 6R3
Tel.: (613)234-4931

Consulate:

3754 Côte des Neiges Rd.
Montréal, Qué. H3H 1V6
Tel.: (514)937-7781, 937-7782

EL SALVADOR
(Embassy of El Salvador)

Embassy:

294 Albert St., Suite 302
Ottawa, Ont. K1P 6E6
Tel.: (613)234-4931

Consulate:

370 St. Joseph Blvd. E.
Montréal, Qué. H2T 1J6
Tel.: (514)842-7053

ETHIOPIA
(Embassy of Ethiopa)

Embassy:

866 United Nations Plaza, Suite 560
New York, N.Y.
USA 10017
Tel.: (212)421-1830

FIJI
(High Commission for Fiji)

High Commission:

One United Nations Plaza, 26th Floor
New York, N.Y.
USA 10017
Tel.: (212)355-7316

Consulate:

1437 West 64th Ave.
Vancouver, B.C. V6P 2H5
Tel.: (604)251-4333

FRANCE
(Embassy of France)

Embassy:

42 Sussex Dr.
Ottawa, Ont. K1M 2C9
Tel.: (613)232-1795

Consulates:

4–834 2nd Ave. N.W.
Calgary, Alta. T2N 0E5
Tel.: (403)270-3243

1299 Joseph-Dandurand
Chicoutimi, Que. G7H 6R6
Tel.: (418)545-5466

Guardian Bldg., Suite 402
10240–124 Street,
Edmonton, Alta. T5N 3W6
Tel.: (403)482-3636

35 Bayview Rd.
Halifax, N.S. B3M 1N8
Tel.: (902)443-5848

250 Lutz, P.O. Box 1109
Moncton, N.B. E1C 8P6
Tel.: (506)855-4303

2 Elysée, Place Bonaventure
P.O. Box 177,
Montréal, Qué. H5A 1A7
Tel.: (514)878-4381

30 Blowers St.
P.O. Box 308
North Sydney, N.S. B2A 3J5
Tel.: (902)794-4800

1110 Laurentides Ave.
Québec, Qué. G1S 3C3
Tel.: (418)688-0430

P.O. Box 3663
Regina, Sask. S4P 3N8
Tel.: (306)545-9912

40 Charlotte St.
Saint John, N.B. E2L 3W9
Tel.: (506)693-1193

17 Yetman Dr.
St. John's, Nfld. A1N 3A7
Tel.: (709)364-7492

102 Saskatchewan Crescent W.
Saskatoon, Sask.

40 University Ave., Suite 620
Toronto, Ont. M5J 1T1
Tel.: (416)977-3131

736 Granville St., Suite 1201
The Vancouver Block
Vancouver, B.C. V6Z 1H9
Tel.: (604)681-2301

3946 Emerald Place
Victoria, B.C. V8P 4T6

210 Rogers St.
Whitehorse, Y.T. Y1A 1X2

GABON
(Embassy of the Gabonese Republic)

Embassy:

4 Range Rd.
Ottawa, Ont. K1N 8J3
Tel.: (613)232-5301, 232-5302

Consulates:

85 St. Catherine St. W.
Montréal, Qué. H2X 3P4

347 Bay St., Suite 700
Toronto, Ont. M5H 2R7
Tel.: (416)362-1288

THE GAMBIA
(High Commission for the Gambia)

High Commission:

c/o Permanent Mission of Gambia to
the United Nations
19 East 47th Street, 15th Floor
New York, N.Y.
USA 10017
Tel.: (212)752-6213

Consulates:

363 St. François Xavier St., Suite 300
Montréal, Qué. H2Y 3P9
Tel.: (514)849-2885

102 Bloor St. W., Suite 510
Toronto, Ont. M5S 1N1
Tel.: (416)923-2935

GHANA
(High Commission for Ghana)

High Commission:

85 Range Rd., Suite 810
Ottawa, Ont. K1N 8J6
Tel.: (613)236-0871

GRENADA
(High Commission for Grenada)

High Commission:

112 Kent St., Suite 1701
Place de Ville, Tower B,
Ottawa, Ont. K1P 5P2
Tel.: (613)236-8952

GUATEMALA
(Embassy of Guatemala)

Embassy:

294 Albert St., Suite 500
Ottawa, Ont. K1P 6E6
Tel.: (613)237-3941, 237-3942

Consulates:

International Trade Centre, Place
Bonaventure
P.O. Box 401,
Montréal, Qué. H5A 1B7
Tel.: (514)861-5919

50 Aberdeen St.
Québec, Qué. G1R 2C7
Tel.: (418)423-0426

67 Yonge St., Suite 608
Toronto, Ont. M5E 1J8
Tel.: (416)459-3727

1400–736 Granville St.
Vancouver, B.C. V6Z 1G7
Tel.: (604)682-4831

GUINEA
(Embassy of the Republic of Guinea)

Embassy:

112 Kent St., Suite 208
Place de Ville, Tower B
Ottawa, Ont. K1P 5P2
Tel.: (613)232-1133

GUINEA-BISSAU
(Embassy of the Republic of
Guinea-Bissau)

Embassy:

211 East 43rd St., Suite 604
New York, N.Y.
USA 10017
Tel.: (212)661-3977

Consulate:

4200 St. Laurent Blvd.,
Montréal, Qué. H2W 2R2

GUYANA
(High Commission for the
Co-operative Republic of Guyana)

High Commission:

Burnside Building
151 Slater St., Suite 309
Ottawa, Ont. K1P 5H3
Tel.: (613)235-7249, 235-7240

Consulate:

505 Consumers Rd., Suite 502
Willowdale, Ont. M2J 4V8
Tel.: (416)494-6040

HAITI
(Embassy of Haiti)

Embassy:

112 Kent St., Suite 1308
Tower B, Place de Ville
Ottawa, Ont. K1P 5P2
Tel.: (613)238-1628, 238-1629

Consulates:

Place Bonaventure, P.O. Box 187
Montréal, Qué. H5A 1A9
Tel.: (514)871-8993

3291 Chemin Ste Foy, Suite 205
Ste. Foy
Québec, Qué. G1X 3V2
Tel.: (418)651-2894

113 Simonston Blvd.
Toronto, Ont. L3T 4L9
Tel.: (416)886-3398

HONDURAS
(Embassy of the Republic of
Honduras)

Embassy:

151 Slater St., Suite 300–A
Ottawa, Ont. K1P 5H3
Tel.: (613)233-8900

Consulates:

1500 Stanley St., Suite 308
Montréal, Qué. H3A 1R3
Tel.: (514)935-9708

1334 Maréchal Foch St.
Québec, Qué. G1S 2C4
Tel.: (418)681-5070

22 Mayhoff Square
Unionville, Ont. L3R 1Y4
Tel.: (416)477-0631

104–535 West Georgia St.
Vancouver, B.C. V6B 1Z6
Tel.: (604)685-7711

INDIA
(High Commission for India)

High Commission:

10 Springfield Rd.
Ottawa, Ont. K1M 1C9
Tel.: (613)744-3751, 744-3752,
744-3753

Consulates:

2 Bloor St. W., Suite 500
Toronto, Ont. M4W 2E
Tel.: (416)960-0751, 960-0752

325 Howe St., 1st floor
Vancouver, B.C. V6C 1Z7
Tel.: (604)681-0644

INDONESIA
(Embassy of the Republic of
Indonesia)

Embassy:

287 MacLaren St.
Ottawa, Ont. K2P 0L9
Tel.: (613)236-7403

Consulates:

425 University Ave., 9th Floor
Toronto, Ont. M5G 1T6
Tel.: (416)591-6613

526 Granville St., 2nd Floor
Vancouver, B.C. V6C 1W6
Tel.: (604)682-8855

IRAN
(Embassy of the Islamic Republic of
Iran)

Embassy:

411 Roosevelt Ave., 4th Floor
Ottawa, Ont. K2A 3X9
Tel.: (613)729-0902

IRAQ
(Embassy of the Republic of Iraq)

Embassy:

215 McLeod St.
Ottawa, Ont. K2P 0Z8
Tel.: (613)236-9177, 236-9178

Consulates:

3019 St. Sulpice Rd.
Montréal, Qué. H3H 1B6
Tel.: (514)937-9143, 937-9144

ISRAEL
(Embassy of Israel)

Embassy:

410 Laurier Ave. W., Suite 601
Ottawa, Ont. K1R 7T3
Tel.: (613)237-6450

Consulates:

550 Sherbrooke St. W., Suite 1675
Montréal, Qué. H3Z 1B9
Tel.: (514)288-9277

180 Bloor St. W., Suite 700
Toronto, Ont. M5S 2V6
Tel.: (416)961-1126

THE IVORY COAST
(Embassy of the Republic of Ivory Coast)

Embassy:

9 Marlborough Ave.
Ottawa, Ont. K1N 8E6
Tel.: (613)236-9919

Consulate:

260 Adelaide St. E., P.O. Box 90
Toronto, Ont. M5A 1N0
Tel.: (416)967-1212 Ext 3338

JAMAICA
(Jamaican High Commission)

High Commission:

275 Slater St., Suite 402
Ottawa, Ont. K1P 5H9
Tel.: (613)233-9311, 233-9314

Consulates:

36 Windermere Crescent
St. Albert, Alta. T8N 3S5
Tel.: (403)459-8440

214 King St. W., Suite 216
Toronto, Ont. M5H 1K4
Tel.: (416)598-3008, 598-3393

11 Wadham Bay
Winnipeg, Man. R3T 3K2
Tel.: (204)269-0094

JAPAN
(Embassy of Japan)

Embassy:

255 Sussex Dr.
Ottawa, Ont. K1N 9E6
Tel.: (613)236-8541

Consulates:

10020–100 St., Suite 2600
Edmonton, Alta. T5J 0N4
Tel.: (403)422-3752, 429-3052

Lindwood Holdings Ltd., Keith Hall
1475 Hollis St.
Halifax, N.S. B3J 1V1
Tel.: (902)429-6530

1155 Dorchester Blvd. W.,
Suite 2701
Montréal, Qué. H3B 2K9
Tel.: (514)866-3429

Haldane House, 2100 Scarth St.
Regina, Sask. S4P 2H6
Tel.: (306)352-2651

1803 Toronto-Dominion Centre,
P.O. Box 10
Toronto, Ont. M5K 1A1
Tel.: (416)363-7038

Annex Office, Suite 1910
Royal Trust Tower, P.O. Box 93
Toronto-Dominion Centre
Toronto, Ont. M5K 1G8

1177 Hastings St. W., Suite 1210
Vancouver, B.C. V6E 2K9
Tel.: (604)684-5868, 684-5869

Three Lakeview Square
185 Carlton St., 5th Floor
Winnipeg, Man. R3C 3J1
Tel.: (204)943-5554

JORDAN

(Embassy of the Hashemite Kingdom
of Jordan)

Embassy:

100 Bronson Ave., Suite 701
Ottawa, Ont. K1R 6G8
Tel.: (613)238-8090

KENYA

(High Commission for the Republic of
Kenya)

High Commission:

415 Laurier Ave. E.
Ottawa, Ont. K1N 6R4
Tel.: (613)563-1773, 563-1774,
563-1775, 563-1776

KOREA

(Embassy of the Republic of Korea)

Embassy:

85 Albert St., 10th Floor
Ottawa, Ont. K1P 6A4
Tel.: (613)232-1715, 232-1716,
232-1717

Consulates:

1000 Sherbrooke St. W., Suite 2205
Montréal, Qué. H3A 3G4
Tel.: (514)845-3243, 845-3244

439 University Ave., Suite 700
Toronto, Ont. M5G 1Y8
Tel.: (416)598-4608, 598-4609,
598-4600

1066 West Hastings St., Suite 830
Vancouver B.C. V6E 3X1
Tel.: (604)681-9581

KUWAIT

(Embassy of the State of Kuwait)

Embassy:

c/o Embassy of Kuwait
2940 Tilden St. N.W.
Washington, D.C.
USA 20008
Tel.: (202)966-0702

Consulate:

1510 Walkley Road
Ottawa, Ont. K1V 6P5
Tel.: (613)731-3242

LAOS

(Embassy of the Lao People's
Democratic Republic)

Embassy:

c/o Embassy of the Lao People's
Democratic Republic
2222 S St. N.W.
Washington, D.C.
USA 20008
Tel.: (202)332-6416, 332-6417

LEBANON

(Embassy of Lebanon)

Embassy:

640 Lyon St.
Ottawa, Ont. K1S 3Z5
Tel.: (613)236-5825, 236-5855

Consulates:

10187–103 Street
Edmonton, Alta. T5J OY6
Tel.: (403)424-0485

227 Bedford Highway,
Halifax, N.S. B3M 2J9
Tel.: (902)443-1666

40 St. Catherine St.
Montréal, Qué. H2V 2A2
Tel.: (514)276-2638, 276-2639

700 Bay St., Suite 1604
Toronto, Ont. M5G 1Z6
Tel.: (416)596-7788

LESOTHO

(High Commission for the Kingdom of
Lesotho)

High Commission:

350 Sparks St., Suite 910
Ottawa, Ont. K1R 7S8
Tel.: (613)236-9449, 236-0960

LIBERIA
(Embassy of the Republic of Liberia)

Embassy:

c/o Embassy of Liberia
5201–16th St. N.W.
Washington, D.C.
USA 20011
Tel.: (202)723-0437

Consulates:

1080 Beaver Hall Hill, Suite 2020
Montréal, Qué. H2Z 1S8
Tel.: (514)871-9121

160 Elgin St.
P.O. Box 466, Stn 'A'
Ottawa, Ont. K1N 8S3
Tel.: (613)232-1781

1011 Burrard Building
1030 Georgia St. W.
Vancouver, B.C. V6E 2Y3
Tel.: (604)681-6418

LIBYA
(Embassy of the Socialist People's
Libyan Arab Jamahiriya)

Embassy:

c/o Permanent Mission of the
Socialist People's Libyan Arab
Jamahiriya to the United Nations
309–315 East 48th St.
New York, N.Y.
USA 10017
Tel.: (212)752-5775

MADAGASCAR
(Embassy of the Democratic Republic
of Madagascar)

Embassy:

c/o Permanent Democratic Republic
of Madagascar to the United Nations
801 Second Avenue, Suite 404
New York, N.Y.
USA 10017
Tel.: (212)986-9491, 986-9492

Consulates:

459 St-Sulpice St.
Montréal, Qué. H2Y 2V8
Tel.: (514)844-4427

335 Watson Avenue
Oakville, Ont. L6J 3V5
Tel.: (416)845-8914

MALAWI
(High Commission for Malawi)

High Commission:

112 Kent St., Suite 905
Tower B, Place de Ville
Ottawa, Ont. K1P 5P2
Tel.: (613)236-8931

Consulates:

245 des Peupliers St.
Montréal, Qué. J3V 2M2
Tel.: (514)670-9007, 461-0277

38 Maple Ave.
Toronto, Ont. M4W 2T7
Tel.: (416)927-7615

MALAYSIA
(High Commission for Malaysia)

High Commission:

60 Boteler St.
Ottawa, Ont. K1N 8Y7
Tel.: (613)237-5182, 237-5183,
237-5184

Consulates:

Box 172, Suite 1010
Royal Trust Tower,
Toronto-Dominion Centre
Toronto, Ont. M5K 1H6
Tel.: (416)869-3886, 869-3887

The Burrard Building, 14th Floor
1030 West Georgia St.
Vancouver, B.C. V6E 3C2
Tel.: (604)687-9444

MALI
(Embassy of the Republic of Mali)

Embassy:

50 Goulburn Ave.
Ottawa, Ont. K1N 8C8
Tel.: (613)232-1501

Consulate:

782 Upper Lansdowne Ave.
Westmount, Qué. H3Y 1J8
Tel.: (514)397-3018

MAURITANIA
(Embassy of the Islamic Republic of Mauritania)

Embassy:

c/o The Permanent Mission of the Islamic Republic of Mauritania to the United Nations
600 Third Avenue, 37th Floor
New York, N.Y.
USA 10016
Tel.: (212)697-2490, 697-2491

MAURITIUS
(High Commission for Mauritius)

High Commission:

c/o Embassy of Mauritius, Suite 134
Van Ness Centre, 4301 Connecticut Ave. N.W.
Washington, D.C.
USA 20008
Tel.: (202)244-1491, 244-1492

MEXICO
(Embassy of Mexico)

Embassy:

130 Albert St., Suite 206
Ottawa, Ont. K1P 5G4
Tel.: (613)233-8988, 233-9272, 233-9917

Consulates:

3100, 300 Fifth Ave. S.W.
Calgary, Alta. T2P 0L3
Tel.: (403)260-9300

430 The Permanent Bldg.
10036 Jasper Ave.
Edmonton, Alta. T5J 2W2
Tel.: (403)424-7201

95 Bessemer Rd.
London, Ont. N6E 1P9
Tel.: (519)681-3331

1000 Sherbrooke St., Suite 2215
Montréal, Qué. H3A 3G4
Tel.: (514)288-2502, 288-4916

380 Saint-Louis Rd., Apt. 1407
Québec, Qué.
Tel.: (418)681-4482

60 Bloor St. W., Suite 203
Toronto, Ont. M4W 3B8
Tel.: (416)922-2718, 922-3196

625 Howe Street, Suite 310
Vancouver, B.C. V6C 2T6
Tel.: (604)684-3547, 684-5725

MONGOLIA
(Embassy of the Mongolian People's Republic)

Embassy:

c/oThe Permanent Mission of the Mongolian Republic to the United Nations
6 East 77th St.
New York, N.Y.
USA 10021
Tel.: (212)861-9460

MOROCCO
(Embassy of the Kingdom of Morocco)

Embassy:

38 Range Road
Ottawa, Ont. K1N 8J4
Tel.: (613)236-7391, 236-7392, 236-7393

Consulate:

1455 Sherbrooke St.
Montréal, Qué. H3Y 1L2
Tel.: (514)937-9460, 937-9469

MOZAMBIQUE
(Embassy of the People's Republic of Mozambique)

Embassy:

1990 M St. N.W., Suite 570
Washington, D.C.
USA 20036
Tel.: (202)293-7146

NEPAL
(Royal Nepalese Embassy)

Embassy:

c/o Embassy of Nepal
2131 Leroy Place N.W.
Washington, D.C.
USA 20008
Tel.: (202)667-4550

NICARAGUA
(Embassy of Nicaragua)

Embassy:

170 Laurier Ave. W., Suite 908
Ottawa, Ont. K1P 5V5
Tel.: (613)234-9361, 234-9362

Consulate:

4 Topaz Gate
Willowdale, Ont. M2M 2Z7
Tel.: (416)221-3092

NIGER
(Embassy of the Republic of the Niger)

Embassy:

38 Blackburn Ave.
Ottawa, Ont. K1N 8A3
Tel.: (613)232-4291, 232-4292, 232-4293

Consulate:

255 St-Jacques St. W., Suite 100
Montréal, Qué. H2Y 1M6
Tel.: (514)845-6126

NIGERIA
(High Commission for the Federal Republic of Nigeria)

High Commission:

295 Metcalfe St.
Ottawa, Ont. K2P 1R9
Tel.: (613)236-0521

OMAN
(Embassy of the Sultanate of Oman)

Embassy:

c/o Embassy of Oman
2342 Massachusetts Ave. N.W.
Washington, D.C.
USA 20008
Tel.: (202)387-1980, 387-1982

PAKISTAN
(Embassy of the Islamic Republic of Pakistan)

Embassy:

Burnside Bldg.
151 Slater St., Suite 608
Ottawa, Ont. K1P 5H3
Tel.: (613)238-7881

Consulates:

2100 Drummond St., Suite 505
Montréal, Qué. H3G 1X1
Tel.: (514)845-2297, 845-2298

8 King St. E.
Toronto, Ont. M5C 1B5

PANAMA

Consulates:

10355–146 St.
Edmonton, Alta. T5N 3A3
Tel.: (403)482-2263

62 Bedford Highway
Halifax, N.S. B3M 2J2
Tel.: (902)443-0011

1500 Stanley St., Suite 304
Montréal, Qué. H3A 1R3
Tel.: (514)845-6016

1 Fanshawe Dr.
Brampton, Ont. L6Z 1A7
Tel.: (416)846-1855

PAPUA NEW GUINEA
(High Commission for Papua New
Guinea)

High Commission:

c/o Permanent Mission of Papua New
Guinea to the United Nations
100 East 42nd St., Room 1005
New York, N.Y.
USA 10017
Tel.: (212)682-6447

PARAGUAY
(Embassy of Paraguay)

Embassy:

c/o Permanent Mission of Paraguay
to the OAS
2400 Massachusetts Ave. N.W.
Washington, D.C.
USA 20008
Tel.: (202)483-6960

Consulate:

1110 Sherbrooke W., Suite 1611
Montréal, Qué. H3A 1G8
Tel.: (514)849-9483

PERU
(Embassy of Peru)

Embassy:

170 Laurier Ave. W., Suite 1007
Ottawa, Ont. K1P 5V5
Tel.: (613)238-1777, 238-1779

Consulates:

2250 Guy St., Suite 304
Montréal, Qué. H3H 2M3
Tel.: (514)932-3692, 932-8645

1200 Bay St., 5th Floor
Toronto, Ont. M5H 2X6
Tel.: (416)963-9696

1151 Hornby St.
Vancouver, B.C. V6Z 1W1
Tel.: (604)669-1347

436 Main St.
Winnipeg, Man. R3B 1A7
Tel.: (204)947-0131

THE PHILIPPINES
(Embassy of the Philippines)

Embassy:

130 Albert St., Suite 607
Ottawa, Ont. K1P 5G4
Tel.: (613)233-1121

Consulates:

111 Avenue Rd.
Toronto, Ont. M5R 3J8
Tel.: (416)922-7181

301–308, 470 Granville St.
Vancouver, B.C. V6C 1V5
Tel.: (604)685-7645

QATAR
(Embassy of the State of Qatar)

Embassy:

c/o The Permanent Mission of Qatar
to the United Nations
747 Third Ave., 22nd Floor
New York, N.Y.
USA 10017
Tel.: (212)486-9335, 486-9336

RWANDA
(Embassy of the Rwandese Republic)

Embassy:

350 Sparks St., Suite 903
Ottawa, Ont. K1R 7S9
Tel.: (613)238-1603, 238-1604

Consulate:

1600 Delorimier St.
Montréal, Qué. H2K 3W5
Tel.: (514)527-2859

SAINT CHRISTOPHER-NEVIS
(Saint Christopher-Nevis High Commission)

High Commission:

112 Kent St., Suite 1701
Place de Ville, Tower B
Ottawa, Ont. K1P 5P2
Tel.: (613)236-8952

SAINT LUCIA
(Saint Lucia High Commission)

High Commission:

112 Kent St., Suite 1701
Place de Ville, Tower B
Ottawa, Ont. K1P 5P2
Tel.: (613)236-8952

SAINT VINCENT AND THE GRENADINES
(Saint Vincent and the Grenadine High Commission)

High Commission:

112 Kent St., Suite 1701
Place de Ville, Tower B
Ottawa, Ont. K1P 5P2
Tel.: (613)236-8952

Consulate:

16 Denmar Rd., Suite 1945
Pickering, Ont. L1V 3E2

SAO TOMÉ AND PRINCIPE
(Embassy of Sao Tomé and Principe)

Embassy:

c/o The Permanent Mission of Sao
Tomé and Principe to the United
Nations
801 Second Ave., Room 1504
New York, N.Y.
USA 10017
Tel.: (212)697-4212

SAUDI ARABIA
(Embassy of the Kingdom of Saudi Arabia)

Embassy:

99 Bank St., Suite 901
Ottawa, Ont. K1P 6B9
Tel.: (613)237-4100, 237-4101,
237-4102, 237-4103

SENEGAL
(Embassy of the Republic of Senegal)

Embassy:

57 Marlborough Ave.
Ottawa, Ont. K1N 8T8
Tel.: (613)238-6392

Consulate:

2472 Bayview Ave.
Toronto, Ont. M2A 2A7

SEYCHELLES
(High Commission for the Seychelles)

High Commission:

53 Bis, Rue François ler,
75008, Paris, France
Tel.: 723-9811

SIERRA LEONE
(High Commission for Sierra Leone)

High Commission:

1701-19th Street N.W.
Washington, D.C.
USA 20009
Tel.: (202)939-9261

SINGAPORE
(High Commission for Singapore)

High Commission:

Two United Nations Plaza
26th Floor
New York, N.Y.
USA 10017
Tel.: (212)826-0840, 826-0841,
826-0842, 826-0843

SOMALIA
(Embassy of the Somali Democratic
Republic)

Embassy:

130 Slater St., Suite 1000
Ottawa, Ont. K1P 5P2
Tel.: (613)563-4541

SOUTH AFRICA
(Embassy of the Republic of South
Africa)

Embassy:

15 Sussex Dr.
Ottawa, Ont. K1M 1M8
Tel.: (613)744-0330

Consulates:

1 Place Ville Marie, Suite 3736
Montréal, Qué. H3B 3P5
Tel.: (514)878-9217

Stock Exchange Tower, Suite 2515
2 First Canadian Place
King and York Streets
Toronto, Ont. M5X 1E3
Tel.: (416)364-0314

SRI LANKA
(High Commission for the Democratic
Socialist Republic of Sri Lanka)

High Commission:

85 Range Rd.
Suites 102, 103, 104
Ottawa, Ont. K1N 8J6
Tel.: (613)233-8449

THE SUDAN
(Embassy of the Democratic Republic
of Sudan)

Embassy:

2210 Massachusetts Ave. N.W.
Washington, D.C.
USA 20008
Tel.: (202)338-8565, 338-8570

SURINAME
(Embassy of the Republic of
Suriname)

Embassy:

c/o Embassy of the Republic of
Suriname
2600 Virginia Ave. N.W., Suite 711
Washington, D.C.
USA 20037
Tel.: (202)338-6980

SWAZILAND
(High Commission for the Kingdom of
Swaziland)

Embassy:

c/o Embassy of the Kingdom of
Swaziland
Suite 441, Van Ness Centre
4301 Connecticut Ave. N.W.
Washington, D.C.
USA 20008
Tel.: (202)362-6683, 362-6684,
362-6685

Consulate:

42 Acadie St.
Aylmer, Qué. J9J 1H7
Tel.: (819)777-1967

SYRIA
(Embassy of the Syrian Arab
Republic)

Embassy:

2215 Wyoming Ave. N.W.
Washington, D.C.
USA 20008
Tel.: (202)232-6313

Consulate:

324 Arlington Crescent
Beaconsfield, Qué. H9W 2K3
Tel.: (514)695-3530

TANZANIA
(High Commission for the United Republic of Tanzania)

High Commission:

50 Range Rd.
Ottawa, Ont. K1N 8J4
Tel.: (613)232-1509

THAILAND
(Royal Thai Embassy)

Embassy:

85 Range Rd., Suite 704
Ottawa, Ont. K1N 8J6
Tel.: (613)237-1517, 237-0476

Consulates:

1245 Sherbrooke St. W.
Suite 1030
Montréal, Qué. H3G 1G2
Tel.: (514)842-0433

Bank of Canada Building
250 University Ave., 7th Floor
Toronto, Ont. M5H 3E5
Tel.: (416)593-2887

736 Granville St., Suite 106
Vancouver, B.C. V6Z 1G3
Tel.: (604)687-1143

TOGO
(Embassy of the Republic of Togo)

Embassy:

12 Range Rd.
Ottawa, Ont. K1N 8J3
Tel.: (613)238-5916, 238-5917

TRINIDAD AND TOBAGO
(High Commission for the Republic of Trinidad and Tobago)

High Commission:

75 Albert St., Suite 508
Ottawa, Ont. K1P 5E7
Tel.: (613)232-2418, 232-2419

Consulate:

365 Bloor St. E., Suite 1202
Toronto, Ont. M4W 3L4
Tel.: (416)922-3175

TUNISIA
(The Embassy of the Republic of Tunisia)

Embassy:

515 O'Connor St.
Ottawa, Ont. K1S 3P8
Tel.: (613)237-0330, 237-0332

Consulate:

511 Place d'Armes, Suite 600
Montréal, Qué. H2Y 2W7

TURKEY
(The Embassy of Turkey)

Embassy:

197 Wurtemburg St.
Ottawa, Ont. K1N 8L9
Tel.: (613)232-1577, 232-1578

UGANDA
(High Commission for the Republic of Uganda)

High Commission:

170 Laurier Ave. W., Suite 601
Ottawa, Ont. K1P 5V5
Tel.: (613)233-7797, 233-7798

UNION OF SOVIET SOCIALIST REPUBLICS
(Embassy of the Union of Soviet Socialist Republics)

Embassy:

285 Charlotte St.
Ottawa, Ont. K1N 8L5
Tel.: (613)235-4341, 236-1413

Consulate:

3655 Ave. du Musée
Montréal, Qué. H1W 1S1
Tel.: (514)843-5901

UNITED ARAB EMIRATES
(Embassy of the United Arab Emirates)

Embassy:

747 Third Ave.
New York, N.Y.
USA 10017
Tel.: (212)371-0480

URUGUAY
(Embassy of Uruguay)

Embassy:

1918 F St. N.W.
Washington, D.C.
USA 20006
Tel.: (202)331-1313

Consulates:

1010 St. Catherine St. W.
Suite 347, 3rd Floor
Montréal, Qué. H3B 3R7
Tel.: (514)866-0217

Toronto Dominion Bank Tower
Suite 2990, P.O. Box 10069
Vancouver, B.C. V7Y 1B6
Tel.: (604)682-0404

VENEZUELA
(Embassy of Venezuela)

Embassy:

294 Albert St., Suite 602
Ottawa, Ont. K1P 6E6
Tel.: (613)235-5151, 235-5153

Consulates:

1410 Stanley St., Suite 600
Montréal, Qué. H3A 1P8
Tel.: (514)842-3417, 842-3418

2 Carlton St., Suite 703
Toronto, Ont. M5B 1J3
Tel.: (416)977-6809, 977-6810

525 Seymour St.
Seymour Bldg., Suite 103
Vancouver, B.C. V6B 3H7
Tel.: (604)685-0561

VIET NAM
(Embassy of the Socialist Republic of Viet Nam)

Embassy:

12–14 Victoria Rd.
London (England)
United Kingdom W85RD
Tel.: 937-1912 and 927-8564

WESTERN SAMOA
(High Commission for Western Samoa)

High Commission:

820 Second Ave., Suite 800D
New York, N.Y.
USA 10017
Tel.: (212)599-6196

YEMEN ARAB REPUBLIC
(Embassy of the Yemen Arab Republic)

Embassy:

Watergate Six Hundred, Suite 860
600 New Hampshire Ave. N.W.
Washington, D.C.
USA 20037
Tel.: (202)965-4760, 965-4761

Consulate:

56 Sparks St., Suite 500
Ottawa, Ont. K1P 5A9
Tel.: (613)230-6136

PEOPLE'S DEMOCRATIC REPUBLIC OF YEMEN
(Embassy of the People's Democratic Republic of Yemen)

Embassy:

c/o Permanent Mission of the People's Democratic Republic of Yemen
413 East 51st St.
New York, N.Y.
USA 10022
Tel.: (212)752-3066, 752-3067, 752-3068

ZAÏRE
(Embassy of the Republic of Zaïre)

Embassy:

18 Range Rd.
Ottawa, Ont. K1N 8J3
Tel.: (613)236-7103

ZAMBIA
(High Commission for the Republic of
Zambia)

High Commission:

130 Albert St., Suite 1610
Ottawa, Ont. K1P 5G4
Tel.: (613)563-0712, 563-0714,
563-0715, 563-0716

ZIMBABWE
(High Commission for the Republic of
Zimbabwe)

High Commission:

112 Kent St., Suite 915
Place de Ville, Tower B
Ottawa, Ont. K1P 5P2
Tel.: (613)237-4388, 237-4389

B

CANADIAN DIPLOMATIC REPRESENTATIVES IN THIRD WORLD COUNTRIES

1. This list has been prepared in alphabetical order using the common name of each country followed by its often very different official name. The real name of Libya, for example, is the *Socialist People's Libyan Arab Jamahirya*.

2. Countries not on this list do not maintain diplomatic relations with Canada. A Canadian citizen visiting one of them can call on the good offices of British High Commissioners, embassies or consulates. (Commonwealth countries exchange High Commissioners rather than ambassadors with each other.)

3. Note that with several countries Canada maintains diplomatic relations but does not have a representative in residence. The address given in such cases is of the Canadian embassy, generally located in a neighbouring country, accredited to the country in question. If necessary, the British mission can be called on in those countries.

ALGERIA
(People's Democratic Republic of Algeria)

Chancery:

27 Bis, rue d'Anjou,
Hydra, Alger
Tel.: 60-66-11

ANGOLA
(People's Republic of Angola)

Embassy:

The Canadian Embassy to Angola,
c/o The Canadian High Commission,
P.O. Box 1430,
Harare, Zimbabwe

ANTIGUA AND BARBUDA

High Commission:

The Canadian High Commission to
Antigua and Barbuda,
c/o The Canadian High Commission,
P.O. Box 404,
Bridgetown, Barbados

ARGENTINA
(Argentine Republic)

Chancery:

Suipacha 1111, 25th Floor,
Brunetta Bldg.,
Suipacha and Santa Fé
Tel.: 312-9081/8

AUSTRALIA
(Commonwealth of Australia)

Chancery:

The Canadian High Commisssion,
Commonwealth Ave.,
Canberra A.C.T. 2600
Tel.: (062) 733-844

BAHAMAS
(Commonwealth of the Bahamas)

High Commission:

The Canadian High Commission to
the Bahamas,
c/o The Canadian High Commission,
P.O. Box 1500,
Kingston 10, Jamaica

BAHRAIN
(State of Bahrain)

Embassy:

The Canadian Embassy to Bahrain,
c/o The Canadian Embassy,
P.O. Box 25281
(Safat), Kuwait City, Kuwait

BANGLADESH
(People's Republic of Bangladesh)

High Commission:

House CWN 16/A,
Road 48, Gulshan,
Dhaka, Bangladesh
Tel.: 600181, 82, 83, 84

BARBADOS

Chancery:

Commonwealth Development
Corporation Building,
Culloden Road,
St. Michael
Tel.: 429-3550

BELIZE

High Commission:

The Canadian High Commission to
Belize,
c/o The Canadian High Commission,
P.O. Box 1500,
Kingston 10, Jamaica

BERMUDA

Commission:

The Canadian Commission to
Bermuda,
c/o The Canadian Consulate General
1251 Ave. of the Americas,
New York, N.Y.
USA 10020

BOLIVIA
(Republic of Bolivia)

Embassy:

The Canadian Embassy to Bolivia,
c/o The Canadian Embassy,
Casilla 1212,
Lima, Peru

BOTSWANA
(Republic of Botswana)

High Commission:

The Canadian High Commission to
Botswana,
c/o The Canadian High Commission,
P.O. Box 1430,
Harare, Zimbabwe

BRAZIL
(Federation Republic of Brazil)

Chancery:

Ave. das Nacoes, Number 16,
Setor das Embaixadas Sul
Brasilia
Tel.: (61) 223-7515

BRITAIN
(United Kingdom of Great Britain and
Northern Ireland)

Chancery:

Macdonald House,
1 Grosvenor Square,
London, W1X 0AB,
England, U.K.
Tel.: (01) 629-9492

BRUNEI

High Commission:

The High Commission of Canada to
Brunei,
c/o The Canadian High Commission,
P.O. Box 10990,
50732 Kuala Lumpur,
Malaysia

BURKINA-FASO

Embassy:

The Canadian Embassy to
Burkina-Faso,
c/o The Canadian Embassy,
01 P.O. Box 4101,
Abidjan 01, Ivory Coast

BURMA
(Socialist Republic of the Union of
Burma)

Embassy:

The Canadian Embassy to Burma,
c/o The Canadian High Commission,
G.P.O. Box 569,
Dhaka, Bangladesh

BURUNDI
(Republic of Burundi)

Embassy:

The Canadian Embassy to Burundi,
c/o The Canadian Embassy,
P.O. Box 8341
Kinshasa, Zaïre

CAMEROON
(Republic of Cameroon)

Chancery:

Immeuble Stamatiades,
Place de l'Hôtel de Ville
Yaoundé, Cameroon
Tel.: 23-02-03, 22-29-22

CAPE VERDE
(Republic of Cape Verde)

Embassy:

The Canadian Embassy to Cape
Verde,
c/o The Canadian Embassy,
P.O. Box 3373,
Dakar, Senegal

CENTRAL AFRICAN REPUBLIC

Embassy:

The Canadian Embassy to the Central
African Republic,
c/o The Canadian Embassy,
P.O. Box 572,
Yaoundé, Cameroon

CHAD
(Republic of Chad)

Embassy:

The Canadian Embassy to Chad,
c/o The Canadian Embassy,
P.O. Box 572,
Yaoundé, Cameroon

CHILE
(Republic of Chile)

Chancery:

Ahumada 11, 10th Floor,
Santiago, Chile
Tel.: 6962256, 7, 8, 9

CHINA
(People's Republic of China)

Embassy:

The Canadian Embassy,
10 San Li Tun Road,
Chao Yang District,
Beijing, China
Tel.: 52-1475, 52-1571

COLOMBIA
(Republic of Colombia)

Embassy:

The Canadian Embassy,
Calle 76, No. 11-52,
Bogotà, Colombia
Tel.: 235-5066

COMOROS
(Islamic Federal Republic of the
Comoros)

Embassy:

The Canadian Embassy to the
Comoros,
c/o The Canadian High Commission,
P.O. Box 30481,
Nairobi, Kenya

CONGO
(People's Republic of the Congo)

Embassy:

The Canadian Embassy to the Congo
c/o The Canadian Embassy,
P.O. Box 8341,
Kinshasa, Zaïre

COSTA RICA
(Republic of Costa Rica)

Chancery:

6th Floor,
Cronos Building,
Calle 3 y Ave. Central
San José, Costa Rica
Tel.: 23-04-46

CUBA
(Republic of Cuba)

Chancery:

The Canadian Embassy,
Calle 30,
No. 518 Esquina a7a,
Havana, Cuba
Tel.: 26421, -22, -23

DJIBOUTI
(Republic of Djibouti)

Embassy:

The Canadian Embassy to Djibouti,
c/o The Canadian Embassy,
P.O. Box 1130,
Addis Ababa, Ethiopia

DOMINICA
(Commonwealth of Dominica)

High Commission:

The Canadian High Commission to
Dominica,
c/o The Canadian High Commission,
P.O. Box 404,
Bridgetown, Barbados

DOMINICAN REPUBLIC

Embassy:

The Canadian Embassy to the
Dominican Republic,
c/o The Canadian Embassy,
Apartado 62302,
Caracas 1060A,
Venezuela

ECUADOR
(Republic of Ecuador)

Chancery:

Edificio Belmonte,
6th Floor,
Calle Corea 126,
Y Amazonas, Quito
Tel.: 458-016, 458-156

EGYPT
(Arab Republic of Egypt)

Chancery:

6 Sharia Mohamed Fahmi
el Sayed
Garden City
Cairo, Egypt
Tel.: 54-3110

EL SALVADOR
(Republic of El Salvador)

Embassy:

The Canadian Embassy to El
Salvador,
c/o The Canadian Embassy,
Apartado Postal 10303
San José, Costa Rica

EQUATORIAL GUINEA
(Republic of Equatorial Guinea)

Embassy:

The Canadian Embassy to Equatorial
Guinea,
c/o The Canadian Embassy,
P.O. Box 572
Yaoundé, Cameroon

ETHIOPIA

Chancery:

African Solidarity Insurance Building,
6th Floor, Churchill Avenue
Addis Ababa, Ethiopia
Tel.: 15 11 00, 15 12 28

FIJI

High Commission:

The Canadian High Commission to
Fiji,
c/o The Canadian High Commission,
P.O. Box 12-049
Wellington North, New Zealand

FRANCE
(French Republic)

Chancery:

The Canadian Embassy,
35, av. Montaigne
75008 Paris VIIe
Tel.: 47.23.01.01

GABON
(Gabonese Republic)

Embassy:

The Canadian Embassy,
P.O. Box 4037
Libreville, Gabon
Tel.: 72-41-54, 72-41-56, 72-41-69

GAMBIA
(Republic of the Gambia)

High Commission:

The Canadian High Commission to
the Gambia,
c/o The Canadian Embassy,
P.O. Box 3373
Dakar, Senegal

GHANA
(Republic of Ghana)

Chancery:

43 Independence Ave.
Tel.: 28555, 28502

GRENADA

High Commission:

The Canadian High Commission to
Grenada,
c/o The Canadian High Commission,
P.O. Box 404
Bridgetown, Barbados

GUATEMALA
(Republic of Guatemala)

Chancery:

Galerias Espana,
6th Floor,
7 Avenida 11-59, Zona 9
Tel.: 321411, 13, 17, 18, 19,
321426, 28, 29

GUINEA
(Republic of Guinea)

Embassy:

P.O. Box 99,
Conakry, Guinea
Tel.: 46-37-32, 46-37-33, 46-36-26

GUINEA-BISSAU
(Republic of Guinea-Bissau)

Embassy:

The Canadian Embassy to
Guinea-Bissau,
c/o The Canadian Embassy,
P.O. Box 3373
Dakar, Senegal

GUYANA
(Republic of Guyana)

Chancery:

High and Young Streets
Gcorgetown, Guyana
Tel.: 72081-5, 58337

HAITI
(Republic of Haiti)

Chancery:

Edifice Banque Nova Scotia,
Route de Delmas
Port-au-Prince, Haiti
Tel.: 2-2358, 2-4231, 2-4919

HONG KONG

Commission:

Office of the Commission for Canada,
14/15 Floors,
Asian House, 1 Hennessy Road
Hong Kong
Tel.: 5-282222, 3, 4, 5, 6, 7 and
5-282422, 3

INDIA
(Republic of India)

Chancery:

7/8 Shantipath,
Chanakyapuri
New Delhi 110021, India
Tel.: 60-8161

INDONESIA
(Republic of Indonesia)

Chancery:

5th Floor,
WISMA Metropolitan
Jalan Jendral Sudirman
Jakarta, Indonesia
Tel.: 510709

IRAN
(Islamic Republic of Iran)

Chancery:

57 Darya-e-Noor Ave.,
Takht-e-Tavoos
Tehran, Iran
Tel.: 623177, 623548, 622310,
623549, 623192, 623629, 622975,
623202

IRAQ
(Republic of Iraq)

Embassy:

47/1/7 Al Mansour
Baghdad, Iraq
Tel.: 542-1459, 542-1932, 542-1933

ISRAEL
(State of Israel)

Chancery:

220, Rehov Hayarkon,
Tel Aviv 63405, Israel
Tel.: (03) 228122-6

IVORY COAST
(Republic of the Ivory Coast)

Embassy:

Immeuble Trade Center,
23 av. Nogues
Abidjan, Ivory Coast
Tel.: 32-20-09

JAMAICA

Chancery:

Royal Bank Bldg.,
30–36 Knutsford Blvd.,
Kingston 5, Jamaica
Tel.: 926-1500, 1, 2, 3, 4, 5, 6, 7

JAPAN

Embassy:

38 Akasaka 7-chome,
Minato-ku,
Tokyo 107, Japan
Tel.: 408-2101, 8

JORDAN
(Hashemite Kingdom of Jordan)

Chancery:

The Canadian Embassy,
Pearl of Shmeisani Bldg.,
SH Shmeisami,
Amman, Jordan
Tel.: 666124, 5, 6

KENYA
(Republic of Kenya)

Chancery:

Comcraft House,
Hailé Sélassie Ave.,
Nairobi, Kenya
Tel.: 334-033, 4, 5, 6

KIRIBATI

High Commission:

The Canadian High Commission to
Kiribati,
c/o The Canadian High Commission,
P.O. Box 12–049
Wellington North,
New Zealand

KOREA
(Republic of Korea)

Chancery:

10th Floor,
Kolon Building,
45 Mugyo-Dong,
Jung-Ku,
Seoul, Korea
Tel.: 776-4062, 4068

KUWAIT
(State of Kuwait)

Chancery:

28 Quaraish Street,
Nuzha District,
Kuwait City, Kuwait
Tel.: 251-1451, 255-5754, 5934,
256-3025, 3078, 3019

LAOS
(Laos People's Democratic Republic)

Embassy:

The Canadian Embassy to Laos,
c/o The Canadian Embassy,
P.O. Box 2090
Bangkok 10500, Thailand

LEBANON
(Lebanese Republic)

Embassy:

The Canadian Embassy to Lebanon,
c/o The Canadian Embassy,
Hotel Al Jalaa, Avenue Mezze
Damascus, Syria

LESOTHO
(Kingdom of Lesotho)

High Commission:

The Canadian High Commission to
Lesotho,
c/o The Canadian Embassy,
P.O. Box 26006, Arcadia
Pretoria 0007, South Africa

LIBERIA
(Republic of Liberia)

Embassy:

The Canadian Embassy to Liberia,
c/o The Canadian High Commission,
P.O. Box 1639
Accra, Ghana

LIBYA
(Socialist People's Libyan Arab
Jamahiriya)

Embassy:

The Canadian Embassy to Libya,
c/o The Canadian Embassy,
C.P. 31, Belvédère
Tunis, Tunisia

MACAO

Commission:

c/o The Office of the Commission for
Canada,
P.O. Box 20264
Hennessy Road Post Office
Hong Kong

MADAGASCAR
(Democratic Republic of Madagascar)

Embassy:

The Canadian Embassy to
Madagascar,
c/o The Canadian High Commission,
P.O. Box 1022,
Dar-es-Salaam, Tanzania

MALAWI
(Republic of Malawi)

High Commission:

The Canadian High Commission to
Malawi,
c/o The Canadian High Commission,
P.O. Box 31313
Lusaka, Zambia

MALAYSIA

Chancery:

7th Floor, Plaza MBF,
172 Jalan Ampang,
50540 Kuala Lumpur, Malaysia
Tel.: 261-2000

MALDIVES
(Republic of Maldives)

High Commission:

The Canadian High Commission to
Maldives,
c/o The Canadian High Commission,
P.O. Box 1006
Colombo, Sri Lanka

MALI
(Republic of Mali)

Embassy:

The Canadian Embassy to Mali
c/o The Canadian Embassy
01 P.O. Box 4101
Abidjan 01, Ivory Coast
Tel.: 22-22-36

MAURITANIA
(Islamic Republic of Mauritania)

Embassy:

The Canadian Embassy to
Mauritania,
c/o The Canadian Embassy
P.O. Box 3373
Dakar, Senegal

MAURITIUS

High Commission:

The Canadian High Commission to
Mauritius
c/o The Canadian High Commission
P.O. Box 1022
Dar-es-Salaam, Tanzania

MEXICO
(United Mexican States)

Chancery:

Calle Schiller No. 529,
(Rincon del Bosque),
Colonia Polanco
11560 Mexico, D.F.
Tel.: 254-32-88

MONGOLIA
(Mongolian People's Republic)

Embassy:

The Canadian Embassy to Mongolia,
c/o The Canadian Embassy,
23 Starokonyushenny Pereulok,
Moscow, U.S.S.R.

MOROCCO
(Kingdom of Morocco)

Chancery:

12, Bis, Rue Jaafar As-Sadik,
Rabat-Agdal, Morocco
Tel.: 713-75, 76, 77

MOZAMBIQUE
(People's Republic of Mozambique)

Embassy:

The Canadian Embassy to
Mozambique,
c/o The Canadian High Commission,
P.O. Box 1430
Harare, Zimbabwe

NEPAL
(Kingdom of Nepal)

Embassy:

The Canadian Embassy to Nepal,
c/o The Canadian High Commission
P.O. Box 5207
New Delhi, India

NICARAGUA
(Republic of Nicaragua)

Embassy:

The Canadian Embassy to Nicaragua,
c/o The Canadian Embassy,
Äpartado Postal 10303
San José, Costa Rica

NIGER
(Republic of the Niger)

Embassy:

The Canadian Embassy to the Niger,
c/o The Canadian Embassy,
01 P.O. Box 4101
Abidjan 01, Ivory Coast
Tel.: 73-36-86/87, 73-37-58

NIGERIA
(Federal Republic of Nigeria)

Chancery:

Committee of Vice-Chancellors
Building,
Plot 8A,
4 Idowu-Taylor St.,
Victoria Island
Lagos, Nigeria
Tel.: 612-382, 383, 384, 385, 386

OMAN
(Sultanate of Oman)

Embassy:

The Canadian Embassy to Oman,
c/o The Canadian Embassy,
P.O. Box 25281 (Safat)
Kuwait City, Kuwait

PAKISTAN
(Islamic Republic of Pakistan)

Embassy:

Diplomatic Enclave,
Sector G-5
Islamabad, Pakistan
Tel.: 821101, 821102, 821103,
821104, 821109, 821302, 821306

PANAMA
(Republic of Panama)

Embassy:

The Canadian Embassy to Panama,
c/o The Canadian Embassy,
Apartado Postal 10303
San José, Costa Rica

PAPUA NEW GUINEA

High Commission:

The Canadian High Commission to
Papua New Guinea,
c/o The Canadian High Commission,
Commonwealth Ave.,
Canberra, A.C.T.,
2600 Australia

PARAGUAY
(Republic of Paraguay)

Embassy:

The Canadian Embassy to Paraguay,
c/o The Canadian Embassy,
Casilla de Correo 1598,
Buenos Aires, Argentina

PERU
(Republic of Peru)

Chancery:

Federico Gerdes 130,
(Antes Calle Libertad)
Miraflores, Lima
Tel.: 444015, 443841

PHILIPPINES
(Republic of the Philippines)

Chancery:

9th Floor,
Allied Bank Centre,
6754 Ayala Avenue, Makati
Manila

QATAR
(State of Qatar)

Embassy:

The Canadian Embassy to Qatar,
c/o The Canadian Embassy,
P.O. Box 25281 Safat
Kuwait City, Kuwait

RWANDA
(Rwandese Republic)

Embassy:

The Canadian Embassy to Rwanda,
c/o The Canadian Embassy,
P.O. Box 8341
Kinshasa, Zaïre

SAINT CHRISTOPHER AND NEVIS

High Commission:

The Canadian High Commission to
Saint Christopher and Nevis,
c/o The Canadian High Commission,
P.O. Box 404
Bridgetown, Barbados

SAINT LUCIA

High Commission:

The Canadian High Commission to
Saint Lucia,
c/o The Canadian High Commission,
P.O. Box 404
Bridgetown, Barbados

SAINT VINCENT AND THE GRENADINES

High Commission:

The Canadian High Commission to
Saint Vincent and the Grenadines
c/o The Canadian High Commission,
P.O. Box 404
Bridgetown, Barbados

SAO TOME AND PRINCIPE
(Democratic Republic of Sao Tome and Principe)

Embassy:

The Canadian Embassy to Sao Tome and Principe,
c/o The Canadian Embassy,
P.O. Box 572
Yaoundé, Cameroon

SAUDI ARABIA
(Kingdom of Saudi Arabia)

Chancery:

Diplomatic Quarter,
Riyadh, Saudi Arabia
Tel.: 488-2288, -0292, -0275

SENEGAL
(Republic of Senegal)

Chancery:

45, av. de la République
Dakar, Senegal
Tel.: 210290

SEYCHELLES
(Republic of Seychelles)

High Commission:

The Canadian High Commission to Seychelles,
c/o The Canadian High Commission,
P.O. Box 1022
Dar-es-Salaam, Tanzania

SIERRA LEONE
(Republic of Sierra Leone)

High Commission:

The Canadian High Commission to Sierra Leone,
c/o The Canadian High Commission,
P.O. Box 54506,
Ikoyi Station,
Lagos, Nigeria

SINGAPORE
(Republic of Singapore)

Chancery:

8th, 9th and 10 Storeys,
Faber House,
230 Orchard Road,
Singapore 9016
Tel.: 737-1322

SOLOMON ISLANDS

The Canadian High Commission to Solomon Islands,
c/o The Canadian High Commission,
Commonwealth Ave.,
Canberra A.C.T. 2600, Australia

SOMALIA
(Somali Democratic Republic)

Embassy:

The Canadian Embassy to Somalia,
c/o The Canadian High Commission,
P.O. Box 30481
Nairobi, Kenya

SOUTH AFRICA
(Republic of South Africa)

Chancery:

5th Floor, Nedbank Plaza,
Corner Church and Beatrix Streets,
Arcadia, Pretoria 0083
Tel.: 28-7062

SRI LANKA
(Democratic Socialist Republic of Sri Lanka)

Chancery:

6 Gregory's Road,
Cinnamon Gardens,
Colombo 7.
Tel.: 59-58-41; -42; -43; -44;
59-87-97

SUDAN
(Democratic Republic of the Sudan)

Embassy:

The Canadian Embassy to the Sudan
c/o The Canadian Embassy,
Kasr el Doubara Post Office
Cairo, Egypt

SURINAME
(Republic of Suriname)

Embassy:

The Canadian Embassy to the
Republic of Suriname,
c/o The Canadian High Commission,
P.O. Box 10880
Georgetown, Guyana

SWAZILAND
(Kingdom of Swaziland)

High Commission:

The Canadian High Commission to
Swaziland,
c/o The Canadian Embassy,
P.O. Box 26006,
Arcadia, Pretoria 0007, South Africa

SYRIA
(Syrian Arab Republic)

Chancery:

Hotel Al Jalaa
Avenue Mezze
Damascus, Syria
Tel.: 664.936/7

TANZANIA
(United Republic of Tanzania)

Chancery:

Pan Africa Insurance Building
Samora Machel Avenue
Dar-es-Salaam
Tel.: 20651/2/3

THAILAND
(Kingdom of Thailand)

Chancery:

Boonmitr Bldg.
11th Floor
138 Silom Rd.
Bangkok 10500

TOGO
(Togolese Republic)

Embassy:

The Canadian Embassy to Togo
c/o The Canadian High Commission
P.O. Box 1639
Accra, Ghana

TONGA
(Kingdom of Tonga)

High Commission:

The Canadian High Commission to
Tonga
c/o The Canadian High Commission
P.O. Box 12-049
Wellington North, New Zealand

TRINIDAD AND TOBAGO
(Republic of Trinidad and Tobago)

Chancery:

Huggins Bldg.
72 South Quay, Port of Spain
Tel.: 62-34787, 62-37254, -8.

TUNISIA
(Republic of Tunisia)

Chancery:

3, rue du Sénégal
Place Palestine, Tunis
Tel.: 286-577, 337, -619, -004, -114

TURKEY
(Republic of Turkey)

Chancery:

The Canadian Embassy
Nenehatun Caddesi No. 75
Gaziosmanpasa, Ankara, Turkey
Tel.: 27-58-03, -04, -05.

UGANDA
(Republic of Uganda)

High Commission:

The Canadian High Commission to
Uganda
c/o The Canadian High Commission
P.O. Box 30481
Nairobi, Kenya

UNION OF SOVIET
SOCIALIST REPUBLICS

Chancery:

The Canadian Embassy
23 Starokonyushenny Pereulok
Moscow, U.S.S.R.
Tel.: 241-9155, 241-3067, 241-5070

UNITED ARAB EMIRATES

Chancery:

Federal Commercial Bank Building
Tourist Club Area
Abu Dhabi
Tel.: 723800

VANUATU
(Republic of Vanuatu)

High Commission:

The Canadian High Commission to
Vanuatu,
c/o The Canadian High Commission,
Commonwealth Ave.,
Canberra A.C.T. 2600, Australia

VENEZUELA
(Republic of Venezuela)

Chancery:

Edificio Torre Europa,
7th Floor,
Avenida Francisco de Miranda,
Chacaito
Tel.: 951-6166, 951-6167, 951-6168

VIET NAM
(Socialist Republic of Viet Nam)

Embassy:

The Canadian Embassy to Viet Nam,
c/o The Canadian Embassy,
P.O. Box 2090,
Bangkok 10500, Thailand

WESTERN SAMOA
(Independent State of Western
Samoa)

High Commission:

The Canadian High Commission to
Samoa,
c/o The Canadian High Commission,
P.O. Box 12-049,
Wellington North, New Zealand

WEST INDIES
ASSOCIATED STATES AND
MONTSERRAT

Commission:

The Canadian Commission to the
West Indies Associated States and
Montserrat,
c/o The Canadian High Commission,
P.O. Box 404,
Bridgetown, Barbados

YEMEN
(Yemen Arab Republic)

Embassy:

The Canadian Embassy to
Democratic Yemen,
c/o The Canadian Embassy,
P.O. Box 22593,
Riyadh 11416, Saudi Arabia

ZAÏRE
(Republic of Zaïre)

Chancery:

Edifice Shell,
Coin av. Wangata et boul. du 30-juin.
Kinshasa
Tel.: 22-706-24,346, 27-839, 27-551

ZAMBIA
(Republic of Zambia)

Chancery:

Barclays Bank North End Branch,
Cairo Road, Lusaka
Tel.: 216161

ZIMBABWE
(Republic of Zimbabwe)

Chancery:

45 Baines Ave., Harare
Tel.: 79-38-01

C

REGIONAL
PASSPORT OFFICES

NEWFOUNDLAND

Fourth Floor
General Post Office Building
354 Water St.
St. John's, Nfld. A1C 1C4
Tel.: (709)772-4616

NOVA SCOTIA

Suite 1210
Barrington Tower
Scotia Square
Halifax, N.S. B3J 1P3
Tel.: (902)426-2770

NEW BRUNSWICK

Suite 601, Kings Place
440 King St.
Fredericton, N.B. E3B 5B9
Tel.: (506)452-3900

QUÉBEC

Suite 215
West Tower
Guy Favreau Complex
200 Dorchester Blvd. W.
Montréal, Qué. H2Z 1X4
Tel.: (514)283-2152

Suite 1000
Place Belle Cour
2590 Laurier Blvd.
Ste-Foy, Qué. G1V 4M6
Tel.: (418)648-4990

ONTARIO

Suite 330
Standard Life Building
120 King St. W.
Hamilton, Ont. L8N 4V2
Tel.: (416)572-2217

Eighth Floor
Government of Canada Building
451 Talbot Street
London, Ont. N6A 5C9
Tel.: (519)679-4366

Suite 1031
Tenth Floor
Atrium on Bay
P.O. Box 171
20 Dundas St. W.
Toronto, Ont. M5G 2C2
Tel.: (416)973-3251

Second Floor (Sub-office)
Government of Canada Building
4900 Yonge St.
Willowdale, Ont. M2N 6A6
Tel.: (416)973-3251

Suite 504
Bank of Commerce Building
100 Ouellette Ave.
Windsor, Ont. N9A 6T3
Tel.: (519)253-3507

MANITOBA

Suite 308
Revenue Building
391 York Ave.
Winnipeg, Man. R3C 0P6
Tel.: (204)949-2190

SASKATCHEWAN

Suite 605
Sixth Floor
Federal Building
101–22nd St. E.
Saskatoon, Sask. S7K 0E1
Tel.: (306)975-5106

ALBERTA

Room 480
Government of Canada Bldg.
220–4th Ave. S.E.
Calgary, Alta. T2G 4X3
Tel.: (403)292-5171

Suite 500
Royal Bank Bldg.
10117 Jasper Ave.
Edmonton, Alta. T5J 1W8
Tel.: (403)420-2622

BRITISH COLUMBIA

610–800 West Pender St.
Vancouver, B.C. V2C 2V6
Tel.: (604)666-1221

Suite 228
Customs House
816 Government St.
Victoria, B.C. V8W 1W8
Tel.: (604)388-0213

D

REGIONAL CUSTOMS OFFICES

ATLANTIC PROVINCES

Customs Office
6169 Quyinpool Rd.
Halifax, N.S. B3J 3G6
Tel.: (902)426-2911

QUEBEC

Customs Office
130 Dalhousie St.
Québec, Qué. G1K 7P6
Tel.: (418)648-4445

Customs Office
400 Youville Square
Montréal, Qué. H2Y 3N4
Tel.: (514)283-2953

ONTARIO

Customs Office
360 Coventry Road
Ottawa, Ont. K1K 2C6
Tel.: 8:00 A.M. to 4:30 P.M.:
(613)993-0534
After 4:30 P.M. and wknds:
(613)998-3326

Customs Office
10 John St. S.
Hamilton, Ont. L8N 3V8
Tel.: (416)523-2891
Evenings & wknds: (416) 679-6202

Customs Office
P.O. Box 5940, Terminal "A"
451 Talbot St.
London, Ont. N6A 4T9
Tel.: 7:00 A.M. to 11:00 P.M. 7 days a
week: (519)679-4131

Customs Office
185 Ouellette St.
Windsor, Ont. N9A 4H8
Tel.: (519)254-9202 (Exts. 254-5)
Evenings & wknds: (519)253-7271

MANITOBA

Customs Office
Federal Building
269 Main St.
Winnipeg, Man. R3C 1B3
Tel.: (204)949-6004

SASKATCHEWAN

Customs Office
204 Towne Square
1919 Rose Street
Regina, Sask. S4P 3P1
Tel.: (306)780-5218

ALBERTA

Customs Office
220–4th Ave. S.E., Ste. 720
Calgary, Alta. T2P 2M7
Tel.: 8:00 A.M. to 4:00 P.M.:
(403)292-4660

BRITISH COLUMBIA

Customs Office
1001 West Pender St.
Vancouver, B.C. V6E 2M8
Tel.: (604)666-0545

E

TRAVEL INFORMATION OFFICES (Department of National Health and Welfare)

NEWFOUNDLAND

Officer-In-Charge
Medical Services
Health and Welfare Canada
Room 410
Sir Humphrey Gilbert Building
Duckworth Street
P.O. Box 5759
St. John's, Nfld. A1C 5X3
Tel.: (709)772-5571

Nurse-in-Charge
Medical Services
Health and Welfare Canada
P.O. Box 368
Gander International Airport
Gander, Nfld. A1B 1W7
Tel.: (709)256-3035

NOVA SCOTIA

Medical Officer-in-Charge
Medical Services
Health and Welfare Canada
3129 Kempt Road
Halifax, N.S. B3K 5N6
Tel.: (902)426-3998

Officer-in-Charge
Medical Services
Health and Welfare Canada
63 Charlotte Street
Sydney, N.S. B1P 1B8
Tel.: (902)564-7290

NEW BRUNSWICK

Nurse-in-Charge
Medical Services
Health and Welfare Canada
89 Canterbury Street
Room 513
Saint John, N.B. E2L 2C7
Tel.: (506)648-4862

QUÉBEC

Medical Services
Health and Welfare Canada
Guy Favreau Complex
200 Dorchester West
Montréal, Qué. H2Z 1X4
Tel.: (514)283-4880

ONTARIO

Medical Officer-in-Charge
Medical Services
Health and Welfare Canada
3rd Floor
55 St. Clair Ave. E.
Toronto, Ont. M4T 1M2
Tel.: (416)966-6245

Zone Director
Medical Services
Health and Welfare Canada
33 South Court Street
Room 350
Thunder Bay, Ont. P7B 2W6
Tel.: (804)345-1443

Regional Director
Overseas and National Capital Region
Medical Services
Health and Welfare Canada
301 Elgin St.
Ottawa, Ont. K1A 0L3
Tel.: (613)990-0641

MANITOBA

Director, Special Services
Medical Services
Health and Welfare Canada
Room 500
303 Main St.
Winnipeg, Man. R3C 0H4
Tel.: (204)949-3616

SASKATCHEWAN

Regional Director
814 Bessborough Tower
601 Spadina Crescent E.
Saskatoon, Sask. S7K 3G8
Tel.: (306)665-4318

ALBERTA

Regional Director
Medical Services
Health and Welfare Canada
401 Toronto Dominion Tower
Edmonton Centre
Edmonton, Alta. T5J 2Z1
Tel.: (403)420-2597

BRITISH COLUMBIA

Zone Director
Medical Services
Health and Welfare Canada
5th Floor
1230 Government St.
Victoria, B.C. V8W 1Y3
Tel.: (604)566-3387

Zone Director
Medical Services
Health and Welfare Canada
581–309-2nd Ave. W.
Prince Rupert, B.C. V8J 3T1
Tel.: (604)627-1381

Zone Director
Medical Services
Health and Welfare Canada
7th Floor
1133 Melville St.
Vancouver, B.C. V6E 4E5
Tel.: (604)666-6196

Zone Director
Medical Services
Health and Welfare Canada
1294-3rd Ave.
Prince George, B.C. V2L 3L4
Tel.: (604)562-6675

F

YELLOW FEVER VACCINATION CENTRES
(Department of Health and Welfare)

NEWFOUNDLAND

District Health Officer
Provincial Department of Health
Forest Road
Public Health Building
St. John's, Nfld.
Tel.: (709)772-5571

NOVA SCOTIA

Medical Officer-in-Charge
Medical Services
Health and Welfare Canada
3129 Kempt Rd.
Halifax, N.S.
Tel.: (902)426-3998

Physician-in-Charge
Cape Breton Health Unit
Provincial Building
Prince Street
Sydney, N.S.
Tel.: (902)564-4447 or (902)564-4448

NEW BRUNSWICK

District Medical Health Officer
Regional Public Health Office
157 Duke St.
Saint John, N.B.
Appointment Tel.: (506)658-2455

PRINCE EDWARD ISLAND

Division of Nursing
Department of Health and Social
Services
Sullivan Building, 1st Floor
16 Fitzroy St.
P.O. Box 2000
Charlottetown, P.E.I.
Tel.: (902)892-5471

QUÉBEC

Département de santé
communautaire
Clinique de vaccination aux voyageurs
1001, rue St-Denis
2e étage
Montréal, Qué.
Tel.: (514)285-6304

Clinique médicale du Chemin de fer
C.N.
935, rue Lagauchetière Ouest
Montréal, Qué.
Tel.: (514)877-5690

Département de santé
communautaire
Hôpital du Saint-Sacrement
1050, Chemin Ste-Foy
Québec, Qué.
Tel.: (418)688-3670

Département de santé
communautaire
Clinique de vaccination des voyageurs
479, boul. Talbot
Chicoutimi, Qué.
Tel.: (418)543-0761

Clinique du voyageur international
Boutique Santé 2000
Carrefour de l'Estrie
3050, boul. Portland
Sherbrooke, Qué. J1L 1K1
Tel.: (819)564-1010

Centre local de services
communautaires de l'Estuaire
180, des Gouverneurs
Rimouski, Qué. G5L 8G1
Tel.: (418)724-7204

Services médicaux d'Air Canada
Aéroport Dorval
Dorval, Qué.
Tel.: (514)636-2973

ONTARIO

Zone Director
Medical Services
Health and Welfare Canada
3rd Floor
55 St. Clair Ave. E.
Toronto, Ont.
Tel.: (416)966-6245

Toronto General Hospital
Travel and Innoculation Clinic
Toronto, Ont. M5G 1L7
No appointment necessary
Tel.: (416)595-3670

Canadian National Railways
Medical Clinic
7th Floor
123 Edward St.
Toronto, Ont.
Tel.: (416)860-2711

Air Canada Medical Clinic
Box 6002, Toronto AMF
Toronto, Ont.
Tel.: (416)676-2400

University Hospital
Immunization Clinic
University Hospital
339 Windermere Rd.
London, Ont.
Appointment Tel.: (519)663-3395

Regional Director
Overseas and National Capital Region
Medical Services
Health and Welfare Canada
301 Elgin St.
Ottawa, Ont.
Tel.: (613)996-4185

Lake Superior Health Centre
National Health and Welfare
Medical Services Branch
106 Cumberland St. N.
Thunder Bay, Ont. P7A 4M2
Tel.: (807)345-1443

Base Surgeon
Canadian Forces Base Kingston
Kingston, Ont. K7L 2Z2
Appointment Tel.: (613)545-5508

Medical Officer of Health
Sudbury and District Health Unit
1300 Paris Crescent
Sudbury, Ont.
Appointment Tel.: (705)522-9200

Base Surgeon
Canadian Forces Base
Trenton, Ont.
Appointment Tel.: (613)392-2811
(Ext. 3641)

Simcoe County District Health Unit
County Administration Centre
Midhurst, Ont.
Appointment Tel.: (705)726-0100
(Ext. 36)

Operating Division
McMaster University
Medical Centre
1200 Main St. W.
Hamilton, Ont. L8N 3Z5
Tel.: (416)521-2100 (Ext. 6307)

MANITOBA

Director, Special Services
Medical Services
Health and Welfare Canada
500 Grain Commissioners Building
303 Main St.
Winnipeg, Man.
Tel.: (204)949-4194

SASKATCHEWAN

Medical Officer of Health
City Health Department
1910 McIntyre
Regina, Sask.
Tel.: (306)522-3621

Medical Health Officer
City of Saskatoon
350–3rd Avenue North
Saskatoon, Sask. S7K 6G7
Tel.: (306)664-9627

ALBERTA

Central Health Clinic
10005–103A Ave.
Edmonton, Alta.
Tel.: (403)428-3444

International Travel Immunization
Clinic
Health Sciences Centre
3330 Hospital Dr. N.W.
Calgary, Alta.
Tel.: (403)283-2758

BRITISH COLUMBIA

Zone Director
Medical Services
Health and Welfare Canada
5th Floor
1230 Government St.
Victoria, B.C.
Tel.: (604)388-3565

Base Surgeon
Canadian Forces Base Comox
Lazo, B.C. V0R 2K0
Tel.: (604)339-2211 (Ext. 2267)

Zone Director
Medical Services
Health and Welfare Canada
7th Floor
1133 Melville St.
Vancouver, B.C.
Tel.: (604)666-3331

Northern Interior Health Unit
1444 Edmonton St.
Prince George, B.C.
Appointment Tel.: (604)563-1631

North Okanagan Health Unit
1277–15 St.
Vernon, B.C. V1T 8S7
Tel.: (604)545-0651

G

DEPARTMENT OF REGIONAL INDUSTRIAL EXPANSION— REGIONAL OFFICES

NEWFOUNDLAND

P.O. Box 8950
Parsons Building
90 O'Leary Ave.
St. John's, Nfld. A1B 3R9
Tel.: (709)772-4884

Local Offices:

Corner Brook, Nfld.
Tel.: (709)634-4477

Goose Bay, Labrador
Tel.: (709)896-2741

PRINCE EDWARD ISLAND

P.O. Box 1115
Confederation Court Mall
134 Kent St., Suite 400
Charlottetown, P.E.I. C1A 7M8
Tel.: (902)436-4846

NOVA SCOTIA

P.O. Box 940, Stn. M
1496 Lower Water St.
Halifax, N.S. B3J 2V9
Tel.: (902)426-2018

Local Office:
Sydney, N.S.
Tel.: (902)564-7007

NEW BRUNSWICK

P.O. Box 1210
Assumption Place
770 Main Street
Moncton, N.B. E1C 8P9
Tel.: (506)857-6400

Local Offices:

Bathurst, N.B.
Tel.: (506)548-8907

Fredericton, N.B.
Tel.: (506)452-3124

Saint John, N.B.
Tel.: (506)648-4791

QUÉBEC

Tour de la Bourse
800, Place Victoria, Bureau 3800
C.P. 247
Montréal, Qué. H4Z 1E8
Tel.: (514)283-8185

Local Offices:

Alma, Qué.
Tel.: (418)668-3084

Drummondville, Qué.
Tel.: (819)478-4664

Québec, Qué.
Tel.: (418)648-4826

Rimouski, Qué.
Tel.: (418)722-3282

Sherbrooke, Qué.
Tel.: (819)565-4713

Trois-Rivières, Qué.
Tel.: (819)374-5544

Val-d'Or, Qué.
Tel.: (819)825-5260

ONTARIO

P.O. Box 98
1 First Canadian Place, Suite 4840
Toronto, Ont. M5X 1B1
Tel.: (416)365-3821

Local Offices:

London, Ont.
Tel.: (519)679-5820

Ottawa, Ont.
Tel.: (613)993-4963

Sudbury, Ont.
Tel.: (705)675-0711

Thunder Bay, Ont.
Tel.: (807)623-4436

MANITOBA

P.O. Box 981
330 Portage Ave.
Room 608
Winnipeg, Man. R3C 2V2
Tel.: (204)949-6162

Local Office:

Thompson, Man.
Tel.: (204)778-4486

SASKATCHEWAN

105–21st Street
6th Floor
Saskatoon, Sask. S7K 0B3
Tel.: (306)975-4400

Local Offices:

Regina, Sask,
Tel.: (306)780-6108

Prince Albert, Sask.
Tel.: (306)764-7169

ALBERTA

Cornerpoint Building
10179–105th Street, Suite 505
Edmonton, Alta. T5J 3S3
Tel.: (403)420-2944

Local Office:

Calgary, Alta.
Tel.: (403)292-4575

BRITISH COLUMBIA

P.O. Box 49178
Bentall Postal Stn.
Bentall Tower IV
1101–1055 Dunsmuir Street
Vancouver, B.C. V7X 1K8
Tel.: (604)661-0434

Local Offices:

Victoria, B.C.
Tel.: (604)388-3181

Prince George, B.C.
Tel.: (604)562-4451

YUKON

Suite 301
108 Lambert St.
Whitehorse, Y.T. Y1A 1Z2
Tel.: (403)668-4655

NORTHWEST TERRITORIES

P.O. Bag 6100
Precambrian Building
Yellowknife, N.W.T. X1A 1C0
Tel.: (403)920-8668, 920-8571

H

REGIONAL OFFICES OF THE CANADIAN HOSTELING ASSOCIATION

NEWFOUNDLAND

Newfoundland Hostelling Association
P.O. Box 1815
St. John's, Nfld. A1C 5P9
Tel.: (709)739-5866

PRINCE EDWARD ISLAND

Prince Edward Island Hostelling
Association
P.O. Box 1718
Charlottetown, P.E.I. C1A 7N3
Tel.: (902)894-9696

NOVA SCOTIA

Nova Scotia Hostelling Association
Sport Nova Scotia Centre
5516 Spring Garden Road
P.O. Box 3010 South
Halifax, N.S. B3J 3G6
Tel.: (902)425-5450

NEW BRUNSWICK

New Brunswick Hostelling
Association
c/o CHA National Office
Tel.: (613)748-5638

QUÉBEC

Québec Hostelling Federation
4545 Pierre de Coubertin
C.P. 1000, Succursale M
Montréal, Qué. H1V 3R2
Tel.: (514)252-3117

ONTARIO

Ontario East Hostelling Association
18 Byward Market
Ottawa, Ont. K1N 7A1
Tel.: (613)230-1200

Great Lakes Hostelling Association
223 Church St.
Toronto, Ont. M5B 1Z1
Tel.: (416)368-1848

MANITOBA

Canadian Hostelling
Association—Manitoba Inc.
1700 Ellice Ave.
Winnipeg, Man. R3H 0B1
Tel.: (204)786-5641

SASKATCHEWAN

Canadian Hostelling Association
Saskatchewan Sport and Recreation
Centre
2205 Victoria Ave.
Regina, Sask. S4P 0S4
Tel.: (306)522-3651

ALBERTA

Canadian Hostelling Association
Northern Alberta District
10926–88th Ave.
Edmonton, Alta. T6G 0Z1
Tel.: (403)432-7798

Southern Hostelling Association
#203, 1414 Kensington Rd. N.W.
Calgary, Alta. T2N 3P9
Tel.: (403)283-5551

BRITISH COLUMBIA

Canadian Hostelling Association
3425 West Broadway
Vancouver, B.C. V6R 2B4
Tel.: (604)736-2674

YUKON

Yukon Hostelling Association
P.O. Box 4762
Whitehorse, Y.T. Y1A 4N6

I

CANADA WORLD YOUTH
REGIONAL OFFICES

BRITISH COLUMBIA

2524 Cypress St.
Vancouver, B.C. V6J 3N2
Tel.: (604)732-5113

PRAIRIE REGION

10765–98 St.
Edmonton, Alta. T5H 2P2
Tel.: (403)424-6411

ONTARIO

627 Davenport Rd.
Toronto, Ont. M5R 1L2
Tel.: (416)922-0776

QUÉBEC

4824, de la Côte des Neiges
Montréal, Qué. H3V 1G4
Tel.: (514)342-6880

ATLANTIC REGION

Third Floor
1652 Barrington St.
Halifax, N.S. B3J 2A2
Tel.: (902)422-1782

GENERAL SECRETARIAT

4824, de la Côte des Neiges
Montréal, Qué. H3V 1G4
Tel.: (514)342-6880

J

AUTOMOBILE CLUBS IN CANADA
(Affiliated to the Canadian Automobile Association)

NEWFOUNDLAND

Newfoundland & Labrador Auto Association
Avalon Mall
54 Kenmount Rd.
St. John's, Nfld. A1B 1W3
Tel.: (709)726-6100

NOVA SCOTIA

Maritime Auto Association
7169 Chebucto Rd.
Halifax, N.S. B3L 1N5
Tel.: (902)453-2320

NEW BRUNSWICK

Maritime Auto Association
Haymarket Sq.
335 City Rd.
Saint John, N.B. E2L 3N6
Tel.: (506)657-3470

PRINCE EDWARD ISLAND

Maritime Auto Association
193A Prince St.
Charlottetown, P.E.I. C1A 4R8
Tel.: (902)892-1612

QUÉBEC

Club Automobile Touring du Québec
1670 Provencher Blvd.
Brossard, Qué. J4W 2Z6
Tel.: (514)465-7770

Club Automobile Touring du Québec
Place du Royaume
1401 Talbot Blvd.
Chicoutimi, Qué. G7H 4C1
Tel.: (418)545-8686

Club Automobile Touring du Québec
456, boul. St-Joseph
Hull, Qué. J8Y 3Y7
Tel.: (819)778-2225

Club Automobile Touring du Québec
1200 St-Martin Blvd. W.
Laval, Qué. H7S 2E4
Tel.: (514)668-2240

Club Automobile Touring du Québec
1425 de la Montagne Street
Montréal, Qué. H3G 2R7
Tel.: (514)288-7111

Club Automobile Touring du Québec
18 Ste-Anne St.
Québec, Qué. G1R 3X2
Tel.: (418)692-4720

Club Automobile Touring du Québec
2600 Laurier Blvd.
Ste-Foy, Qué. G1V 2L1
Tel.: (418)653-2600

Club Automobile Touring du Québec
2433 King St. W.
Sherbrooke, Qué. J1J 2G7
Tel.: (819)556-5132

Club Automobile Touring du Québec
1295 Aubuchon St.
Trois-Rivières, Qué. G8Y 5K4
Tel.: (819)376-9393

ONTARIO

Hamilton Auto Club
393 Main St. E.
Hamilton, Ont. L8N 3T7
Tel.: (416)525-1210

OML-Eastern Ontario Club
2300 Princess St.
Kingston, Ont. K7M 3G4
Tel.: (613)546-2679

OML Mid-Western Auto Club
836 Courtland Ave. E.
Kitchener, Ont. N2C 1K3
Tel.: (519)576-1020

OML-Ottawa Club
1354 Richmond Rd.
Ottawa, Ont. K2B 7Z3
Tel.: (613)820-1890

CAA Peterborough
238 Lansdowne St. E.
Peterborough, Ont. K9J 7X7
Tel.: (705)743-4343

OML-Niagara Peninsula Club
76 Lake St.
St. Catharines, Ont. L2R 6S3
Tel.: (416)688-0321

OML-Elgin Norfolk Club
1091 Talbot St.
St. Thomas, Ont. N5P 1G4
Tel.: (519)631-6490

OML-Nickel Belt Club
Regent Place
1769 Regent St. S.
Sudbury, Ont. P3E 3Z7
Tel.: (705)522-0000

OML-Northwestern Ontario Club
585 Memorial Ave.
Thunder Bay, Ont. P7B 3Z1
Tel.: (807)345-1261

OML-Toronto Club
2 Carlton St.
Toronto, Ont. M5B 1K4
Tel.: (416)964-3111

CAA-Auto Club-Windsor
1215 Ouellette Ave.
Windsor, Ont. N8X 1J3
Tel.: (519)255-1212

MANITOBA

Manitoba Motor League
870 Empress St.
Winnipeg, Man. R3G 3H3
Tel.: (204)239-6455

SASKATCHEWAN

Saskatchewan Motor Club
200 Albert St. N.
Regina, Sask. S4R 5E2
Tel.: (306)543-5677

ALBERTA

Alberta Motor Association
11230–110th St.
Edmonton, Alta. T5L 4J7
Tel.: (403)474-8660

BRITISH COLUMBIA

British Columbia Auto Association
9899 W. Broadway
Vancouver, B.C. V5Z 1K5
Tel.: (604)732-3911

HEAD OFFICE

Canadian Automobile Association
1775 Courtwood Cresc.
Ottawa, Ont. K2C 3J2
Tel.: (613)226-7631

K

AUTOMOBILE AND TOURING CLUBS IN THE THIRD WORLD
(affiliated with the Canadian Automobile Association)

This list mentions certain countries that are not part of the Third World (Japan, France, United Kingdom, etc.) since they often are on travellers' routes.

ALGERIA

Fédération Algérienne du Sport Automobile et du Karting
99 Blvd. Salah Bouakouir
Algiers

Touring Club D'Algérie
1 rue Al-Idrissi
Algiers

ARGENTINA

Automovil Club Argentino
1850 Avenida del Libertador
Buenos Aires

Touring Club Argentino, Esmeralda
605 Tucuman 781-3
Buenos Aires

AUSTRALIA

Australian Automobile Association
212 Northbourn Ave.
Canberra

Royal Automobile Association of South Australia
41 Hindmarsh Square
Adelaide

Royal Automobile Club of Queensland
Corner of Ann & Boundary Streets
Brisbane

Automobile Association of the Northern Territory
79–81 Smith St.
Darwin

Royal Automobile Club of Tasmania
Corner Murray & Patrick Streets
Hobart

Royal Automobile Club of Victoria
123 Queen St.
Melbourne

Royal Automobile Club of Western Australia
228 Adelaide Terrace
Perth

National Roads & Motorists' Association
151 Clarence St.
Sydney

Royal Automobile Club of Australia
89 Maquarie St.
Sydney

BOLIVIA

Automovil Club Boliviano
Avenida 6 de Agosto No. 2993
San Jorge Casilla 602
La Paz

BRAZIL

Automovel Club do Brazil
Rua do Passeio 90
Rio de Janeiro

Touring Club do Brazil
Praca Maua-Estacion Maritima
"Berilo Neves"

BURUNDI

Club Automobile Burundi
P.O. Box 544
Bujumbura

CUBA

Automovil y Aero Club de Cuba
Malecon 217, Bajos
Havana

ECUADOR

Automovil Club del Ecuador
avenida Eloy Alfaro 218 y Berlin
Quito

EGYPT

Automobile et Touring Club d'Egypte
10, rue Kasr el Nil
Cairo

EL SALVADOR

Automovil Club de El Salvador
Alameda Roosevelt y 41
Av.-Sur 2173
San Salvador

ETHIOPIA

Automobile Club Eritreo
Via Giustino de Jacobis n.4-6-8
Asmara

FRANCE

Automobile-Club de France
6–8 Place de la Concorde
Paris

Association Française des
Automobilistes
9, rue Anatole de la Forge
Paris

GHANA

The Automobile Association of Ghana
1 Valley View
Labadi Rd.
Christianborg
Accra

GREAT BRITAIN

The Automobile Association
Fanum House
Basing View
Hampshire
Basingstoke

GREAT BRITAIN (suite)

The Royal Automobile Club
RAC House
Lansdowne Rd.
Croydon
London

Camping & Caravanning Club
11 Lower Grosvenor Place SW1
London

GUATEMALA

Club de Automovilismo y Turismo de
Guatemala
15, Calle "A" 1251 Zone 1
Guatemala

HONG KONG

Hong Kong Automobile Association
Marsh Road
Wanchal Reclamation
Hong Kong

INDIA

Federation of Indian Automobile
Associations
76 Vir Nariman Rd. Churchgate
Reclamation
Bombay

Automobile Association of Eastern
India
13 Promothesh Barua Sarani
Calcutta

Automobile Association of Southern
India
187 Anna Salai
Madras

Automobile Association of Upper
India
14-F Connaught Place
New Delhi

U.P. Automobile Association
32-A
Mahatma Gandhi Marg
Allahabad

INDONESIA

Ikatan Motor Indonesia
Gedun KONI Pusat
Senayan
Djarkarta

IRAN

Touring et Automobile Club de la
République islamique d'Iran
Martyr Dr Fayazbaksh 37
Tehran

IRAQ

Iraq Automobile and Touring
Association
Al.Mansour
Baghdad

ISRAEL

Automobile and Touring Club of Israel
19 Petah Tikva Road
Tel Aviv

IVORY COAST

01 B.P. 3883
Abidjan

JAMAICA

The Jamaica Automobile Association
14 Ruthwen Road
Kingston

JAPAN

Japan Automobile Federation
3-5-8 Shiba-Koen
Minato-Ku
Tokyo

Touring Club of Japan
Daini-Maijma Bldg.
5F 1-9 Yotsuya
Shinjuku-ku
Tokyo

JORDAN

Royal Automobile Club of Jordan
Wadi Seer Cross Roads (9th Circle)
Amman

KENYA

The Automobile Association of Kenya
AA Nyaku House
Hurlingham
Nairobi

KOREA

Korea Automobile Association
Room 405
Hanam Bldg.
1-150, Yoido-Dong
Youngdungpo-Ku
Seoul

KUWAIT

The Automobile Association of
Kuwait and the Gulf
Airport Rd.
Khaldiyah
Kuwait

Kuwait Automobile and Touring Club
Airport Rd.
Khaldiyah
Kuwait

Kuwait International Touring &
Automobile-Club
Airport Rd.
Khaldiyah
Kuwait

LAOS

Royal Automobile Club du Laos
Vientiane

LEBANON

Automobile et Touring Club du Liban
Avenue Sami Solh
Imm: Kalot
Beyrouth

MALAGASY

Automobile-Club de Madagascar
Rue Ravoninahitriniarivo
Alarobia
Antananarivo

MALAYSIA

The Automobile Association of
Malaysia
Jalan Datuk Sulaiman
30, Taman Tun Dr. Ismail
Kuala Lumpur

MEXICO

Asociacion Mexicana Automovilistica
Orizaba 7
Colonia Roma
Mexico City

Asociacion Nacional Automovilistica
Miguel E. Schultz 140
Mexico

MOROCCO

Royal Automobile Club Marocain
Ain Diab
Av. Cote d'Emeraude/rue Mimizan
Casablanca

Touring Club du Maroc
3 Avenue de l'Armée Royale
Casablanca

NEPAL

Automobile Association of Nepal
Traffic Police
Ramshah Path of opp. Sinhdwar
Kathmandu

NEW ZEALAND

The New Zealand Automobile
Association Inc.
98 Lambton Quay
Wellington

NIGERIA

Automobile Club of Nigeria
24 Meray Eneli Surulere
Lagos

OMAN

Oman Automobile Association
P.O. Box 402
Ruwi-Muscat

PAKISTAN

Automobile Association of Pakistan
175/3 Shah Jamal
Near Mazar
Baba Shah Jamal
Lahore

The Karachi Automobile Association
Standard Ins. House
1 Chundriger Road
Karachi

PAPUA NEW GUINEA

Automobile Association of Papua and
New Guinea
GPO Box 5999
Boroko

PARAGUAY

Touring y Automovil Club Paraguayo
25 de Mayo y Brasil
Asuncion

PERU

Touring y Automovil Club del Peru
Avenida Cesar Vallejo 699
(Lince)
Lima

PHILIPPINES

Philippine Motor Association
683 Aurora Blvd.
Quezon City

PUERTO RICO

Federacion de Automovilismo de
Puerto Rico
Minillas Sta
San Juan

QATAR

Automobile et Touring Club of Qatar
Beda Road
Doha

RWANDA

Auto-moto club du Rwanda
Hotel Méridien Umubano
B.P. 822
Kigali

SAUDI ARABIA

P.O. Box 276
Damman

SENEGAL

Automobile Club du Sénégal
Place de l'Indépendence
Dakar

Touring Club du Sénégal
Place de l'Indépendence
Building Air d'Afrique
Dakar

SINGAPORE

The Automobile Association of
Singapore
336 River Valley Road
Singapore

SOUTH AFRICA

The Automobile Association of South
Africa
66 de Korte St.
Braamfontein
Johannesburg

SRI LANKA

Automobile Association of Ceylon
40 Sir M.M.M. Mawatha
Galle Face
Colombo

THAILAND

Royal Automobile Association
Thailand
151 Rachadapisek
Road Bang Chen
Bangkok

TRINIDAD AND TOBAGO

Trinidad and Tobago Automobile
Association
14 Woodford St.
Newton
Port of Spain

TUNISIA

National Automobile Club de Tunisie
29 Avenue Habib Bourguiba
Tunis

Touring Club de Tunisie
15 Rue d'Allemagne
Tunis

TURKEY

Turkiye Turing ve Otomobil Kurumu
364 Sisli Meydani
Istanbul

UNITED ARAB EMIRATES

Automobile and Touring Club for
United Arab Emirates
Box 1183
Sharjah

Automobile Association for United
Arab Emirates
Abu Dhabi

Automobile Association for United
Arab Emirates
Dubai

UNITED STATES OF AMERICA

American Automobile Association
8111 Gatehouse Rd.
Falls Church, Va.

URUGUAY

Automovil Club del Uruguay
Avds. del Libertador Lavalleja y
Uruguay
Montevideo

Touring Club Uruguayo
Avenida Uruguay 2009–2015
Montevideo

Centro Automoviliste del Uruguay
Bulevar Artigas 1773
Esquina Dante
Montevideo

U.S.S.R.

Federacia Automobilnogo Sporta
Intourist
16, Marx Prospect
Moscow

VENEZUELA

Touring y Automovil Club de
Venezuela
Centro Integral ''Santa Rosa de
Lima''
Locales 11, 12–14
Caracas

VIET NAM

Automobile-Club du Viet Nam
17 Duong Ho Xuan Huong
Ex-rue Colombie
Saigon

YUGOSLAVIA

Auto-moto Savez Jugoslavije
Ruzveltova 18
Belgrade

ZAÏRE

Federation Automobile du Zaïre
Av des Inflammables No. 25
Kinshasa

ZIMBABWE

Automobile Association of Zimbabwe
Samora Machel Ave. 57
Harare

L

CHRONOLOGY OF THE AUTHOR'S TRAVELS

1946:

Mexico, Guatemala, El Salvador, Honduras, Costa Rica, Panama, Colombia, Venezuela, Ecuador, Peru, Bolivia, Chile.

1947:

Argentina, Uruguay, Brazil, Guyana, Trinidad, Dominican Republic, Haiti, Cuba.

1948:

Great Britain, France, Spain, Gibraltar, Morocco, Algeria, Niger, Nigeria.

1949:

Chad, Central African Republic, Cameroon, Congo, Zaïre, Zambia, Rhodesia, Botswana, Republic of South Africa, Lesotho, Malawai, Tanzania, Kenya, Uganda, Sudan, Egypt.

1950:

Hawaii, Japan, South Korea, Philippines, Hong Kong, Macao, Vietnam, Cambodia, Thailand, Malaysia, Singapore, India

1951:

Pakistan, Afghanistan, Iran, Iraq, Jordan, Palestine, Lebanon, Syria, Turkey, Greece, Yugoslavia, Austria, Federal Republic of Germany, Switzerland, Italy, Vatican, France.

1952:

France, Algeria, Morocco, Mali, Senegal, Guinea, Upper Volta, Ivory Coast, Ghana.

1953:

Togo, Dahomey, Nigeria, Cameroon, Central African Republic, Uganda, Kenya, Ethiopia, Lebanon, Italy, Austria, Federal Republic of Germany, France.

1955:

France, Poland, Belgium, Ireland.

1958:

Sweden, France.

1959:

Guatemala.

1960:

Great Britain, People's Republic of China, U.S.S.R., France.

1962:

France, Portugal, Italy, Switzerland.

1963:

Haiti, Puerto Rico, France, Federal Republic of Germany, Tunisia, Libya.

1966:

Bulgaria, Rumania, Czechoslovakia, Hungary, Federal Republic of Germany, Belgium.

1968:

Netherlands, Tunisia, Federal Republic of Germany, Malta, France.

1969:

Algeria, France, Ivory Coast, Federal Republic of Germany, Finland, Norway, Denmark.

1970:

Switzerland, Israel, Cyprus, Greece, Great Britain, France, Monaco.

1971:

Mexico, France, Tunisia, Cameroon, Italy, Malaysia, Hong Kong, Federal Republic of Germany, Sweden.

1972:

France, Tunisia, Morocco, Senegal, The Gambia, Federal Republic of Germany, Italy.

1973:

Italy, Cameroon, Tunisia, Malaysia, Great Britain, Costa Rica, Honduras, Belize, Luxembourg, Federal Republic of Germany, Belgium, France.

1974:

Fiji, Australia, Indonesia, France, Belgium, Ivory Coast, Senegal, Algeria, Tunisia.

1975:

Great Britain, France, Indonesia, India, Sri Lanka, Malaysia, Philippines, Ivory Coast, Tunisia, El Salvador, Guatemala, Honduras.

1976:

Mexico, Guatemala, El Salvador, Dutch West Indies, Haiti, Colombia.

1977:

Tanzania, Ivory Coast, Senegal, Mexico, Peru, Bolivia.

1978:

Mexico, Guatemala, El Salvador, Colombia, Panama, Peru, Bolivia, Trinidad and Tobago, Guyana, Haiti, India, Bangladesh, Burma, Sri Lanka.

1979:

Malaysia, Indonesia, Philippines, Mali.

1980:

Senegal, Mauritania, France, Mexico.

1981:

Costa Rica, Ecuador, Peru, Paraguay, Bolivia, Colombia, Senegal, Morocco.

1982:

Saudi Arabia, India, Sri Lanka, Singapore, Philippines, Indonesia, Australia, Papua New Guinea, Fiji, Colombia, Ecuador, Bolivia, Senegal, Mali, Guinea.

1983:

Togo, Morocco, Egypt, Sudan, Kenya, Somalia, Djibouti, Seychelles, Sri Lanka, Zaïre, Dominican Republic.

1984:

Brazil, Ecuador, Singapore, Brunei, Indonesia, Belgium, Rwanda, Dominican Republic, France, Pakistan.

1985:

India, Sri Lanka, Thailand, Australia, Vanuatu, Fiji, Zaïre.

1986:

Malawi, Swaziland, Mauritius, Madagascar, Kenya, France.